DIGITAL MARKETING IN THE AGE OF AI

4 Steps to Digital Marketing Success

A guide for business leaders who want to get found and get heard.

Thomas Young

Attention:
Thomas Young
Intuitive Websites
115 Wilcox Street
Castle Rock, CO 80104
720-934-8409

Website: www.IntuitiveWebsites.com
Email: info@intuitivewebsites.com

ISBN 979-8-9907328-3-4
Ingram SPARK Paperback edition

Ordering Information:
Special discounts are available on quantity purchases by corporations, associations, and others. For details, contact the Author at the address above.

High Praise for
Digital Marketing in the Age of AI

"*Digital Marketing in the Age of AI* is a must read for any business leader looking to take their digital marketing efforts to the next level. The Four-Step Process outlined is an invaluable guide to developing a successful digital marketing strategy. Coupled, as it is in Tom's book, with a strong emphasis on leveraging the power of AI, your enhanced digital marketing plan will drive results."

~ Sam Reese, Chief Executive Officer, Vistage Worldwide

"Over the last 10 years there has been a dramatic shift in the way buyers want to buy and recent Gartner research showed that 72% of B2B buyers prefer a rep-free buying experience. This book will help you make the critical shift to serving buyers the way they want to buy to drive sales funnel success effectively and efficiently using AI."

~ Karen Hayward, Managing Partner, Chief Outsiders

"I conduct over 500 coaching meetings with CEO's and Key Executives each year and have found that Thomas Young has been an incredible resource for my clients. His book helps executives understand how AI can help their business in marketing and all other aspects. This is a must read!"

~ Carl Arnold, Best Practice Chair, Vistage International

"To say marketing is in the midst of revolution is severe understatement. Tom has made himself the leading expert on using AI to supercharge your marketing. He treats AI as just a tool (although a super-exiting one) for effective implementation of the other lessons he has already taught us about the digital marketing revolution. This holistic approach shows us that AI is not just the latest "shiny new object," but an essential means for executing the strategies we already know."

~ Jim Casart, Founder and Owner, Team-80

"I run my own business. I'm super busy every day. Why should I care about AI now before its standardized? Because if you don't, it will be like trying to communicate to your customers via email and not owning a computer. Whether we like it or not, busy, or not, AI is here. Tom's expertise and easy to read style is critical to business in, and beyond."

~ Harlow Russell, President and Founder, Awesome 3D Cards

"Tom's methods are always innovative, and his latest book is no different. This book teaches you to execute and leverage AI into your digital marketing by implementing the Four-Step Process. His approach and ideologies have certainly helped the growth of my firm."

~ Jason Wiggam, CEO and Founder, Wiggam Law

"Tom's relentless focus on simplifying our message down to a few key taglines was really key for helping us to better communicate the powerful savings we deliver for our clients."

~ Kristen Russell, President, Fall River Benefits

"Contrary to the hype, AI is neither a silver bullet nor the end of the world. AI is simply a tool—or even a weapon in a deft marketer's hands. Digital Marketing in the Age of AI outlines a practical and demystifying framework for incorporating AI into everyday digital marketing activities in a way that is both accessible and incredibly useful.

~ Kevin Shutes, Consultant, Fractional VP of Sales

"You may be wondering will AI take my job? No, people who know how to use AI will take your job. This is your wakeup call. Marketing teams that do not use AI are at a serious disadvantage. Tom provides simple steps to get you started immediately, as you're reading. Best Book on the subject I've seen."

~ Dick Sanger, Vistage Group Chair

"This book captures the critical issues and the steps any organization needs to take to finally get a website that works."
~ Tony Veltri, CEO, Veltri Inc.

"To have a website that outpaces your competition you need to be two steps ahead! With this simple Four-Step Process, this book shows you how!"
~ Dustin Carreon, CEO, Freelance Electronics

"Thomas Young gives all business owners a precious gift: four easy to comprehend steps on how to whip our lazy, underperforming websites into shape. Never again will you have to settle for a mediocre website."
~ Henry DeVries, co-author of
How to Close a Deal Like Warren Buffett

"Thomas's approach is spot on. He has helped us make our websites more relevant to our audience, easier to navigate and much better in terms of look and function. With Tom's assistance we have grown our presence on the web, and it has translated into more revenues. The data covered in this book is exactly what he did with us to help FitGolf on the web. Thanks, Tom!"
~ David Ostrow, CEO, FitGolf

"Since my business opened almost seven years ago, my biggest source of new clients has been the internet. Tom Young's strategies have taken my web presence to an entirely new level, which has directly improved my bottom line. This book is full of creative, productive, and effective ideas for getting a bigger slice of the internet referral pie."
~ Lisa S. Jenks, MD, Owner and Medical Director,
Genesis MedSpa

"This book gets to the essence of how to win at digital marketing. The book reviews the pros and cons of different approaches and provides an action plan to get it right."
~ Mikki Williams, CSP, CPAE, Vistage Speaker,
Executive Speech Coach

"Here's what I like about this book: It's comprehensive. It works as an outline for thinking through a web strategy. Tom's knowledge of the business shows through. Tom's book is a comprehensive overview of all the steps required to build a successful website strategy."

~ Lisa Rogge, Vistage Chair

"This is a great book. It helped to read about the Four-Step Process while we are transitioning through it. We have seen excellent results. I highly recommend this book."

~ Jimmy Thompson, CEO, Card Lock Company

"Digital Marketing in the Age of AI" was the answer to our biggest dilemma. We were committed to a traditional marketing strategy that left our company void of sales and an empty pipeline. The changes that seemed obvious were not easily embraced, leaving our company at a standstill. When we implemented the Four Steps, calls started coming in from an unlikely source…our once dormant, newly revitalized website. Thank you for the directional change and this book that has changed our business."

~ Steve Fleming, CEO, Alpine Technology Corporation

"This book helped us understand what really mattered to our website users. The importance of giving your users what they want instead of what you think is best for them cannot be overstated. We all want the fanciest website with the most information about us or our companies, but in some cases that could drive your users away. Tom's book really helped Vistage develop a clear strategy for addressing our user base and put us on the path to developing our most successful website yet."

~ Andy Ramirez, Vice President of Digital Products,
Vistage International

"Thomas Young knows websites better than anyone I know. He has honed his craft of developing, analyzing, and refining websites and online marketing for so many years that his book is only a fraction of what he could share, given enough time and space. Tom brings to this eminently practical book a perspective that goes beyond mere layout and design to understanding the basics of how humans use this highly evolving medium and what it takes to analyze and refine what we throw out there so that it keeps up with real people's interests. Use Tom's book as your guide to this changing world."

~ Kent Wilson, Vistage Chair

"As a small business that began in the heart of a recession, digital marketing was an overwhelming necessity for our company. We followed Tom's Four-Step Process and saw results firsthand. This book was THE cornerstone of our online success, without a doubt.

~ Travis Turner, Broker/Owner, Turner Associates

"We are all about systems at our company. I appreciated Tom's Four-Step Process and detailed information to help us capitalize on our internet marketing efforts. The key business points and Action Items for business leaders will help us focus on the right areas for success. I'm excited to start implementing these strategies today to help us rise above the competition."

~ Lain Chappell, CGB, CGR, CAPS, President,
Solid Rock Custom Homes

Table of Contents

Dedication

This book is the result of more than 25 years of work in digital marketing. It wouldn't have been possible without the support and teamwork from my team at Intuitive Websites. A special shout out to Adrian Collins, our Creative Director, and Kerianne Leffew, both valuable members of our leadership team.

A special thanks to the Vistage organization and the support from many Vistage Chairs and members over the years. A big thanks to the team at Chief Outsiders for their support. I have great appreciation for the many clients of Intuitive Websites and the trust they place in me and our team. I'm grateful for the many lessons learned from each project.

I would like to dedicate this book to my two sons, Bryce and Blake, to my mother, Gloria, and to Lori, my wife, for her patience and support on this journey.

Foreword

Artificial Intelligence (AI) has been around for more than a decade, regulating traffic lights, removing "red eye" from photos, and even reading X-rays. But the "large language model" engines take it to another level. You can write an essay, or a song, or even create art in seconds by typing a few words into a prompt box.

The impact it's having on marketing, and digital marketing in particular, is hard to overstate. It's like having all the best consultants from McKinsey, Bain, and Deloitte on retainer. Ask them anything.

AI can identify your best customers, tell you what and why they buy, and how to find them. It can write a sales script, build a pitch deck, and articulate customer benefits you've never thought about. It can analyze the reputation of your company and your competitors and show you how to win.

Of course, digital marketing is more than just an e-mail list. B-to-B buyers want to do business with trusted advisers, so you have to deliver useful content, to an engaged audience, on a regular cadence. You've built a website, a YouTube channel, a Facebook following, accounts on X, Instagram and LinkedIn, a newsletter, a blog AND a podcast. And I'm guessing it's not working. It's costing a bundle, and you can't track the ROI.

AI can simplify and streamline all of that while delivering immediate, measurable results.

You may be wondering, "Is AI going to take my job?"

No. People who know how to *use* AI are going to take your job.

This book will show you how.

~ Orvel Ray Wilson, CSP. Co-author of *Guerrilla Selling*

Introduction

This is not your typical AI book. Nor is it your typical digital marketing book. While others talk in broad terms about AI and digital marketing, this book is grounded in what works, with very clear and specific recommendations on how to use AI to improve your marketing today.

This book gets to what matters in AI for marketing and how to actually use it.

This book is a comprehensive approach to what works in digital marketing. I'm not going to write about how AI works; I'm going to show you **how to use AI to grow your company's sales**. The book gives you a tested Four-Step Process grounded in strategy, content, marketing and ROI. Thanks to this Four-Step Process, the book is comprehensive but not overwhelming.

This work draws from over 25 years of digital marketing experience with more than 1,000 companies. You'll find dozens of action items ready to implement at your company. These are specific things you can do *today* to drive results.

Your awareness of these strategies, tools and tactics will give you an advantage over competitors and help you perform at high levels.

Thanks for letting me join you on your digital marketing journey and get ready to take your results to the next level.

My Story...

Growing up, I loved sports and was always competitive by nature. In high school and college, I was the captain of the swim team and a national qualifier. After I graduated and started in business, I realized an MBA would be a great next step and found myself leading sales and marketing teams in my early 30s. I loved the competitive nature of sales and marketing and how you set goals and get wins like a competitive athlete.

In the late 90s, just as the Internet was growing in popularity, I started a sales and marketing consulting business. One of my early projects was a user testing program for IntraWest Resorts. For two years I traveled around the US and Canada testing how people use websites to book ski vacations. This was an eye-opening experience as I learned firsthand what people want from websites and digital marketing.

During user sessions, it was common to hear people say they wished websites were more "intuitive." In 2004, I launched our agency, Intuitive Websites, with the primary goal of helping companies build great websites that were intuitive for visitors to use and met their needs.

Twenty years later, Intuitive Websites is going strong.

With the emergence of AI, our clients have the opportunity to take their websites and digital marketing to a new level. That's why this book is so important. AI is a game changer for sales and marketing teams, and this book will be your guide.

ChatGPT is Dumber Than it Looks

That's not true for a screwdriver.

Or a table saw or even a spatula.

These are useful tools, but they don't pretend to be well-informed or wise. They're dumb, and they look dumb too.

That's one reason that tools are effective. We use them to leverage our effort, but we don't trust them to do things that they're not good at.

The reason AI language models are dumb is that they don't actually know anything; the model is simply calculating probabilities. Not about the unknown but about *everything*. Each word, each sentence, is a statistical guess.

I've switched mostly to claude.ai because it's more effective and less arrogant, but it's still guessing.

If a guess is good enough, you're set. If it's not, plan accordingly.

In my experience, the most useful approaches to AI are:

Ask clearly bounded questions, where you can easily inspect the results.

Don't let AI make decisions for you. Instead, challenge it to broaden your options.

Take advantage of the fact that it doesn't have feelings and use its honesty to get useful feedback.

Don't ignore AI because it's dumb. Figure out how to create patterns and processes where you can use it as the useful tool it's becoming.

~ Seth Goden

CHAPTER 1:
Why This Book is Needed

Digital marketing is at the core of marketing. Companies that do digital marketing grow faster than those that don't, and those who do it well will thrive.

Digital marketing comprises many things: websites, SEO, YouTube channels, LinkedIn profiles, email marketing, marketing automation, social media and more. Digital marketing works best when you have a plan and a process.

In the age of AI, digital marketers must embrace technology to take things to a new and higher level. This book will help you get there. We will keep our focus on how to use AI to supercharge your marketing and grow your business around a proven Four-Step Process.

AI Has Changed Digital Marketing

I'll start with a confession. Parts of this book were written with AI. Can you guess which parts? Probably not, because ultimately, a human pulls it all together to produce a finished product.

This book will lay out a plan for incorporating AI into each part of your Four-Step Process for digital marketing success. AI works best when it merges seamlessly into what you're already doing well, and each of the Four Steps reviewed in this book can be enhanced using AI.

AI is an incredible tool for generating content, analyzing data, writing website code, conducting marketing research, market planning, persona development and so much more.

Marketing teams who are not using AI are at a serious disadvantage and will lose market share to competitors who are. You must have a plan for incorporating AI into your digital marketing or miss huge opportunities for growth.

AI Enhances What You Already Do Well

By far the greatest advantage of AI is that it enhances what you already do well. It's not a magic bullet, but there's a major advantage to moving faster and improving how you do your job, no matter what your role in marketing. At the same time, AI in the hands of an amateur can spell disaster!

Use the concepts in this book as guidelines for how you use AI to get results. One of the primary uses of AI will be to generate first-draft content. This is content that, once reviewed by a human, can be used to share your thought leadership with the world. You will also learn to use AI to better understand your target customers to better meet their needs.

AI is Timeless

The goal of this book is to give you timeless AI strategies that will work for years to come, no matter what the latest AI app or tool can do. We do make some assumptions about the future of AI based on what it's doing today and suggest ways to supercharge digital marketing using the current AI tools and those to come.

AI in Marketing is Storytelling

Marketing is about connecting with your prospective customer where they are in their life story. AI helps you create and support that story.

AI tools have gotten a bit of a bad rap when it comes to information, data, and history. If you go to Microsoft's ChatGPT and try to create a history of something that happened, you can get what they call *hallucinations,* where the AI will actually *make up a story that did not happen.* There was an embarrassing example of a law firm submitting their defense argument to ChatGPT and asking it to list the applicable cases. It soon became apparent that all of the citations were fake. Sometimes AI can be so eager to answer your question that it just makes stuff up. In this case, the judge gave the attorney a stiff reprimand and a $5,000 fine.

We've seen it happen. And when you correct it, it doesn't go back and say, "Sorry, I got my facts wrong." It just goes back and changes the story. This has resulted in many people being turned away from the real power of AI, which is the use of storytelling in marketing.

Don't let an early bad experience with AI put you off using it. Marketing is not about communicating facts, information or history. Marketing is about connecting with people so they have an emotional response and purchase from you. It's about people connecting with you as a guide or a resource in their lives. And this is where AI is fantastic because it's a great tool for storytelling. It creates a story around your marketing and your brand. Even asking AI the simple question, "What are the benefits of buying from my company?" can yield fantastic results.

It's creating a story; yes, it's making stuff up, and that's what it's really good at. It can actually help you with your digital marketing by making stuff up! In fact, that's what we do when we market our business, we make stuff up. We make up our business and hope what we make up has value for people who want to buy from us.

There are many aspects of business where AI is not going to help, but it will certainly help you in marketing because AI is about putting words together that communicate a story, and that's what we must do in marketing. Microsoft's ChatGPT and Google's Gemini have proven to be fantastic marketing tools to support the storytelling process.

What is AI and How Does it Work?

AI is like spell check on steroids. It predicts the word that comes next, just like spell checkers can go into a database and find the correct spelling of a word, and grammar checkers can help you figure out the order of words in a sentence, or auto complete can suggest the next word in your text message. AI has taken this to a whole new level.

This is fantastic for marketing professionals because it creates story-based copy. You want to use stories to connect with your customers, and you want to connect with customers where they are in their life story.

It's even surprising the engineers who are creating these large language models. The AI is learning because it can take all the combinations of words and sentences and see the patterns in how people use them. Every day, these AI tools become better marketing tools for your company.

AI's Been Around for a While

The dream of intelligent machines dates back centuries, but the term "Artificial Intelligence" emerged in 1956. Pioneering figures like Alan Turing laid the groundwork with theoretical models, while others, like Warren McCulloch, explored the brain's electrical processes. Early research focused on replicating human reasoning and problem-solving, leading to machines that could play checkers or chess. Advancements in computing power and algorithms have accelerated the development of more and more powerful tools. When ChatGPT was released in November 2022, it became the *fastest-growing consumer software application in history*.

And it's Everywhere

The past decade has witnessed a surge in AI applications, weaving themselves into the fabric of our daily lives:

Personalization: AI algorithms power recommendation systems on streaming services, e-commerce platforms and social media, suggesting content, products and connections tailored to individual preferences.

Smart Assistants: Virtual assistants like Siri, Alexa and Google Assistant leverage AI for voice recognition, natural language processing and task automation, offering hands-free control over various aspects of our digital lives.

Image and Speech Recognition: AI advancements have revolutionized how we interact with devices. Facial recognition unlocks smartphones, while speech recognition powers voice search, voice commands for smart devices and real-time translation tools.

Content Creation: AI is assisting in creative endeavors like generating marketing copy, composing music and even writing different creative text formats.

Cybersecurity: AI is employed to detect and prevent cyberattacks, analyze security threats and identify suspicious activities in real-time, protecting individuals and organizations.

Predictive Analytics: AI algorithms analyze vast datasets to predict future trends, customer behavior and potential risks, enabling informed decision-making in various sectors.

Robotics and Automation: AI is driving advancements in robotics, enabling automation in diverse fields like manufacturing, logistics and healthcare, with robots performing tasks with increased precision and efficiency.

Financial Services: AI powers fraud detection in financial transactions, personalized financial advice and algorithmic trading, transforming how we manage our finances.

Healthcare: AI is making inroads in medical diagnosis, drug discovery and personalized treatment plans, assisting healthcare professionals in improving patient care and outcomes.

Self-Driving Cars: While still under development, self-driving cars use AI for perception, navigation and decision-making, paving the way for a future of autonomous transportation.

These are just a few examples, and the list continues to grow as AI continues to evolve and permeate various aspects of our lives.

AI's Learning and it's Getting Better

ChatGPT developed a bad reputation at first because of its tendency to "hallucinate." It was so eager to provide a response to the prompt that it would fabricate stories, facts and even legal precedents, causing problems for some early adaptors. If you've had one of these experiences, don't let it dissuade you.

Every year, AI produces better content, gives us better information and tells better stories. Where it gets a bit confused at times is when we have to know the difference between a story and the facts, so for now, AI is more about a conversation.

Think of AI as your own personal consultant, helping you do what you do well even better. In fact, when thinking about the questions and comments you put into the AI chat prompt, think about how you might have a conversation with a consultant.

The Current State of AI

As of this writing, AI is in the exploration and discovery phase. As with personal computers in the 70s, we're still in the very early stages of learning what AI can do. But just like the Internet and mobile phones, AI will be a mainstay. In the next 10 to 20 years, we'll just rely on AI to do more and more things for us, and it'll be an excellent tool.

It's going to change consumer behavior and then it's going to make our lives easier. That's what all technology ultimately does. If technology is challenging and confusing, we ignore it. We just don't use it. We leave that for the techy folks. But when it makes our lives easier, we embrace it.

And this is how AI is changing our everyday life. When technology can predict what the local weather's going to be and adjust your thermostat accordingly based on your preferences, you're going to love that. When the map in your car can take you to the destination that it knows you're going to because you've been there before, and it's in your calendar, then you're going to love AI.

It's also going to help you better understand the needs of your customers and then present those customers with content that meets their needs and promotes your products and services. It will do this in a way that creates engagement: helping potential customers learn more about your brand, talking to them about your products and services and assisting them with making online purchases, scheduling appointments with sales teams, submitting forms, and subscribing to email newsletters. It will be doing things that grow your business.

The rise of AI automation is driving how fast marketers can move. Not only can you meet the needs of users, but you can also move quickly to meet those needs. It no longer takes days to write a blog post. It doesn't take weeks to write eBooks; you can crank those out in hours. AI will make sure the content you write really meets user needs.

AI is Changing Everything

You either use AI chat tools or you don't; chances are you're using it already and don't even know it.

AI has been impacting technology advancements for over a decade. It's baked into your web browser, your tablet, your TV and the apps you download. It's the "smart" in your smart phone. It drives manufacturing systems, fast fashion design, and even self-driving cars. AI will soon be part of every household appliance in your home.

The focus of this book is on the use of AI in marketing. And boy, is it changing marketing! Still, a common mistake in marketing is failure to do marketing! It's amazing how often we hear from companies that tell us they don't do *any* marketing. We recently launched a new project for a company called Bulldog Bags. They're a $50 million manufacturer of paper and plastic bags, the sort you use all the time. They produce packaging for everything from birdseed to dog food to carrying home the groceries.

Bulldog grew their business from a start-up selling mattress bags to more than $50M in annual sales through a great reputation and personal selling. They recently opened a new production facility, then realized, "What's going on here? Things have really slowed down. We're not getting the leads we used to. We're not closing new business. We want to be a $100 million company, but how are we going to get there if we don't have new leads?"

Well, now they've started doing digital marketing, and we're using AI to supercharge their ability to move fast, get a marketing plan executed and get their new website launched.

It's not optional because those who do not actively embrace AI are going to be left behind. Your competitors are going to leap ahead, and you won't even know why because people search anonymously. You'll notice you're getting less traffic, fewer leads, and less engagement on your website. That lost traffic is going over to your competitors who are leveraging digital marketing and AI tools like ChatGPT and Gemini.

A lack of digital marketing knowledge is not an excuse, and the same goes for AI. Not having a login to the latest version of ChatGPT or Gemini doesn't give you a free pass. There's no excuse for not getting out there and learning how to use AI.

Get Started with AI in Your Marketing

AI is shaking things up, and for good reason! Companies that embrace AI are reaping a variety of benefits, putting them ahead of the curve in an increasingly competitive landscape. Here are some key advantages of AI in digital marketing:

Persona Development

AI can be used to create detailed and highly accurate personas of your target customers. You can also use AI to find where these personas research online and determine what they want to read. You can use these personas to highly personalize your content to meet their needs and drive movement in your sales funnel.

Benefits and Risks

AI can help you create checklists of the benefits most important to the personas you are targeting in your marketing. It can also help you understand the risks they are taking by buying from your company.

Data Analysis and Insights

AI excels at analyzing vast amounts of data quickly and efficiently, uncovering hidden patterns that humans might miss. This can provide valuable insights into your customers' behavior, preferences and trends. AI can analyze past purchase history and website interactions to predict what customers are likely to want or need next. This enables you to proactively make personalized recommendations and offers, boosting engagement and closing sales. Predictive modeling helps you forecast future trends and customer behavior, enabling more informed decision-making.

Personalization

AI algorithms can analyze visitors' behavior and preferences to deliver personalized content, recommendations, and ads, increasing engagement and conversion. It even allows the creation of dynamic content that adapts to user interactions, ensuring a more personalized and relevant experience. Content your personas want to read in their buying journey.

Chatbots and Virtual Assistants

AI-powered chatbots, like Microsoft Copilot, can provide instant and round-the-clock customer support, answering queries, resolving issues and guiding users through the sales funnel. Chatbots can enhance the user experience by providing interactive and conversational interactions, product recommendations or technical support, reducing friction and making the customer journey more seamless.

Customer Segmentation

AI can dynamically segment audiences based on various criteria like company size, job title or last date active, allowing for more precise targeting. It can be used to get inside the minds of your customers by speaking to them in the language they understand.

Ad Campaign Optimization

AI can optimize advertising budgets by analyzing data in real time, ensuring that ads are delivered to the most relevant and high-converting audiences. AI algorithms can dynamically adjust bidding strategies to maximize the impact of advertising campaigns.

Email Optimization

AI can analyze user behavior to send personalized emails that speak to specific interests, improving open and conversion rates. Smart CRM products like HubSpot can deliver email sequences based on user interactions, streamlining communication. You might use this to confirm delivery of your product, then ask for a review, or remind customers when they're ready to re-order.

Content Creation and Curating

AI tools can assist in content creation, generating first-draft text, images or even videos so your content team can produce more content. They can get better ideas for articles and blogs. They can optimize content for SEO. They can have their content proofread. They can keep the voice of their content consistent. AI can even analyze user preferences, then recommend relevant content, improving user engagement.

Create Content by Channel

Digital content takes many forms, and AI can adapt your content for websites, blogs, social media, emails, eBooks, webinars, YouTube videos and more.

Enhanced Security

AI can help identify and block fraudulent activities in digital marketing, protecting both your company and your customers from potential threats.

Generate and Code New Tools

AI can write the software you need to create unique features within your website, like an estimator tool, ROI calculator, interactive submission forms and more.

Accelerate Teamwork

Ultimately, every company needs to execute with a team. That team needs the tools to execute, and AI is one of the best tools for enhancing what you already do well and supercharging it so you get much stronger performance from your marketing team.

The uses of AI in marketing are only limited by your imagination.

Build a Team, Make a Plan, and Beat Competitors

Marketing leaders are fighting several battles when launching and managing a winning digital marketing program. They're fighting on two fronts. The first is outperforming their competition, and the second is developing an effective digital marketing team. This book will show you how to win both those challenges and use AI to supercharge your efforts.

This book is not necessarily written for digital marketing professionals, although they'll get tremendous value. It's written for business owners or key managers who are leading digital marketing efforts for their companies but are *not* going to handle design or technology issues directly. Their job is to make sure that digital marketing delivers results. They must also provide direction to a team of experts who will be doing the work by following a strategic digital marketing plan. This book is a starting point for those efforts and presents a proven process for getting results from your website and your digital marketing.

The book is for leaders at all levels interested in gaining a comprehensive understanding of how to generate leads and grow sales through digital marketing. It's not a technical book but rather a strategic book that helps you ask the right questions and set a strategic groundwork for digital marketing success. The right strategy wins in digital marketing and gets you found and heard above the noise.

This book is important because many business leaders turn over strategic digital marketing decisions to team members without taking time to learn the fundamentals of digital marketing. Those fundamentals are necessary to set direction for this work and to drive results. They're also needed so business leaders can write a digital marketing plan and set the right priorities.

A Proven Process Gets Results

Smart business leaders and managers know that companies with excellent processes get better results. Yet, most companies fail to follow a proven system for digital marketing. They often take advice from people who are not thinking strategically about their business, which leads to poor results. It's also common for digital marketing teams to just wing it or to guess at what users want.

This book lays out a proven Four-Step Process for getting results from your digital marketing efforts:

Step 1: Digital Strategy

Step 2: Strategic Communication

Step 3: Inbound Marketing

Step 4: Conversions and ROI

Each Section of this book will explore each of these steps in detail.

The Internet and your company website are critically important resources that can drive success or failure for organizations looking to increase sales, get more leads and retain customers and clients. That's why a strategic process is critical to success, and just "winging it" will not bring adequate returns on your time and money.

Use the Four-Step Process

AI tools greatly improve the effectiveness of these Four Steps

Each step of the process can be measured for specific ROI, probably better than any other sales or marketing effort performed at your company. You will learn how to prioritize and assign digital marketing tasks best suited for driving results for each of the Four Steps.

The only factors that may create resistance to your achieving your goals will be market forces outside of your control and the motivation of the people executing the work. That's not to say you won't have roadblocks along the way, but this book will help you cover the fundamentals and help you rest assured that you're doing the right things to grow your business.

Making the Complex Simple

This book will simplify what can be complex and overwhelming for many people. The Four-Step Process breaks down digital marketing into simple and clear sections to help the business leader develop action plans and assign tasks to the right people. This assures the work gets done and that you see results.

People often feel overwhelmed by digital marketing, and having the Four-Step roadmap makes the complex simple. AI can help as well. In fact, you can go to the AI tools and ask, "How do I take this complex thing and make it simple?"

While the focus of this book is primarily on your website, it takes a comprehensive approach, including social media and other digital channels that contain content about your business. The book uses the term "digital marketing" to refer to this approach across multiple channels.

The chapters in this book can stand alone, but they're best taken together for a thorough and comprehensive experience. Too often, business leaders focus on only one part of digital marketing and miss the big picture when it's *the comprehensive approach that drives the greatest return*. For example, just being found on the first page of a Google search is not, by itself, a winning strategy. SEO is only one part of driving growth and must be supported with excellent execution, great content, landing pages that convert, data tracking and more.

Simplifying the world of digital marketing into Four Steps will help you understand the big picture. This book is your blueprint for a digital marketing plan that drives results with the support of AI.

AI is the Future of Marketing

At a recent talk to a group of CEOs, I reviewed the website for Keystone Natural Family Medicine, a natural healthcare clinic based in Arizona. The key message for the clinic's website was, "No Insurance, No Problem!" I asked the question, "Is this *really* the most important concern for your prospective patient? Perhaps getting and staying *healthy* might be a stronger concern?"

I opened up ChatGPT and asked about the benefits people want from a natural health clinic that does not take insurance. The list of benefits it generated was extensive and had *nothing* to do with the clinic accepting health insurance. These are the benefits they must feature on the homepage to connect with prospective patients.

Here are the benefits as listed by ChatGPT:

- **Personalized Care**: Such providers often spend more time with their patients compared to traditional medical practices. This allows for a more personalized approach to healthcare, focusing on the patient's individual needs and lifestyle.
- **Holistic Approach**: Natural medicine providers typically focus on treating the whole person rather than just the symptoms. This holistic approach can lead to better long-term health outcomes by addressing the root causes of health issues.
- **Alternative Treatments**: They often offer alternative treatments that may not be available in conventional medicine. This can be particularly beneficial for patients seeking non-traditional or less invasive treatment options.
- **Preventive Care Focus**: Natural medicine providers often emphasize preventive care, helping patients maintain good health and potentially avoid more serious health issues in the future.
- **No Insurance Limitations**: By not dealing with insurance, the provider may have more freedom in the types of treatments they can offer, as they are not restricted by insurance policies or protocols.

- **Direct Patient-Provider Relationship**: The absence of insurance can simplify the relationship between the patient and provider, often resulting in more transparent pricing and avoiding the complexities of insurance billing.
- **Emphasis on Lifestyle and Nutrition**: Natural medicine providers often place a significant emphasis on diet, exercise, and lifestyle changes as integral components of treatment, which can lead to improved overall well-being.

I then asked ChatGPT, "What would *motivate* a person to seek treatment from a natural medicine clinic that does not accept insurance to pay for treatments?"

Here is the response:

- **Dissatisfaction with Conventional Medicine:** Some individuals may not find relief or satisfactory results with conventional medical treatments and thus turn to natural medicine for alternative solutions.
- **Preference for Holistic Approach:** Many people prefer a holistic approach to health, focusing on the whole person (mind, body, and spirit), which is often a key aspect of natural medicine.
- **Interest in Preventative Care:** Natural medicine often emphasizes preventative care and lifestyle changes, which can appeal to those looking to maintain or improve their health proactively.
- **Desire for Personalized Care:** Natural medicine clinics often provide more personalized care, spending more time with patients and tailoring treatments to individual needs and preferences.
- **Belief in Natural Remedies**: Some individuals have a strong belief in the efficacy and safety of natural remedies and treatments compared to pharmaceuticals and conventional treatments.

- **Chronic Health Conditions:** Patients with chronic conditions that haven't responded well to traditional treatments may seek alternative options in natural medicine.
- **Recommendations and Research:** Personal recommendations, along with independent research, can lead individuals to explore natural medicine as a viable treatment option.
- **Limited Side Effects:** Natural treatments are often perceived as having fewer side effects compared to conventional medical treatments, which can be a significant motivator.

Amazing! This is how the clinic can use AI to better connect with prospective patients. These are the messages that the clinic must communicate on their homepage.

AI and Ethics

There have been some questions about the ethical use of AI in marketing. And at this point, AI has no role in marketing without a human driving the success.

If you're just cutting and pasting and putting out content generated by AI, then I don't think you're being completely ethical and you may be hurting your company. You're not doing your brand justice. Most readers can tell. There are AI tools that will detect an AI fake, and there are AI tools that promise to turn AI text into undetectably human style. There are even AI trolls continuously scanning the Internet for copyright infringement. Make sure to fact check AI content and use it as a first draft.

The ethical way to use AI is to support what you do well by using it for research, stimulating your thinking, and generating *first-draft content.*

This book will prepare you for what AI is going to do in marketing and how it will make companies more competitive. It's going to give you a framework so you can use AI tools to improve what you already do well, build an AI-focused marketing team and supercharge your business.

AI Applications in Digital Marketing

We're going to show you how AI tools can be used in each of those Four Steps to supercharge your marketing. You want to ease into using AI by building it into your Digital Marketing Plan.

If you do that, then AI will be able to help you in so many ways.

Digital Marketing Starts with Awareness

The strategies and action items in this book will help you grow sales.

Digital marketing requires a team, and the techniques in this book will be applied by a mix of professionals, from content writers to graphic designers, marketing specialists, SEO experts and more.

Awareness drives growth because you will move your team to ask the right questions and get results. You may find it impossible to track exactly where the growth comes from because many factors work together to drive results. This includes improved website data, a website that's engaging and easier to use and effective digital content. This book will show you how to bring together these strategies to drive results, win against competitors, and find talent. You'll find ways to grow your business from strategic, well-planned, and well-executed digital marketing.

Here are a few things you can expect:

- Specific action items to generate leads and get new sales from digital marketing.
- The tools to implement the Four-Step Process for driving digital marketing results.
- How to measure those results and determine return on investment.
- Ways to leverage AI to supercharge your digital marketing.
- How to build a digital marketing team to develop and implement tactics.

Awareness Comes from Questions

Smart business leaders must ask the right questions. Those questions move your team to action and toward your intended marketing outcomes. If you're looking at data, you already have some insights into digital marketing, and you're asking questions of your team. That keeps you aware, and unless you have that awareness, you're not going to move anyone to action. You'll keep doing the same things you've been doing.

Go look at your website (many CEOs and business leaders don't even look at their websites) and then go to your team and say, "Hey, I have a few questions about our website data and I want to start moving strategically toward improvement."

Here are a few of the right questions to ask:

- How do we increase company sales with digital marketing?
- What are our digital marketing priorities? How do we use AI to move fast and get results?
- Digital marketing feels overwhelming. How do we simplify our work?
- How do we prepare an effective digital marketing plan?
- Who is going to do this work, and how do we build a team to get this work done?
- Who is going to write content for our website?
- How do we track our return on time and money spent on digital marketing?
- How do I know which strategy for online marketing will work the best?
- How do we measure success?
- How do we get found on Google and other search engines?
- How can we get inside the head of our website visitors to better meet their needs?
- Is there a process to get results that has worked well for others?
- How do we leverage AI in our marketing to get measurable results?

Develop an Action Plan

The recommendations in this book come from more than 25 years of marketing experience, and it would be a waste of time if you didn't translate them into action. Most chapters include a list of action items you can complete as part of your digital marketing plan, which can then be delegated to your team. The book also includes a list of resources and digital marketing worksheets that can be used to develop action plans that will get results. Your first action item is to read this book and share it with your team!

Your AI Action Plan

As of this writing, the two most important AI tools on the market are Open AI's ChatGPT (supported by Microsoft, a major investor), and Google's competing offering, Gemini. Start by opening accounts with Open AI. You can start using ChatGPT for free, but for a small fee the paid version is a better.

If you have a Gmail address or a Google Workplace account, you can start using Google Gemini right now and also upgrade to a paid version.

Currently, the paid versions of these AIs produce more comprehensive results and are worth the investment.

CHAPTER 2:
Four Steps to
Digital Marketing Success

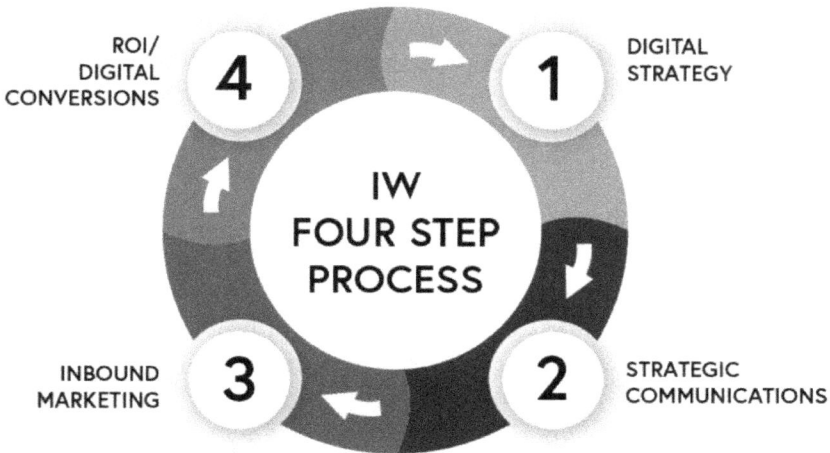

A Process for Results

At the core of this book is a Four-Step Process for digital marketing results. Each of these Four Steps is covered in detail in the following chapters. This is the process business leaders must implement to be successful at digital marketing and cut through the digital noise to get found and get heard:

1. **Digital Strategy**
2. **Strategic Communication**
3. **Inbound Marketing**
4. **Conversions and ROI**

Each step has been developed over the past 25 years and is fundamental to website and digital marketing success. The purpose of the Four Steps is to take the complexity out of marketing, with its many action items and options, and make it simple and easy to follow. These steps form the foundation for how websites get market share and attract visitors that convert to sales. The Four Steps get you found and get you heard.

The Four Steps can also be used as a blueprint for your digital marketing plan. In fact, you'll find that going through the Four-Step Process forces you to consider the focus and strategy of your current business and marketing plans in general. This speaks to the value and comprehensive nature of digital marketing and how important it is to your company. In fact, your company website is like a business plan that's visible to the world!

Before going into greater detail in the coming chapters, here's an overview and brief description of each step.

STEP ONE: Digital Strategy

Digital strategy defines your *translation of value* to your target market and lays out the roadmap for how you're going to reach your marketing and business goals. It sets the direction for all of your website and digital marketing efforts.

It's important to be clear on the website's objectives and how conversions take place online. Digital marketing guru Heather Lutze calls this "The Path to Purchase." Starting with the "Trigger Event," what steps do your customers follow when buying a product like yours? It's best to create a written strategy that clearly defines this path for your marketing team.

Strategy answers the all-important questions about *why* your company is even doing marketing and what you *expect to gain* from those efforts. This digital marketing strategy is spread across all digital marketing channels and may also include offline strategies that coordinate with digital marketing.

MET Printers, a full-service commercial printer based in Vancouver, Canada, executed a winning digital strategy. When MET came to us they had a homepage built around a flashy video with quick edits to communicate their value. Unfortunately, for website visitors, the video gave them a headache and hurt their eyes! The only people happy with the video were the video production company.

We identified that the key value of MET was in their *comprehensive approach* to printing and the high-quality products that showcase their capabilities. We changed out the homepage with new content, images and graphics that communicated their direct value, and within a few days, MET closed a customer order that paid back their investment may times over. When you communicate your value, prospective customers respond.

How to Use AI Tools in Step One - Strategy

AI tools can help you translate value by giving you an understanding of the *benefits* people are looking to get and the risks people face as they're anonymously researching your company online.

You can use AI to identify all the benefits and all the risks of your products and services. AI tools will generate a checklist of benefits and risks for your customers so you know the exact value they're looking to find.

You can then use AI tools to gain a competitive advantage by understanding what your competitors are doing and where they're positioning themselves.

Go to Gemini.Google.com and enter the prompt: "What are the benefits and risks of using [insert your product or service.]" It will highlight things you already know and likely articulate issues you've never considered. AI will ultimately provide a great benefits checklist that drives your strategic value and key marketing messages.

AI can also write a relevant and executable digital marketing plan. This can supercharge your translation of value by gaining a thorough understanding of what your customers really want and why they buy.

STEP TWO: Strategic Communication

Step two is the process of *communicating* to your target market your defined strategy. It's how you translate value. This includes your website, key digital content, taglines, photography, graphics, video and more. This step is the tangible expression of your digital marketing strategy, and it's an area where AI really shines.

AI-generated text can articulate your core message in ways that are short and succinct or deeply detailed, in terms that your customers use and understand. It can suggest topics of interest for newsletters, articles, blogs and videos. It can even create first-draft copy to get your content development team started, and an AI-powered search can help fact-check items before you publish.

How to Use AI Tools in Communicating Your Strategy

Most people hate to write, and even the best writers struggle with first-draft content. AI can create volumes of great first-draft marketing content and is a great tool for writing content for digital marketing. Even though all AI-generated content must be reviewed by a human, it's still one of the biggest advancements in the history of technology. AI solves both these pain points and removes the excuses people have for not writing digital content. Much more to come on this in future chapters.

STEP THREE: Inbound Marketing

Step three comprises all the activities needed to *bring visitors* to your website and to engage them with your brand and your content. This step gets a lot of attention, and many digital marketers put Step Three at the *top* of the list of digital marketing activities. In reality, there is no need to send traffic to a website until your strategy is well-defined and your website is a clear expression of that strategy. This is also important because driving traffic takes time and money. Step Three is not Step One! Get your strategy and your message in order before driving people to your website.

Inbound arketing is about how to find these people, your target market, and how to get your brand found in their research. It's the process of *attracting* people to your brand.

Inbound marketing is supercharged by AI. A common problem we see is "the sample size of one." This happens when people feel like the way *they* use the Internet is how *everybody* uses it, but they don't. People use the Internet in many ways. Not everybody goes to Google to do research. Not everybody's on LinkedIn, and not everybody reads their email. But some people do, right? Some people love LinkedIn, and some people love their email. You have to meet users where they are and not let that sample size of one get in the way. AI is a powerful tool for getting this formula right.

AI is the opposite of a sample size of one. It's the sample size of all human knowledge. All the thoughts that people have recorded, and all the various perspectives represented on the Internet are being digested by AI tools. That's how the language-based model collects information. To really use common sense in marketing, you want to use AI to attract people to your brand.

How to Use AI Tools in Inbound Marketing

From content generation to social calendars to SEO and much more, AI helps lay the groundwork leading to inbound marketing action items that can make a difference in your sales.

STEP FOUR: Conversions and ROI

The final step brings the first three together, and it's the most important. This step involves a process for tracking digital marketing results in your digital stats and then holding meetings to review digital marketing efforts, online conversions and methods for tracking ROI. This step will suggest modifications to the digital marketing strategies and action plans to improve conversions and drive a strong, measurable return. In this step, you set priorities for the team based on clear data and feedback from your target market and current customers.

How to Use AI Tools in Step Four

Conversions and ROI not only happen because you're using AI in the first three steps but also because you can use AI to analyze data. If you have a website that's producing at a sub-optimum level, you can put those notes into the AI tool and ask for recommendations on how to improve. This could be as easy as, "Hey, I've noticed that our website has a high bounce rate," or, "Hey, I've noticed that our website gets a lot of traffic from China but not traffic from the US. How can we fix that?" The AI tools will give you suggestions to make that happen. You still need the team to execute, but the AI tools can help them develop solutions more quickly.

Common Sense is Not So Common

When you first read these Four Steps, you may think they're common sense and that you're following them already. Common sense is not so common in the world of digital marketing.

Most companies do not follow these steps but rather wing it or take direction from a strong personality on their marketing team. This is a major reason why so many websites perform poorly.

In addition, many people get too close to their digital marketing work and use a sample-size-of-one approach that can cause your efforts to miss many of your targeted segments. Just because you prefer how *you* do things online does not mean your target market will do the same.

You must live inside the head of your target audience and understand how they interact with your brand online to truly get digital marketing results.

This is what the best marketers on the planet do.

Follow Each Step in Order

The steps should be followed in order, beginning with Digital Strategy. Many mistakes happen because the steps are not followed properly, such as sending traffic to a website with a poor strategy or having a site that's hard to navigate. Digital marketing begins with setting the proper *strategy* and then *executing* on content that reflects that strategy. After the first two steps are done in order, the focus should be *driving traffic and getting people to read your content*. Step four is the ongoing process of *tracking results* and modifying the strategy to improve.

AI is probably the best tool on the planet right now for delivering targeted digital marketing action items that drive results. AI has this amazing ability to create a checklist. If you have a checklist of excellent digital marketing action items, you have your homework in place and you can get your team moving.

The Four Steps Drive Action Items

In this book, you will gain a deep understanding of each of these Four Steps, along with specific action items. These can be delegated to team members for implementation. In fact, you will even learn how to build a team that will act in each area. This is often a challenge because of the various skill sets that digital marketing requires. The solution is to follow the action items within each step and let the process drive the ongoing work.

Take a closer look at the Four-Step Process and commit each step to memory so you can get digital marketing wins and grow your business.

These steps work, as R&B Wire Products learned firsthand.

R&B Wire Products

R&B Wire Products is a leading manufacturer of industrial laundry carts. Their digital marketing strategy prior to implementing the Four-Step Process was to have a basic website with a few key products.

"We never thought our website could produce sales at a level worth the investment we would have to make to build a new e-commerce website. Most of our sales come from our distributor network, and we didn't think customers would want to buy at full retail prices when they can purchase our products at 20% less from a distributor," reported Ralph.

As it turns out, customers *will* pay more to buy directly from the manufacturer on a website they trust with full access to all available products. Distributor websites are often poorly developed and hard to use. Also, coding every product for SEO increased traffic by 30% annually, leading to higher sales.

"It is sure nice to see a record sales month, especially after the great year we had last year. This is a very pleasant surprise," said Ralph Moore, R&B's Sales and Marketing Director.

They also tackled a high cart abandonment rate head-on by instituting a cart abandonment email program with excellent results. "If a customer doesn't complete their purchase, we follow up with an email reminding them about the product of interest. Many of these website users come back and buy," said Ralph.

The key to success for R&B was keeping things simple and focusing on the products. As part of their digital strategy, they designed and developed an easy-to-use e-commerce website to target buyers of industrial wire carts and baskets. They also included the full complement of products found nowhere else on the Internet. R&B allowed website visitors to buy without a login and included all of their products *with their accessories*. Up-selling accessories and using shipping incentives to improve conversion rates also helped increase their sales.

Hundreds of products were coded to get found for key industry search terms. By coding every product page for SEO, they achieved a page-one ranking in Google for such searches.

They scheduled monthly meetings to analyze sales data and make changes as needed. A follow-up on all visitors who abandoned their shopping carts with a personalized email and description of the products left in their carts was critical to this success.

Consistent annual increases in sales and website traffic built the brand and helped grow the company on and off the Internet with multiple months of record-breaking sales.

STEP 1: DIGITAL STRATEGY

CHAPTER 3:
Digital Strategy

The Translation of Value

Volumes have been written on business and marketing strategy. It's not the goal of this book to discuss the details of how to develop a business strategy or marketing strategy. The focus here is on developing a successful digital *marketing strategy* that either involves a *translation* of your current business success to digital marketing or a *new* digital marketing strategy to grow sales.

Setting a digital strategy helps you clarify and understand how digital marketing can be used to market your business better and increase sales. Also, it's very difficult to lead the implementation of a digital strategy without understanding the fundamentals of digital marketing. Here are a few of the first steps you can take to develop or fine-tune your digital marketing strategy.

Translate Current Business and Marketing Plans

Most successful businesses have a strong business plan that drives their success. Within this plan will be a sales and marketing plan to drive revenues. The best way to execute a strong digital marketing strategy is to *translate what works well* in your current offline marketing plan to online efforts. Your current marketing plan is the starting point for your digital marketing strategy, along with an understanding of what's worked offline in the past.

Many businesses have a hard time with this translation. The key is simplifying what works into a few powerful taglines for your website's homepage and navigation. This will be discussed in more depth, and it's the process of defining what you do really well, then translating that to your website content.

AI and the Translation of Value

Your strategy is the *translation of value*, telling the world the benefits you're going to provide them and the kind of great work or service or product you sell.

AI supports the translation of value by helping you *understand your benefits*.

Many companies are so close to their services or products that it's hard to see their company through the eyes of customers. They don't really understand the benefits people pursue from their company and the benefits they should emphasize.

AI tools today can help you *generate a list of those benefits.* And what's fascinating is every time I use ChatGPT to research benefits, the list gets better. ChatGPT is learning how to improve upon very focused benefits no matter what industry or marketplace you're in. We use AI to understand benefits because those benefits are the translation of value.

Think of it like this. AI will create a comprehensive *checklist of benefits* so the benefits you think are important can be supplemented by what AI thinks. It will be challenging to come up with a *complete* list on your own

Of course, the best way *to confirm your benefits is by talking to your customers* and asking them for feedback about why they buy from you. I recommend you limit this discussion to the *three key benefits* that you focus on in your homepage and key website landing pages.

What do people have to *risk,* either if they make the wrong decision when buying or if they make **no** decision? There are risks to both. AI can help you understand risks because, in addition to key benefits, you also want to talk about the risks of taking the wrong action or taking *no* action.

AI is here to support you by getting your arms around what your future customers think is truly valuable.

Pillars of Thought Leadership

Digital marketing success is driven by content, and at the core of your content must be your pillars of thought leadership. *Thought leadership comprises key areas of business knowledge your company knows better than anyone.* It's what you do very well and the things you know that set you apart from your competitors.

You don't have to be better; you must be different. These pillars of thought leadership attract customers to your company and are a key expression in the translation of value. Your thought leadership is how you translate value around benefits and risks. AI can help you write the pillars of thought leadership and content based on these pillars.

Digital Marketing Plan

Writing a digital marketing plan is an important step toward developing a winning digital marketing strategy. It may be necessary to begin writing the plan based on the Four Steps and watch the strategy evolve as you work through the plan's details. There's great benefit in writing down your strategy because even a one-page written plan is better than no plan at all. AI can actually prepare digital marketing action plans. We're going to dive deeper into this in Chapter 11.

Your digital marketing plan defines the strategy and the key action steps needed to make that strategy a reality. Even a one-page plan is better than nothing! Include a digital marketing plan in your overall business and marketing plans. Use the outline in the Appendix to write your internet marketing plan and set direction for the digital marketing team.

Inside the Head of Website Users

The starting point for developing a digital marketing strategy is understanding what people want from your online presence and how to meet those needs. The better you understand the needs of the website users, the better you can set a strategy that works. Website users are looking for ease of use, simplicity, and convenience. They are looking to avoid pain, have fun, and reduce the risks of making a bad decision.

Your website is a representation of your business. Your website users will have high expectations for your website, just as you do for the sites you visit. Take time to think about *why* you use digital content and take time to get inside the head of your website users. This understanding plays a key role in setting your digital marketing strategy and in using feedback from your visitors to modify that strategy.

Go ask a dozen of your best customers this question, "Why do you buy from us?" Use those answers to form the basis for understanding your translation of value. AI helps us get inside the head of website users by creating personas. And we're going to talk more about personas as well coming up.

Research Competitors

The Internet makes the strategies of your competitors fairly transparent. You can see what your competitors are doing and review their websites across industries. As you do this, you'll find best practices, along with many worst practices. Take those best practices and modify them to improve your own. In fact, you should research websites across market segments and consider indirect competitors as well. The most successful websites apply the best online practices, and so they lead the field. Be cautious of copying websites with a very strong brand because they often play by a different set of rules.

Competitive analysis is very important in the early stages. Take time to review other websites and include your observations in your digital marketing plan. Once you start using AI to generate these lists of benefits and build your personas, it really brings clarity to how you research competitors.

Your challenge is to have the best website in your marketplace based on the content that translates value for users.

Research Keywords

Keyword research is the process of determining the phrases and keywords people type into search engines when looking for your products or services. This is essential to search engine optimization.

However, it's also an excellent research method for testing assumptions and preparing your strategy. Looking at search results in Google and from other search engines is a great way to understand how people use the web in your market segments. You'll find resources for keyword research in later chapters and the Resources section at the end of this book.

You can use AI tools to identify the keywords that people are likely to use to find you. Use a prompt like, "What are the top 10 keywords that people use to find [product] or [company]?" Narrow it further with, "What are the top 10 keywords people use to find [your company name]?"

The Conversion Process

Identifying the behavior of visitors to your website and how they contact your company is also a key to developing and defining your digital strategy and website content. Make a list of how website users will interact or buy from you and ask questions about how and why they take steps toward a purchase. Your conversion rate will only be as good as your digital marketing strategy and the content that moves them to action or deeper into your sales funnel. This is something Turner Associates executed so well to grow their real estate firm and eventually sell to the international firm of Engel & Voelkers.

Turner Associates

Many real estate agents struggle with digital marketing. The best excel in this competitive market. Realtors often turn over digital marketing responsibilities to their broker agency, such as RE/MAX. This often results in a website based on a template and poor-quality digital marketing. You can't blame them—real estate marketing may be the most competitive industry online. One real estate company broke this mold by following the Four-Step Process, and the results speak for themselves.

The company started as a small father-and-son residential real estate company.

"Why not look as big as Zillow in our local markets?" asks Travis Turner, the founder of Turner Associates.

Turner designed their residential real estate website to look as attractive as the best website in the target market, even though it's highly competitive. The website made their company look large and they learned from market leaders. They leveraged their great-looking, professional website to compete on a national level, giving potential clients access to relevant information. This was important because many people moved to Turner's area from military relocation, a business move, or to live in Colorado and enjoy the lifestyle.

Turner downplayed the mass market and instead found their niche in online searches, including marketing to prospective customers moving to their city soon. They did this by generating content for local neighborhoods to capture web searches for those neighborhoods.

Turner designed a website loaded with content about the neighborhoods where their homes are sold. They made it easy to contact the firm and responded immediately to all requests. Turner backed up their digital content with excellent listings on the website and social media. They wrote content about what it's like to work with their experienced team. They used Google Ads campaigns to target people moving to their town and provided free access to all the homes listed in the area. They were always quick to respond to inquiries and build trust with new clients who found them online.

The Turner team experienced a significant increase in clients, home listings, closed home sales and income for the company and its partners. Also, local home buyers and sellers got access to excellent agents they may not have otherwise found. They were able to expand their business into new cities and build a team of realtors throughout the state.

"People want their needs met, and our website does that better than any other local real estate company. People call me directly from the website and are surprised that they're talking to the owner. They love that level of attention, and we respond very quickly to all inquiries," says Travis.

Turner reviewed their website data every month, looking for opportunities to tweak their strategy and make website improvements. The return on their efforts has been phenomenal—they're investing less than $50,000 per year in digital marketing and seeing a six-figure return.

"We did not have huge expectations for digital marketing," Travis says. "We expected a well-designed and easy-to-use website, but the results have exceeded everything we could have hoped for. The website continues to drive new inquiries that convert into customers."

Turner's success secrets include staying disciplined and following the Four Steps. Their strategy utilized a website with a highly professional look that rivals any other real estate website.

"The growth we have seen from our new website has changed our company," says Travis. "It has been the best return of any marketing we have done over the years and is a huge support to our sales process."

While many realtors fear the huge national websites, Turner competes with them head-on. He's not afraid to invest in digital marketing while many of their competitors invest very little.

"We've increased our financial commitment to marketing online significantly, and we're happy to do it because of the results we see," said Travis.

The best news of all is the firm was acquired by a large national firm, providing a nice payday for the owners and allowing them to continue to build on their digital marketing successes.

What You Must Know About Digital Marketing

The first thing you must know about digital marketing is that you are at a significant disadvantage if you don't understand the fundamentals. This is true in all aspects of business. You must be aware. Awareness of your digital marketing will drive growth.

If you're not using AI tools, your competitors will have an advantage. Many people who I've talked to through Vistage signed up for ChatGPT, played around with it a bit, didn't like the results and then dropped it and never went back.

Well, you can't do that. Learn how to use the tools. That's why this book is so important. You want to get this book in the hands of your people *so they can understand how to use AI tools in their digital marketing strategy.*

What business leaders must know about AI in particular is that we're going to use it to discover *benefits*. We're going to use it to understand *risks*. We're going to use it to write *taglines*. We're going to use it to write *first-draft* marketing plans and digital marketing plans. And we're going to use AI to *test assumptions* and *have a marketing conversation.*

Company leadership should ultimately be responsible for digital marketing success because they drive the strategy of the company. They're in the best position to ensure that their strategy is communicated properly online. They must make sure the website does its job as a branding tool and is strategically on target. Leaving these questions in the hands of others can be a recipe for disaster.

These problems occur when business leaders lack the fundamental knowledge needed to drive digital strategy and implementation. Digital marketing ignorance is no longer an excuse for not getting involved in online marketing. Choosing to get involved will lead to a significant competitive advantage for your company. Many of your competitors will not take the time to learn digital marketing fundamentals. This is especially true when it comes to using AI tools. Take advantage of AI now while your competitors miss out or lack the understanding of how to get results using AI.

The Basics of Digital Marketing

It's critical to understand the fundamentals. Here are a few questions you need to be able to answer:

- What are visitors looking to see and read on our website?
- What type of research do we need to conduct to better know our online visitors?
- How does the website brand our company?
- How is Google important to our business?
- Why is Google the most important search engine, and how does it work?
- What are Google Ads, and how do they work?
- What are the keywords people use to find our website?
- How popular and competitive are those keywords?
- How do visitors convert and become customers?
- How can I use website data as a key performance indicator (KPI) for the company?
- What's the best web development platform for our company? Why?
- How can I build a team to get all this work done?
- How do I measure results?
- How can AI tools help us write better digital content?
- How do AI tools help us better understand our target market and develop personas?

All the answers and more will be found in the coming chapters.

Strategy Questions

After you learn more about digital marketing and develop your digital marketing strategies, you can ask the following questions:

- What percentage of total revenue can be generated from the website and digital marketing?
- What is the ROI from digital marketing and the company website?
- How does the website brand the business?
- Are we missing opportunities from digital marketing?

- How can AI be leveraged to drive digital marketing results?

Seven Successful Digital Marketing Strategies

Digital marketing strategies can certainly be unique to each business. One size does not fit all. There are many examples of digital
marketing strategies that have proven successful in driving strong
ROI. Most of these strategies fall into one of the seven areas below
or a combination of these strategies.

Here is an overview of each of the seven strategies for successful
digital marketing. You will learn more in the coming chapters.

1. Branding and building trust in target markets

All websites should do this, and for some websites, this is the primary marketing strategy. Branding is what your website visitors
think about your website and company when they visit the site. It's
the power of the first impression, and it's a strategy in itself. The
importance of online branding and the impact your efforts leave on
visitors should be well-defined in your digital marketing plan and
consistent across all digital marketing channels. Take time now to
write down how you will approach online branding and use what's
worked offline to support this strategy.

You can measure the success of this strategy through increased
website visitors and overall engagement with your company website. Both metrics not only measure the popularity of your brand but
are also leading indicators of growth.

2. Converting website visitors into sales leads

Just about all websites should have a process for converting visitors
into prospective customers. This is a very common strategy and
very important because, in both B2C and B2B markets, most people
research online before buying.

There are several steps needed to develop a website that produces
leads. An online brochure with basic content will *not* convert prospects at an acceptable rate. Also, there's no need to drive traffic to

a content page that lacks a strategy for interaction and a path to purchase. This happens best when the conversion process, your sales funnel, is driven by your overall digital marketing strategy.

Converting website visitors into leads is movement in your sales funnel, which is measured by page visits and key conversion tracking like web form submissions and phone calls. Increasing your conversion rate will grow your sales.

3. Selling products or services directly online

This is straightforward e-commerce. If it's possible to sell products online, then your website should have that ability. You'll be surprised at what people are willing to buy on a website, and don't assume they won't buy your products directly. Selling directly through your website is the ideal online conversion point.

4. Building a competitive advantage

Make sure your website is the best in your marketplace. Look at what others are doing online and do it better. Keep in mind many of the things that make your site valuable are not expensive. Some strategies to improve your website over a competitor's are adding written content, photos that tell your story, and other value-added items that meet the needs of your visitors. Content makes a website valuable, and it's one of your best competitive advantages.

5. Supporting the sales team

Cold calling and other prospecting techniques are more difficult than ever, if not impossible. Salespeople need every advantage they can get to close more sales. A great website that generates leads and provides excellent content is a salesperson's best friend and will grow sales. Website visits can also be used as key benchmarks and steps in the sales process. A website demo of your services and products, a free online audit of a prospective customer's needs, great content and other items can help move prospects more efficiently through your sales process and closer to a sale. Your prospect has many options, and a visit to your website is a key milestone in their buying process.

6. Becoming a content and thought leader

Content will not only set your site apart and generate leads but also position your company as a thought leader in your market. Many executives are pioneers and leaders in their industry, but their websites fail to support those positions. This is often because the site lacks a focused content marketing plan. There are many benefits to the development and placement of excellent online content. Google rewards websites with excellent content and visitors become leads based on the content they see and read online. Content marketing will drive results and deserves your attention.

7. Building a loyal following

The final strategy involves building followers who allow you to connect online with your target market. This includes building an email list, driving followers to your various social media platforms, getting readers to subscribe to your email newsletter and more. Digital marketing is the perfect way to build loyal followers in ways that no other marketing channel can. People can find the companies that suit them best for products, services and information, and companies can easily and very cost-effectively market to these followers. This does not happen by chance. It takes excellent project management and planning to make this work.

8. Bonus Step: Recruiting team members and new employees

What you do well in your digital marketing and how you present your brand to the world also attracts the best employees. Some companies rely too much on LinkedIn, Monster, or other Internet tools and apps to recruit people, rather than working enough on their website.

If you're trying to recruit employees, you need to have a great website that follows all the guidelines in this book.

Your homepage should have a *section for employee recruitment* and a *robust employee recruitment page*. Don't just put a link or two on the page and a couple photos of happy employees. Really show what it's like to work at your company and describe your culture.

For years we've helped Veltri Trucking recruit drivers. They did this by showing potential drivers the culture and what it was like to work at Veltri through multiple channels: their website, dedicated web pages, social media and email marketing. They also made it *easy for folks to apply for jobs* at Veltri. They didn't have to jump through a lot of hoops. They could talk to someone quickly if they were interested.

All the fundamentals of digital marketing work for employee recruitment as well. Don't make the mistake most people make, which is to just give lip service to recruiting and not really go into great depth.

Potential Results from Digital Marketing and AI

The potential results are determined by your expectations for ROI from sales and marketing efforts. All the strategies we've discussed will drive marketing results and deliver a healthy return on your time and money. Include ROI goals in your digital marketing plan as a target to measure success.

Start with Proper Expectations

Setting your expectations is the starting point for the digital marketing plan and the overall online strategy.

Here are a few key questions to ask as you start the process:

- What percent of total revenue can be generated from the website and digital marketing?
- What is the ROI from marketing on the web?
- How does the website brand the business?
- Are we missing opportunities?

No Quick Fix to Digital Marketing or AI

There's no quick fix in digital marketing, and the return you receive is equal to the work you put in. However, the return is usually greater than other forms of marketing. This is because of the number of people you can reach and the ease with which people can research your company, learn about your products and services and make contact. It's also true because you can *track all this activity* and determine what works. All of this happens with a relatively small investment, considering the potential return.

There's no quick fix with AI. It takes strategy and great prompts to get the marketing results you want from AI tools. It's best to use AI to strengthen the skills you already have and to be careful when using it for a new skill set because you may not know if it is hallucinating!

The Benefits of Digital Marketing

Digital marketing offers several key benefits not seen in other forms of sales and marketing. Here are a few potential results you should see from a successful digital marketing program:

- Trackable and effective ROI from marketing investments.
- The strongest ROI of any marketing or sales investment.
- Sales lead conversion rates of 5-10% from key website landing pages.
- A website visitor conversion rate of up to 5% for direct online sales.
- The ability to reach an unlimited audience with your message and content.
- A very low-cost method for reaching thousands of people via email marketing.
- The most powerful branding tool for your company.
- The easiest way for people to research your products and services, make contact and inquire about your company.

What is NOT a Digital Marketing Strategy?

Don't listen to team members just because they have some digital marketing experience. This book will help you develop the skills needed to know the difference between poor strategies and strategies that actually grow sales through online marketing.

The Myths of Digital Marketing

As you analyze your digital marketing strategy and develop your strategic plan, it will be easy to confuse some of the things you're currently doing online as strategy, or you may be misled into thinking that these approaches work online. These mistakes often result in underperforming websites. Here are ten common approaches that often pass for strategy but just don't work.

Get a website up fast — quick, cheap, and we're done.

Many business leaders take the approach of getting something up fast and end up launching an incomplete website. While this is better than nothing, it must have a plan for ongoing improvement, or it could damage your brand. Websites are never really complete and require regular updates. You may launch a new website, but it's always under construction and should be improved and updated regularly.

A bargain website generally leads to poor results and can hurt your brand. An expensive website can also crash and burn. It's the right *strategy* that drives the results.

Everyone else has a website, so we need one too

Websites should define your competitive advantage and clearly communicate what separates your company from the competition. Having a copycat website will not differentiate you or grow your market share. Don't build a website just because everyone else is doing it. Build a website to position your company above the competition. Take what's *unique* to you and your loyal customer base and incorporate *that* into your digital presence.

Use the company brochure for the website

Brochures do not make good websites. Website visitors will leave quickly if they sense the website's main purpose is to sell or promote.

The site's content must deliver value by helping people do their job better or improving the quality of their lives. Brochure copy is often made up of large blocks of text with interchangeable, marketing-speak content that no one reads. That's the last thing you want. Toss out the company brochure and use your website to communicate your marketing strategy in ways that attract visitors.

Our IT department or design agency handles the website

Rarely should the IT department or the graphic designers lead digital marketing strategy. Digital marketing strategies must come from the highest levels of your leadership. Delegate those tasks to people who have strategic marketing and sales experience, or do it yourself. You can learn about the different roles people play in successful digital marketing in the coming chapters.

I haven't been to our website in weeks

What you give attention to in digital marketing drives results. It's always surprising to see how many business leaders have never seen their company websites. Chances are, if you're not regularly visiting your website, you see it as dormant and not very important. The work on your company website is never done. Design, development and content updates are an ongoing part of digital marketing. Also, make time to review your website stats. They are the key indicators of your marketing and business performance.

We don't need a website

This strategy is very difficult to justify in today's digital environment, where the majority of buyers do research online before contacting a company. Every company needs a website. It's at the core of your marketing efforts.

Customers know what we do and understand our website

Your website should be easy to use and understand; don't take this for granted. Anyone who comes to your website should quickly understand what your company does and how you add value.

Never assume people understand your website just because *you* understand it. Companies have their own internal language which customers don't always understand. This is true of even your most loyal customers. Make it easy for people to quickly comprehend what you do, who you do it for, and how they benefit.

Follow the ten-out-of-ten visitor rule: Ten-out-of-ten visitors who come to your website should be able to easily explain the value you bring to clients and customers. Don't make assumptions. Get feedback from your website visitors.

Our customers don't use websites or social media

This is probably a false assumption. Get inside the head of your website's users and you'll find ways they can use your website as a resource. Look at your website stats and you will see hundreds, if not thousands, of people are visiting your website every month.

A large percentage of website visitors will use your website to research your company, and that percentage is growing. The question to ask in this case is: How can we take advantage of digital marketing to grow our business?

Another take on this myth is the business leaders who proclaim, "I don't read email and I hate getting spam, so our company doesn't do email marketing."

Valuable emails get read, saved, shared and acted upon. You can expect open rates of up to 30% when you email a targeted list. You send emails to these contacts and you can also reach them through SEO, social media and other tactics.

We don't have the time or the budget

This is really an excuse for not doing your homework. Digital marketing has the best ROI and tracking ability of just about any sales or marketing expense. The best question to ask in this case is, "What opportunities are we missing?"

Our sales leads don't come from our website

That just means that you're missing the opportunity to generate more sales leads. Generating leads from a website happens when the digital strategy implementation falls in line with the research you conduct about your target market and key personas. Leads won't come unless you work at it, but digital marketing leads can be very profitable. These efforts should not happen in a vacuum but through coordinated efforts with your sales team. Some of your best sales leads may come after they've been referred to your website by offline marketing, referrals from your customers or your sales team!

Don't assume people won't be researching your company, find your website and reach out to buy. Test your assumptions against data and the results will surprise you.

Digital Marketing Blind Spots

What you don't know about digital marketing may be hurting your ability to generate leads, close sales, and gain market share. The good news is with awareness comes the opportunity for change and growth.

Do what you've always done, and you'll get the same results. This is often true in digital marketing because many companies do what they know, and they stay in their comfort zone. They fail to implement key digital marketing tactics needed to grow their company.

Let's look at five digital marketing blind spots you must correct to drive growth.

1. The "Lack of Digital Marketing and Website Awareness" Blind Spot

Many marketers have seen digital marketing flourish in the past few years but have yet to understand what's happening or how to take advantage of it. These business leaders rarely visit their company website or review digital marketing metrics and data.

Although this group has dwindled in size over the years, they're still prevalent, and their lack of attention results in missed opportunities for growth and, in some cases, a shrinking company.

Get access to Google Analytics and you can have the data shared with you every month. Look at total monthly visitors, the pages they visit, and the website traffic sources to gauge your digital marketing effectiveness. Focus on specific pages that provide conversion opportunities, optimizing high-performing ones and refining others. You can feed the data from Google Analytics into the AI prompt box with the question, "What are some ways we could improve these numbers?"

Identify where website traffic originates (organic search, social media, etc.) to focus and fine-tune your efforts. Make sure to track people who contact your company by setting up automated responses to acknowledge and thank them for their interest.

Also, visit your company website at least once a week to see what the outside world is seeing. Question your team about the data and strive for constant improvements.

2. The "Know-It-All" Blind Spot

A closed mind is a beautiful thing to lose. Success in digital marketing requires an open mind and the ability to test new approaches and learn.

This blind spot is growing as younger people come into the workforce. These people were part of the digital revolution and grew up with the Internet but lack a comprehensive view of what really works in digital marketing. They tend to focus on handling digital marketing themselves and focus on what they know.

Digital marketing requires a variety of skill sets, and it is nearly impossible to know it all. The result of this blind spot is trying something and then giving up when it doesn't work as expected. We often hear that a particular digital marketing tactic has *never* worked. Today things have changed, and we see that a *variety* of marketing tactics working *together* in harmony is the key to driving the best results.

Embrace a comprehensive digital marketing plan. Don't rely on just one or two tactics to get results. Explore new digital channels and cover the essentials:

- A great website that meets the needs of users
- Optimization to get found in Google search
- Social media posts and a content calendar
- Great content loaded with benefits for readers

- Email marketing and monthly newsletters
- AI-generated lists, such as benefits and risks, personas, and first-draft content

3. The "Do-it-Yourself (DIY) Digital Marketing" Blind Spot

Marketing is a discipline and requires a team, a comprehensive approach and the attention of experts. A DIY approach will dilute your ability to focus on what you do well. You most likely don't do your own taxes or legal work. Marketing requires the same input and attention from experts. Build a digital marketing team and leverage experts to get results and complement your in-house marketing team.

Talk to experts and get feedback. You can book a time with an expert at IW and get an assessment of your current team and tactics.

4. The "Sample Size of One" Blind Spot

Many business leaders think that how *they* use the Internet is how *everyone* else uses it. This is a significant blind spot in digital marketing. They need to get out of their heads and into the heads of their prospective customers. This is how the best marketers on the planet approach digital marketing.

People buy for their own reasons. Find out why and how people buy from your company and meet them where they are on the Internet.

Talk to your customers and prospects about how they use your website, Google, social media and email to research and make buying decisions. Ask customers why they buy from you and share those perceived benefits on your website.

5. The "Ignoring AI" Blind Spot

Using AI to enhance your digital marketing is a must. Many markets are yet to embrace ChatGPT and how it can be used in marketing. This is a major blind spot as their competitors who use AI will save time and better communicate to their prospects using this fantastic tool.

Get access to ChatGPT or Google's Gemini. Use it to write personas, get key benefits, write blogs and other digital content, analyze data and much more.

A New Generation of Digital Marketers

What's needed is a new generation of digital marketers who focus on strategic intent and translating value with great content. They build a team of experts to leverage inbound marketing with great results in Google, social media, email marketing and other channels.

They understand websites are now the centerpiece of marketing for most companies and digital marketing is essential to attract new customers. This new generation is great with data, and they use metrics to drive tactics and make informed decisions. They embrace learning and the constant changes happening in digital marketing. They're open to testing ideas and leveraging AI tools to improve their work.

Finally, they build a team and leverage the knowledge of experts. This removes blind spots and generates a flow of ideas to leverage the potential of digital marketing.

Get rid of blind spots to build your awareness and reach higher success with your marketing. Goetzmann Homes of Colorado Springs removed a major blind spot and had a record sales year.

Goetzman Custom Homes

Katie Smith, of Goetzmann Custom Homes, was amazed. In her many years selling homes, she had never before seen this happen. An out-of-state customer flew into town and walked into their model home, ready to sign a contract.

"Don't you want to see the floor plan before we start the contract?" Katie asked.

"Nope," said the customer, "I saw everything I needed on your website and I'm ready to build a home with your company."

Katie was able to see the results of an effective digital marketing strategy firsthand. This new customer bought a $750,000 home based on his internet research.

"The impact [on] our brand has been incredible. Our website strategy is paying off," reported Katie. The strategy involved a closer alignment between target market needs and website design, along with hundreds of quality photos highlighting homes built by Goetzmann.

"Prospective buyers love our website, and the photo galleries are very popular. People can view those photos and imagine living in one of our homes," explained Katie. "This has increased inquiries and increased engagement by website visitors."

Custom home builder websites can be hit or miss. Some are well-designed and others are a mess, rarely communicating properly with their target market. The key strategy for Goetzmann was to understand the target market for new homes. Then they were able to more effectively draw those people into their website and eventually into the model home where they could experience Goetzmann quality. The sales team was able to take over from there. They understood that word-of-mouth is very valuable in building custom homes, and qualified website visitors bring a great return. Website traffic coming from offline marketing sources is highly valuable.

Executing Strategy with a Digital Marketing Plan

Goetzmann's marketing team learned that a successful digital marketing plan starts with understanding your target market and knowing your goals and what you hope to accomplish. User Testing and marketing research will get you started, but it's the actual execution of your plan with winning, measurable tactics that drives growth.

This plan defines your digital marketing strategy and is the blueprint for all digital marketing projects, including design and development efforts, traffic generation, and conversions. All the elements of your digital marketing strategy are included in this plan.

Yeah, you can go to AI and create a digital marketing plan outline, and it'll look a lot like this plan. But make sure that the elements of human creativity and awareness are part of that.

You can't just take the stuff from ChatGPT and follow it blindly. I think it's interesting because in my talks, some members of the audience assume they can just take what AI gives them and use it as-is. Well, that's not how it works. Take what AI gives you and use it as *a tool to enhance what you're already doing.* Use it as a *checklist* to make sure you've covered the bases. Use it as a *plan* to get started and as a rough *first draft.* Don't use it as the finished product.

This is a great way to feel like you've got a comprehensive plan from a real marketing pro who's done this for 20 years. Then you can use AI in each of these areas to *expand* upon each part of the plan and make them more comprehensive.

The Digital Marketing Plan will answer the following questions:

- How do our digital marketing efforts result in sales growth?
- What percent of total revenue can be generated from the website and digital marketing?
- What is our target ROI from digital marketing?
- How does our website and digital content brand the business?
- What opportunities are we missing with our current digital marketing?
- What are our specific action items for web strategy, design and development, traffic generation, performance monitoring and ROI?

Digital Marketing Plan Outline

Here are the major sections and outline for your digital marketing plan using the Four-Step Process. We will be going deeper into each step later in the book.

STEP ONE: Strategy

Strategy — This includes a detailed description of the strategy behind the website and all your online marketing. It should answer the following questions:

- What is the purpose of the website?
- How does the website and digital content translate value?
- What is the branding strategy for the website?
- How will users convert on the website?
- How can the website use simple and clear content with a call to action and a sales funnel to drive conversions?

Website Goals and Objectives — This includes the monthly and annual goals and expected results from the website, such as total visits, leads per month or sales revenue. At a minimum, the following areas should be included:

- Total website visitors
- Engagement rates
- Search engine traffic to your website
- Referral traffic
- Conversion rate
- Total conversions

Target Market — This section describes the key market segments targeted by the website and their conversion points. It also includes the secondary markets in each market segment and their location, as digital marketing is very effective at targeting site visitors by geography. It should also include a description of the target market's demographics and psychographics.

Psychographics describe your target market's key characteristics, personality, values, and related lifestyle variables. This provides direction for the website's taglines, navigation, content, design, usability and more.

The objective is to describe the ideal market segment and then develop a website that meets their needs. Include any user behaviors that are unique to your target market. Include the results of your market research in this section to help verify your strategy and the needs of your target market.

Competitive Analysis — This section is a thorough analysis of competing websites targeting similar market segments. Include several industry-leading websites to learn about best practices as well as lower-performing ones, which will provide many examples of what not to do on your site. This is an essential part of your digital marketing plan and most business leaders do not spend enough time reviewing and monitoring competitor websites and strategies. This can help you avoid loss of market share.

Taglines and Content Strategy — The strategy section should include a tagline that's a summary of your company's key value and ties into the strategy. This may include several taglines and ideas for content in general.

Products and Services — Much of the most valuable content on the site will be descriptions of your products and services. Your digital marketing plan describes the themes and organization for this content throughout the web. Include a path-to-purchase for how visitors can inquire about or buy your services or products directly through the website.

STEP TWO: Strategic Communications

Just as commercial or residential buildings are designed by an architect, so should you develop a blueprint for your website content. These are the specific instructions you turn over to your design and development team as they build the website.

Site Map — The site map is an outline of the navigation structure for the website including the main navigation. The site map can be used to create a wireframe design for the website. This is a critical part of the website design and should be included in your digital marketing plan before the site goes to the design phase.

Website Wireframe – The website pages must be laid out in a wireframe before these pages go to the design and development step. Your wireframe is comprised of content sections, headers, bullet points, captions, brief blocks of text and all the written content to be placed on your homepage and key interior pages.

Website Design — Detailed design instructions are included here for the graphic designer. Design elements are driven by the needs of the target market, not the needs of the designer. This section should include specific instructions and perhaps even a wireframe of the website navigation so your graphic design team can develop an initial homepage layout. The following elements should be reviewed in this section:

- Logo design
- Colors and graphic elements
- Photos and images
- Navigation menus
- Secondary navigation and footers
- Fonts and content layout
- Layout recommendations and usability

Website Development — This section is an overview of the various technology platforms for the site selected in part by how many visitors you expect and the site's overall strategy. Consider ongoing updates when selecting a platform along with the amount of outside help versus internal resources needed for regular site updates.

Content Management System — WordPress is the industry standard and recommended for the majority of content-based websites. This allows anyone on your team to update the website from a browser. This section should define the use of website plugins, forms, e-commerce solutions, integration with current software and other technologies as needed. WooCommerce is an excellent tool for e-commerce websites using WordPress as their CMS.

STEP THREE: Inbound Marketing

Traffic Generation — Many types of traffic generation action items are included in this section. It includes search engine optimization details, social media, content strategies, search engine advertising and more.

The most important traffic generation channels to review:
Offline Traffic Generation — This includes all the offline methods used to send visitors to your website. Traffic from this source is usually measured as direct traffic and can be the highest converting traffic of any traffic source.

Search Engines — This includes search engine optimization (SEO), pay-per-click (PPC) advertising, keyword analysis and research and all other efforts to get found in the search engines. Google is far-and-away the dominant search engine on the web. This part of your plan outlines how to get found in those search engines for important keyword search terms.

Email Marketing — A plan for email marketing is included in this section.

Website Referrals — Building links from other websites that are frequented by your target market that can link to your website.

Social Media — This includes your content strategy for Facebook, LinkedIn, Google+, YouTube, Instagram, Pinterest, and other social media.

Content Marketing — Your plan for content distribution throughout the web and your use of content on your website and in social media to pull traffic into your website.

Other Traffic Generation — Include other suggestions that can result in traffic generation opportunities here.

All these traffic generation channels should be measured closely in your web stats and monitored for ROI. Traffic generation is the most expensive of the digital marketing steps and you must have a plan in place for measuring conversions.

STEP FOUR: Monitoring ROI and Tracking Results

Website Data and ROI Objectives — This section defines how web data is used and the process for regular website updates and ongoing content generation. Monthly meetings should include sample agendas and team member responsibilities. Websites are never finished. They're ongoing sales and marketing channels for your business that never stop working. This is a good section for ROI and conversion worksheets to help you track and measure results.

Colorado Academy Summer Camps – the Four Steps in Action

"Our previous website was designed by the parents of a summer camper. It was too internally focused, and new parents didn't know how to use the website to register their child," reported Gwen Davis, marketing director for Colorado Academy Summer Camps. "We were losing valuable new customers."

Their strategy changed to better understand how parents use the website to research the camps and register their children. This was accomplished through user testing, resulting in easier-to-use navigation and better-organized content. This increased online registrations and better met the needs of website visitors.

"We launched the new website in February, and by the end of March registrations were well ahead of last year and on track to set a record for this year," said Gwen.

"Many people hear about us through word-of-mouth and visit us on Facebook, but they all end up on our website to research our camps and register their kids," explained Gwen. Following the Four-Step Process resulted in a higher-producing website and increased registrations.

"Our summer camp registrations are at record levels, and we know an easier-to-use website has been a huge factor in this increase," said Gwen.

Here is what Colorado Academy Summer Camps learned:

Get inside the head of your target market and understand how they will use your website to research and register. Conduct user testing to get this right and avoid designing your site from an internal point of view.

Keep the navigation simple and focus on the key content needed for visitors to better understand your services and products.

Use social media to drive for word-of-mouth content distribution and to improve search engine placement.

Include key conversion points in the website's main navigation menu and track conversions from new site visitors.

Use AI to Develop a Winning Strategy

AI supports each part of the Four-Step Process and makes you a better marketer. You can use AI to make marketing decisions faster, execute tactics before your competitors, measure results in real time and modify marketing efforts in ways that help your company grow.

AI is a digital marketing must-have tool to help you:
- Determine your benefits and risks to understand your company's real value from the perspective of your customers.
- Build Personas, identifying your best prospects, what they want to know and how to find them.
- Develop content that your key personas want to read when they're researching.
- Write headers and taglines that engage your target market.
- Write digital content that they can use in their buying journey to drive online conversions.
- Understand how to find your target market in their preferred channel.
- Support the buyer's journey and nurture your sales funnel.
- Analyze data and current results to find areas for growth.

And more!

AI is one of the *fastest growing* technologies in history. It sure is going to be one of the fastest growing technologies ever implemented in history. It's *going to power so many different things,* from software applications to apps on our phones to what's happening with websites. It's going to continue to grow exponentially.

We won't always know that AI is there. We're not going to see a little logo that says. "Powered by AI," but it will be.

AI is a resource for enhancing what you already do well. AI is not necessarily great as a tool to train you in things you don't know. The reason that's important is because AI creates stories, it *hallucinates,* and it can deliver faulty data and information.

In marketing, the *story* is so important, and AI is a great resource for marketing content. However, you've *got to know marketing and you need a strategic sense of what your marketing is about.* Otherwise, AI can send you in the wrong direction.

Many people are still not using these AI tools, and if they are, they're not using them well. I've been on Zoom calls with folks and watched them put prompts into the AI tools, and they either just don't get the prompts quite right or they get them completely wrong. They think the prompts are kind of like a Google search, or they don't realize that they're *talking* to AI, and so they make the prompts too technical or too straightforward without enough detail.

The best way to use prompts in AI is to write as if you're having a conversation. It's like having your own personal marketing consultant available 24-7.

Use AI to help solve your biggest marketing challenges and ask it clear, direct, and common-sense questions.

Our client, Wiggam Law, increased their lead generation efforts by 100% with an excellent website and solid digital marketing to build awareness and drive traffic. However, their close rate was only 6%. We logged into ChatGPT and asked this question: "After maximizing the effectiveness of their website and digital content, how can a tax resolution attorney improve their close rate from leads generated from their website?

Here is the response:

"Once a tax resolution attorney has optimized their website and digital content for lead generation, further improving the close rate from these leads involves refining the client engagement process, personalizing interactions, and employing strategic follow-up practices. Here are advanced strategies to consider:

1. Implement Advanced Lead Tracking and Analytics:

Use advanced analytics to track the journey of leads through the website. Understand which pages or content are most influential in leading to conversions. This insight can help in refining the content strategy and focusing efforts on what works best.

Set up conversion goals in analytics tools to measure the effectiveness of different pages or sections of the website in real-time.

2. Enhance Personalization Through Automation:

Utilize marketing automation tools to personalize communication with leads based on their actions on the website. For example, if a lead downloads a guide on a specific tax issue, follow up with an email offering additional information on that topic or a free consultation to discuss their situation further.

Personalization should extend to all touchpoints, including emails, phone calls, and even retargeting ads.

3. Improve Lead Nurturing Programs:

Develop a structured lead nurturing program that keeps potential clients engaged over time. This can include a series of emails that provide valuable information, check-ins from the attorney or staff and timely reminders about the benefits of addressing their tax issues promptly.

Segment your leads based on their interests, needs and where they are in the decision-making process, tailoring the nurturing content accordingly.

4. Strengthen Client Relationship Management (CRM) Practices:

Use a CRM system to manage all interactions with leads and clients efficiently. A good CRM can help ensure no lead falls through the cracks and that each lead is followed up with appropriately.

Analyze CRM data to identify patterns and insights that can inform strategies for improving conversion rates, such as the most effective communication methods or the best times to contact leads.

5. Offer Flexible Communication and Consultation Options:

Provide multiple channels for leads to engage with you, such as phone, email, live chat and video consultations. Flexibility can make a significant difference in conversion rates.

Consider offering after-hours or weekend consultations for clients who cannot meet during regular business hours.

6. Utilize Social Proof Strategically:

Beyond featuring testimonials and reviews on your website, consider how social proof can be integrated into your communication with leads. For example, sharing success stories during follow-up emails or consultations can help build trust and demonstrate expertise.

7. Optimize the Consultation Experience:

Ensure the initial consultation process is streamlined, informative and free from pressure. Use this opportunity to provide genuine value, understand the client's needs deeply and establish a connection.

Prepare personalized advice or insights even at this early stage to demonstrate your capability and understanding of their situation.

8. Engage in Continuous Training and Improvement:

Invest in regular training for yourself and your team on sales techniques, client communication and empathy. Understanding how to connect with and persuade potential clients effectively is crucial.

Continuously review and refine your sales and consultation processes based on feedback, successes and failures.

9. Leverage Client Feedback:

Collect and analyze feedback from leads who did not convert to understand their reasons. Use this feedback to adjust your process, communication or offerings.

10. Adjust Your Offerings Based on Client Needs:

Regularly review and adjust your service offerings to ensure they meet the evolving needs of your target market. Offering flexible pricing options or tailored service packages can also help improve conversion rates.

Improving close rates is an ongoing process of testing, learning and refining. By focusing on personalized, client-centered strategies and leveraging technology for better insights and automation, a tax resolution attorney can significantly improve their conversion rates from website leads."

Amazing! Implementing these ideas will improve their conversion rates and take Wiggam Law's revenues to a higher level.

Use AI in digital marketing in the following areas:

Use it for *determining benefits and risks*. What are the very specific benefits that people get from buying your products and services? What are the *risks* people take if they get a buying decision wrong or if they make no decision?

Use AI to *write personas* so you can identify your target market and their preferences, what kind of content they want to read and where they read this content. Then you can *prepare that content* for them *in the channel they prefer* and in a form they want to read.

Use AI to write *first-draft* content that you can modify.

You can also write *content that's super engaging,* and that engaging content would generally be website *taglines and headers,* content headers, and pieces of text that are shorter than twelve words, so they draw people in.

Then you can create content that the online researcher can use to make decisions, reach out to one of your salespeople or even buy directly from your website.

This is where AI supercharges your marketing.

When you use AI, you'll start to gain a competitive advantage as you do these things better than your competitors. You'll get inside the minds of your customers, and you can write executable marketing plans and content using AI as a guide.

Then you can *better meet user intent*. AI is a great tool for understanding user intent. You can do persona research to best understand what people want when they're on a website page. If you know what people want on a website page and you better meet their needs, they're *more likely to move through a sales funnel* and become your customers.

You can *create checklists, eBooks, webinars, white papers, outlines and scripts for videos.* This means you can move faster than ever before to get content published. You can get more people into your funnel which will help drive growth.

AI can also *write that code* for your website. *Digital tools, calculators,* and things that people have to give you an email address to get access to. Those tools can be built, installed on your WordPress website, and generate leads.

Once again, the art and science of writing prompts for AI tools is a new profession that's coming up in the future. People are going to be hired to be Chief AI Officers, and they're going to be very good at using AI tools to improve productivity.

Great prompts to use in ChatGPT and Gemini

Here are a few great marketing questions to ask your favorite AI tool.

- What are the benefits of _____?
- What are the risks of _____?
- What is the ROI of _____?
- How to find the target market for _____?
- Can you write and code a website tool for _____?
- Write a homepage tagline for _____.
- Write a marketing persona for _____.

Fill in the blank with your industry, your marketplace, your customers, your personas, and more. Try variations of things to fill in the blanks.

AI-generated personas require a soft touch.

We must be empathetic and understanding of our personas. AI tools can help us in this, but this is also a mindset for us. And the mindset is that people want to work with companies they trust, companies that have empathy for their current position and understand the pain and gain.

They understand the pain they're going through and the things they want to accomplish. They want digital content for value, not to be sold. One of the things I see in marketing professionals is if we don't use AI tools to get at core benefits, then we end up writing marketing-speak copy that goes nowhere. We must have great digital content focused on value and benefits. Remember, people believe what they want to believe. The Internet revolution that we've seen in the last 20 years has created ecosystems of people living in their own silos, believing what they want to believe. This is a benefit for you because you want to attract customers who believe in your brand. This is true with your targeted personas. That's why the persona work is so important. When you write content that connects with them, they are much more likely to buy from you and they will be that great customer that you want.

People are more important than brands to build trust. AI content must be written as a first draft, a human will be responsible for the final content. A person will edit that content and when they post the content, they'll have their name associated with it because people are thought leaders that move the brand forward.

You build trust with those individual people. We do these things to move people through a sales and marketing funnel. People want things quickly and easily because they are impatient, and the Internet has driven this need to want it *now*.

Doing these things drives higher levels of engagement for your brand.

Suavecito Tequila had just won a national contract with Total Wine and Liquor. The leadership team at Suavecito knew that a great website and digital strategy must be in place to support growth in retail stores. We designed and launched a new website that did just that and met the needs and wants of the key personas important to Suavecito. Engagement on the website increased and Suavecito Tequila went on to have the best sales year in the history of the company.

AI, Digital Content and Story

The bottom line is that AI is great for marketing content, and content is the core of what you need to do in digital marketing because marketing today is about *story*. Story is the idea of how you connect with customers where they are in their life story.

Daniel Miller writes in his best-selling book, *Building a Story Brand*, "Your company is the guide helping your customers defeat their villains and get what they want from their own personal life story. How do you connect with customers as their guide when you are the hero going through their own journey?"

To do that, you want to use the steps outlined in this chapter.

AI is a fabulous tool for this. No matter how AI technology changes over time, the concepts in this chapter will always be foundational for getting great digital marketing results from AI.

We've always wanted to see a return from marketing and sales. We always want that. Now, with AI, you have a tool that's going to help supercharge your results and it's going to help improve the return on your efforts.

Action Items:

- ❑ Write a strategic digital marketing plan following the outline in this book.
- ❑ Make sure there is a connection between your goals and your digital marketing strategy.
- ❑ Set very specific conversion rate goals for the website that will drive sales revenues.
- ❑ Compare online potential results with the cost and potential results of traditional, offline sales and marketing.
- ❑ Complete the ROI worksheet in this book.
- ❑ Pick a primary website strategy or combination of strategies from the list above.

❑ Write a digital marketing action plan to implement the right strategy and include your approach to the selected strategies in your plan.

❑ Develop ROI and success indicators to measure the results of each strategy.

❑ Talk to your sales team and include their input in the website development process to drive leads and complement their sales process.

❑ Develop a content marketing plan as part of your digital marketing plan.

❑ Develop multiple channels for building a loyal following, starting with an email newsletter sign-up and monthly content-rich email newsletters.

Roll up your sleeves and get to work leading a team that will maximize your return from digital marketing and help your company thrive in the age of AI.

CHAPTER 4:
Websites are the Core of Customer Value

How a Website Meets the Needs of Your Market

If you've had a successful business for any length of time, you've figured out how to meet customer needs. Successful companies must be good at doing this, both online and offline. For many companies, the challenge is to translate offline success online, grow sales and stay competitive. This, then, is the key ingredient for your successful digital marketing strategy. Meet customer needs online the same way you meet their needs offline. However, this is easier said than done. Here are a few suggestions to help you meet this challenge and better meet customer needs through digital marketing.

Start With an Understanding of Benefits and Risks

Make the time to identify your target market's needs. Use AI to develop a thorough checklist of benefits and risks in your marketplace. Talk to your sales team to help you clearly understand how you can help your target market do their job better or improve the quality of their lives. The good news is your business already does this! Identify these hot buttons and use them as key benefit statements on your website's homepage and throughout the site's content. Start with the two or three most important benefits and incorporate that message on your homepage. This is what sets you apart and engages visitors.

Translate What You Already Do Well

Use content on your website to communicate your unique competitive advantage or how you are different and better than other companies in your field. This should be clearly stated in your homepage tagline, with photography, graphics and captions. Avoid the temptation to write generic copy. Rather, get into the details of what makes your company stand out and do it briefly and to the point.

Keep it Simple

It's not easy to keep it simple. Digital marketing simplicity is strategic and takes discipline. It's also what your prospective customers want. Website users are looking for simple and clear content with a call to action. In fact, visitors are more likely to select your company if their evaluation is made easier by spending time on your website. They're also more likely to select your company if they feel that working with you is easier than working with your competitors.

Simplicity should be guided by your target market and what your customers value. It also takes courage to keep it simple and test ideas to see what works rather than using too much content. Focus on *three key messages* in your landing pages.

Don't Make Them Think

Users want to get what they need from websites without having to think too much about it. The process should be intuitive and simple. One of the leading books on website usability is actually called *Don't Make Me Think,* by Steve Krug, and I highly recommend it.

Here are a few guidelines to follow to help website users think less:
- Limit the number of clicks and scrolls on the website.
- Limit the site to three levels deep at the most.
- Focus navigation on the following four key areas: Products & Services, Resources, About and Contact.
- Make sure users never get lost as they navigate.
- Users should not have to leave and go to another website.
- Use photos, visual elements and scannable text with captions.
- Include easy-to-find contact information and locations.
- Help people solve their problems and improve their lives.

Digital Marketing Research

Talk to your website visitors to confirm their needs and take time to conduct user testing. This can be done cheaply and effectively on the website UserTesting.com. Ultimately, it's hard to meet user needs unless you analyze visitor data, talk to users and conduct user testing. Do the research and remove the guesswork.

Don't Use an AI Tool to Build Your Website

Your website needs to be crafted by a marketing professional. AI tools can be used to **enhance** your website, give it better content, more thorough content, clear value and list great benefits. But it's that *human touch* that is needed to *communicate your brand promise.*

People have a keen ability to discern what's been created by a machine and what's been created by a person. There's nothing that can replace a human laying out an original design with intention and creative thought. We can tell when graphics have been created by an AI tool because they just don't quite look like what you get from a person. And this is one of the areas where AI tools can't yet match human creativity. You can certainly see that when you watch videos created by AI, especially videos of animated people; you can just tell it's an animation. AI hasn't quite been able to tackle that yet.

What AI *can* do is give you a first draft and explore possibilities. For example, I prompted Gemini to "Create a cartoon in the style of *The New Yorker* magazine of a chimpanzee, smoking a cigar, while sitting behind a massive desk, in front of windows with an expansive city view."

There you have it.

Your Team Needs to be Able to Edit Your Website

It's still common to talk to people who are not able to edit their company website. Your website is the core of your marketing, so your team must be able to add content, make updates and keep the site fluid. Websites are not brochures. They're not one-and-done, gone to the printer. No, websites should be constantly updated and modified. Your people are going to need to make those changes.

Don't build websites that are owned by your developer or a third party like Wix, SquareSpace or GoDaddy. *They* own it. These companies offer a variety of templates and drag-and-drop editors, but ultimately, they severely limit your options. You're likely to wind up with a website that looks like everyone else. When you build your website on platforms like these, you actually *don't* own the website. If you read their Terms of Service, you're paying to *lease* the website, and if you ever want something different, or if you ever want to move it to a different hosting service, it can be difficult and expensive.

Build your website on a platform that you control. That's why we like WordPress. It's super robust, has lots of themes (a starter template) and functional plug-ins available, and it's easy to edit. When you have a WordPress site, you own it. You create the code. It's your intellectual property, and it's much more robust than the options that you have outside of WordPress. You can take a WordPress website and host it anywhere.

Digital Marketing and Branding

Digital branding is an essential website strategy and something your website does the minute it begins to attract visitors. In fact, your company website may have no other purpose than to brand your business. How your company is presented online may be your *most* important piece of branding. This is especially true for those experiencing your brand for the first time. Let's take a closer look at a few important elements of successful online branding and how to incorporate them into your online marketing strategy.

AI is Making Brands So Much Better

The whole brand experience is going to get so much better with AI. Brands are going to be much more intuitive in understanding the needs of their customers because now they have this great AI technology to help them. Some brands will use AI to produce better marketing, better messaging and better offerings. Some brands will also *incorporate AI into their products*, and how they deliver to customers.

Think about it. *How are you using AI to make your customer experience better*? You can use AI to create a *chat option* on your website where people can interact with an AI tool 24/7 to get information about your products and services.

Are you using AI *in your software*? AI can help write code for your website. You can have better code for forms or interactive features like an estimate calculator. AI is going to make brands much stronger, while the brands that don't get on that bandwagon are going to be left behind. It doesn't matter what product or service you're selling because the consumer wants a great product or service. AI is a tool to help you get there, and the people who use it effectively are going to win.

Some CEOs are driving initiatives around AI, while other companies are asking, "Oh, do we really need that? What is it again? I don't understand it, and I don't have a login." Those companies are going to struggle.

A Simple Branding Review

There are many misconceptions about branding and a range of opinions about how to define branding. If you ask ten people, "What is branding?" you're likely to get ten different answers. The most basic way to look at branding is to think of it as the answer to this question, "What do people think about our company?"

More specifically, what do people think about when they visit your website or social media presence on the Internet?" That's digital branding.

You can use AI to serve as a focus group to give you insights into your business reputation and suggest areas for improvement. For example, we prompted Gemini with the question, "What do people think about the company Intel?"

The response was:

"Opinions on Intel are mixed these days. Here's a break-down of some common viewpoints:

Positive:

- **Legacy and Brand Recognition:** Intel has a long history of innovation and brand recognition in the chip-making industry. They are a trusted household name for many consumers.

- **Future Potential:** Intel is investing heavily in new manufacturing facilities and research areas like AI. This could lead to significant growth, especially if they can catch up to competitors.

- **Undervalued Stock:** Some investors believe Intel's stock price doesn't reflect its true potential and could be a good long-term investment.

Negative:

- **Falling Behind Competitors:** AMD has been steadily gaining market share on Intel in recent years, particularly in CPUs.

- **Manufacturing Issues:** Intel has faced delays in its manufacturing processes, which has hurt their ability to compete.

- **Frequent Platform Upgrades:** Some users dislike that Intel frequently changes its motherboard sockets, making CPU upgrades less economical.

Overall, Intel is a company at a crossroads. They have the potential to rebound, but they face stiff competition and need to execute on their plans."

Keep in mind that when prospects are doing online research, they're using these same tools to ask similar questions. How people experience you online is the key factor driving their perceptions of how they will experience your products and services.

How to Build Your Reputation Online

An effective marketing strategy is to actively drive your reputation. Make a list of 25 words that you *hope* people would use to describe your firm: responsive, reliable, high-quality, excellent service, easy to work with, great value, local, leading-edge, personable, friendly, helpful, [fill-in-the-blank] specialists. You get the idea. Then, consistently imbed these keywords into *all* of your digital marketing content throughout your website and across social media.

Everything on Your Website is Branding

Everything on your website and in your social media content is branding. Photos, colors, graphics and content all form an impression. That impression is branding, and that's why so much thought must be given to your website and content.

Do not add elements just to have them on the website. Every part of your site should convey a clear and deliberate message. If "a picture's worth 1,000 words," then think hard about *every* image on your website. What does it say? Does it say anything? Is the story it tells consistent with your message?

Adding unnecessary elements only leads to clutter and confusion, which hurts your brand. People will quickly leave a confusing or cluttered website and will rarely come back. Visitors make a connection between the branding coming from your website and your ability to deliver services or quality products. Basically, if you have a bad website, you are likely to produce bad products and services.

Websites Make a Company Transparent

A website is your business plan for the world to see. Companies can no longer hide behind their brand as they did in the past with ads and marketing-based content. Your target market is looking for depth and clarity. The company website exposes the business and puts the prospective customer in charge. Consumers are very smart and can see through the malarky. Be direct and honest because the Internet is transparent.

Your Website is a Silent Brand

Most visitors will never connect with you directly or provide feedback. They don't make a lot of noise. They're more likely to vote with a click and leave than provide feedback on their experience. However, there are a few key indicators of a website's general branding experience with users. Website users leave evidence of their visit, which can be found in Google Analytics; total website visits, website engagement and overall bounce rate are key measurements of your online brand. Website engagement is measured by the number of *pages visited,* the *time* spent on the website and any *actions* taken by the user. The *bounce rate* is a measurement of users leaving your website immediately after only visiting one page, which indicates a lack of interest.

Declining visits, low engagement and a high bounce rate are negative indicators. If you are not watching your web stats, your brand could be deteriorating, and you would never know it until you see revenues decline. This is the power of digital branding.

All these metrics are leading indicators for what is to come. Companies with websites that have growing traffic and high engagement rates are growing faster than those that don't.

An External Versus Internal Focus

People come to your website with an *intention* and a strong focus on getting value. They're looking for information to solve a problem or to get something done. The better you understand user intentions, the better you can drive conversions and movement in your sales funnel. See your website from your customer's point of view. It's not easy and it may be your greatest marketing challenge.

Most websites are developed from a very strong internal perspective. Avoid these internal biases. This is often seen in website navigation titles and content. Your website must have an external focus to adequately brand your value to visitors.

Photos Can Hurt or Help Your Online Brand
Photos tell a story, and users will look at those photos before any other part of the website, especially photos of *people*. This drives your key messaging. Avoid clip-art imagery or stock photos with no captions, and instead, use real photos from your company, along with captions that tell your brand story and describe the photo. Copying images from the Internet can also expose you to liability for copyright infringement, and the penalties can be egregious. The last thing you need is a lawsuit.

Ranking in Google is Branding
Google has changed branding. The top of the scroll of Google search results defines the brand for that search term. Pick the search terms most relevant in describing your company. There are many ways to do this, and you can read more about it in Chapter 7 where we discuss traffic generation.

Establish a Voice for Your Brand Online
Content is a key part of online branding. You must have a content strategy and plan for regular content updates and blog posts. Keep in mind that this content must be *consistent* to avoid brand confusion and must come from *one central voice or theme*. The voice of the brand in your online content must make sense to your target market. If your target customers are engineers, then speak the language of engineering and give them data, numbers, facts and specs. If your target customers are realtors, then make it social and fun. The key is to meet the needs of your online researchers and keep your content themes consistent.

Digital Content is Changing Branding
Digital content is growing in its use and reach. Telling the story of your company is critical to developing your online brand and connecting with your customers. If you don't tell your story, people will make one up. This is true whether it's a ten-word tagline or a thousand-word article. The future of online branding is digital content.

Action Items:

- ❏ Find out how visitors are responding to your website.
- ❏ Set up and review Google Analytics and get feedback from visitors.
- ❏ Work to get the right type of qualified traffic.
- ❏ Develop a great tagline and photos with captions that communicate your brand.
- ❏ Develop an online content strategy and find the team to implement it.
- ❏ Research which keywords will get your website to the top 10 in Google search results.
- ❏ Write website content that is going to be helpful to your customers.
- ❏ Write in the language of your prospective customers.

Understanding Your Customers in the Age of AI

AI can help you get inside the minds of your customers by developing personas. A persona is *a fictional representation of your ideal* customer. You can create personas by looking at your current customer base and asking, "Which of these customers do we want more of? Which customers are profitable, great to work with, fun people and who love our products and services and will be advocates for our company?"

How do we find more people like them? Well, I can tell you right now, there are more people like them out there, and they are identified as marketing personas. Great marketers look for the similarities in their target market, the things they have in common, and build a profile of this ideal customer. And guess what? AI can do that for you. It does it really, really well. And it's been doing it better every time we've tested it.

So how do you create a persona? Well, you simply go into ChatGPT or Gemini and use the prompt to ask, "Please create a persona for [_____]." Fill in the blank with the services or products you're marketing. AI will then describe *a typical customer who would buy your products and services now.* This is an amazing resource for marketers looking to grow their company.

Let's go back to the natural health clinic, Keystone Medicine, that targets patients who are willing to pay out of pocket rather than through health insurance.

ChatGPT created this persona of an ideal patient:

Persona: Emily Johnson

> **Age:** 35
>
> **Occupation:** Graphic Designer
>
> **Location:** Phoenix, Arizona
>
> **Healthcare Preferences:** Strongly prefers natural and holistic approaches to health.
>
> **Medical History:** Emily has dealt with chronic digestive issues and mild anxiety for several years. She has tried various conventional treatments but found them either ineffective or accompanied by undesirable side effects.
>
> **Lifestyle:** Emily is an active individual who enjoys hiking and yoga. She is also a vegan and is very conscious about her diet and environmental impact.
>
> **Beliefs and Values:** Emily believes strongly in the body's ability to heal itself when given the right natural tools and environment. She prefers treatments that align with her lifestyle and values, such as herbal supplements and acupuncture.
>
> **Insurance:** She has health insurance but is aware that it covers only a limited range of natural treatments. Despite this, she is willing to pay out-of-pocket for treatments she believes are more beneficial for her health.

Health Goals: Her primary goals are to manage her digestive issues and anxiety without relying on pharmaceuticals and to maintain her overall wellness through preventive care.

Experience with Healthcare: Emily has had mixed experiences with conventional healthcare providers and feels that her concerns and lifestyle choices are often not taken into consideration.

Seeking in a Natural Medicine Clinic: Personalized care, a holistic approach to her health issues and a healthcare provider who respects and aligns with her lifestyle choices and beliefs.

Financial Consideration: While cost-conscious, Emily is prepared to invest in her health and is willing to allocate a portion of her income towards treatments that she feels are more effective and align with her beliefs."

Then you can ask the AI tool two very important questions. First, "How do we find this persona?" and second, "What kind of digital content do they want to read?"

Where are they online? What do they research when making buying decisions? We use these questions to create digital content that will attract Emily to our website and social media platforms.

Here is what ChatGPT reports on how we find Emily online:

"Finding personas like Emily online for your natural medicine clinic involves a combination of targeted digital marketing strategies and understanding the platforms where your ideal audience, like Emily, is likely to engage.

Here's how you can go about finding Emily:

1. Social Media Targeting:
Platforms like Facebook, Instagram and Pinterest are great for reaching individuals interested in holistic health and

natural lifestyles. Utilize targeted ads focusing on interests such as yoga, veganism, natural remedies and holistic health.

Join groups or communities related to natural health and participate in discussions to increase visibility.

2. Content Marketing:

Create blog posts, videos and infographics about topics relevant to Emily's interests and needs, like natural remedies for digestive issues and anxiety, the benefits of holistic healthcare and preventive health tips.

Optimize your content for search engines (SEO) with keywords that Emily might use when searching for natural health solutions.

3. Influencer Collaborations:

Collaborate with influencers who embody Emily's lifestyle and values. This could be health and wellness bloggers, yoga instructors or vegan lifestyle influencers.

Influencers can provide authentic endorsements and reach a dedicated audience that trusts their recommendations.

4. Email Marketing:

Build an email list by offering valuable resources like free guides or webinars on topics that would interest Emily.

Use personalized email campaigns to nurture relationships and keep your clinic top of mind.

5. Online Communities and Forums:

Participate in online forums like Reddit or Quora in sections dedicated to natural health, holistic lifestyles, and similar interests.

Offer helpful advice and information to establish credibility and attract individuals like Emily.

6. Paid Search Advertising:

Use Google Ads to target specific search terms that Emily might use.

Include keywords related to natural medicine, holistic health clinics and alternative treatments for specific health concerns.

7. Partnerships with Related Businesses:
Collaborate with businesses that Emily might frequent, such as health food stores, yoga studios or eco-friendly product retailers, for cross-promotion.

8. Analytics and Feedback:
Utilize analytics tools to track the success of your strategies and understand where your traffic is coming from.
Regularly gather feedback through surveys or social media to refine your approach."

Remember, the key is to consistently provide value and engage authentically with the community. Building trust and demonstrating expertise in natural medicine will attract personas like Emily to your clinic. Then you can start with those tactics of finding your best personas and build a winning digital marketing plan."

The best marketers on the planet are using AI to get inside the heads of their prospective customers. You can use AI to supercharge your knowledge and make it accurate.

Market Research and User Feedback

The Internet and AI have changed marketing. Business leaders should be aware of two of the most profound changes. The first is the ability of marketing staff to collect highly accurate data from your target markets. The second is the ability to accurately measure the impact and return of various digital marketing strategies.

This was impossible to this extent prior to the web. Online marketers know more about their online consumers than ever before, thanks to AI tools, Google Analytics, HubSpot and other statistical tools. They can also track conversion sources more accurately, along with what's needed to drive sales.

There's been two or three big changes in technology. One of the biggest changes in digital marketing was the advent of *Content Management Systems*, or CMS, which allows you to edit your own website. While several CMSs have come and gone, WordPress ended up being the market leader because it was an open-source system. We jumped on the WordPress bandwagon really early.

The next big change was *mobile*, and mobile was also then tied to WiFi. Remember when you used to have to plug in? So now you have WordPress, WiFi and mobile 5G, which enable mobile websites with connectivity available pretty much everywhere in the world. These are *huge* changes.

Not much else has changed. I mean, computers have gotten faster, and our mobile devices are better. WiFi and 5G are faster. But AI is the next big leap in technology. AI can support you in so many ways with all the things that you do with user testing and market research.

This has led to a tremendous boost in the accuracy of market research. The Internet and your company website now provide unique opportunities to further get inside the head of your target customer, understand how they use your website, and why they behave the way they do. Business leaders should have a basic understanding of how to use the Internet and their websites to collect valuable market research data.

Here are a few online market research techniques you can use to improve your digital marketing results.

User Testing

User testing is a very powerful form of marketing research. It's the process of observing your website visitors perform basic tasks on your website, monitoring their actions, and collecting data. User testing can vary widely in scope and depth. It can go from a formal study in a user testing lab with eye tracking to a very simple over-the-shoulder review of a user as they navigate around your website.

There are several steps that must be followed to run a successful user testing session, including:

Task Selection — This is the process of determining the actual tasks users will perform in each session. This can include researching services and products or actually completing an online transaction or conversion.

User Recruitment — Here the targeted users are recruited and scheduled.

Technology Selection — The technology used to record the sessions. There are many options available to record desktop computer screens.

Session Facilitation — This is the process used to facilitate the actual testing session.

Review and Analysis — This final part of the process is used to determine the changes needed to improve the site's usability and better meet the user's needs. These are the final recommendations that come from observing the user testing sessions.

There are several principles to follow when conducting user testing. Here are a few to keep in mind:

Recruit a minimum of five to seven users and group them by market segment and similar attributes. Combining market segments will lead to mixed results. Only five to seven users are needed to provide significant feedback in effective user testing.

- Make sure the facilitator does not help the users complete tasks, even if a user asks for help. Facilitators should listen and only ask questions. Users should be asked to answer their own questions and show the facilitator what they would do on the website to get an answer or solve a problem.
- Ask the users to think out loud as they navigate around the website. Otherwise, most users won't talk, and it will be hard to know their intentions.

- Always record your sessions so you can watch the user a second time and see what you missed.
- Watch out for user testing subjects who are looking to please you or be nice. It's common for users to blame themselves when they can't complete a task online.
- Encourage the users to be honest, speak their minds and do what they would do in real-life situations.
- Don't ask users to provide their opinion. People will tend to give positive or neutral feedback. It is much better to have them attempt a task and monitor their progress.
- User testing can be repeated multiple times to test assumptions and ensure your improvements are getting the results you expected.
- The best user testing results come when the researcher removes possible biases and remains neutral.

User testing works well for a variety of tasks on just about any type of website.

Here are a few common tasks that provide great insights when performing user testing:

- Find information on a service or product you might buy from this company.
- Look for location information and how to contact the company.
- Review a few competitor websites and research their offerings.
- Search for the website in Google.
- Make a purchase on the site directly.
- Complete a form on the website.
- Research the website's content and blog and provide feedback.
- Sign up for an email newsletter.
- How would you describe the website to others?

AI and Market Research

AI can support you with these things in so many ways.

You can use AI to *create the questions* you're going to ask in your research. You can ask AI to help you create a *user testing plan* or have it *analyze the results of surveys* and focus groups and help you with action items. Just like everything else, AI works best when it's a compliment. It helps you do what you already do well so much better. You want to use market research tactics as a compliment to what you're already doing.

Not only can AI help you *plan* the research, but it can also help you execute the research, *analyze* the results of that research and give you some ideas you may not have captured. Here are a few key objectives to gain insights from market research and user testing.

Review your statistics in Google Analytics and talk with your marketing team to come up with a complete set of tasks that your website users are most likely to complete online.

UserTesting.com

This is a must-visit website for the serious digital marketer. This website allows you to recruit users for brief fifteen-to-twenty-minute user-testing sessions. The users find your website and follow your instructions to complete assigned tasks. The sessions are recorded so you can see their mouse movements and hear their reactions as they navigate. All this is done at a very affordable price and is a quick and inexpensive method for getting user feedback.

User Surveys and Focus Groups

Surveys and focus groups are two additional market research formats that you might consider. These research methods take more expertise and skill to conduct, and it's recommended that you find a market research company to conduct these studies. A strong bias often exists when these types of research methods are conducted internally, which may not produce the most relevant feedback.

STEP 2: STRATEGIC COMMUNICATION

CHAPTER 5:
Strategic Communication

Key Elements that Communicate Value

Website design can be overwhelming. It can pull you into uncharted areas of graphic design and user psychology, where emotions rule and what works best is often missed. Business leaders tend to rely on the input of others when it comes to getting this work done. If they miss the mark, this can lead to negative impressions and usability issues that do not reflect the proper strategic direction. These issues can then lead to an underperforming website.

Although AI can provide insights into what works best and help with first-draft content, ultimately, a human will drive the unique aspects of a website that will make it successful. To get it right, you must start with the fundamentals.

Business leaders must understand the fundamentals of website design to best lead their company's digital marketing efforts. You must know enough to provide direction and to make sure your strategic vision for the website doesn't get lost in the design process. It's a mistake to turn this vision over to graphic design or website development professionals because they will not understand your vision without your direction. They are most likely to duplicate what they've done on other projects, which may not be the best approach for your website.

Five Areas of Website Design

These five key areas break down the design process into a more manageable overview. These elements are discussed in more depth in upcoming chapters and will help simplify what can be a very complex project. Business leaders must be aware of each area and be able to provide direction to their digital marketing team in each of these five areas.

1. Navigation and the Site Map

Most designers don't start with a site map, but they should because it's a critical part of any website. The site map is the navigation structure that includes all the links, tabs and methods for the user to move around the website. It gets more attention from visitors than any other element. Keep navigation simple and use link titles that are easily understood. Avoid pull-down menus if possible, and only use one main navigation system that's global on all site pages. Your navigation is strategic and should be limited to only the most important content.

Your site map and website navigation structure are also indexed by Google and other search engines. Websites with intuitive and well-structured navigation systems get ranked higher in potential customers' searches. This will continue to be a benefit as AI tools scan websites and use your navigation structure to make sense of your content.

All business websites must have these four navigation areas for users: *products and services, resources, about* and *contact*. These four areas comprise everything anyone needs to know about your company and help streamline navigation for mobile users.

2. Graphic Design

This encompasses the look and feel of the website and consists of graphics, images, fonts and other design elements. Design for your target market and not for internal needs or the preferences of your graphic design team. Many designers will over-design as they work to impress their boss or client. We've seen many *gorgeous* websites that are completely useless. The design should not get in the way of the site's usability or its ability to communicate the clear value you offer. Simple, professional designs get better results. Avoid clutter and graphics that look like ads, especially as navigational elements. Users do not click on ads, and they make the site appear cluttered. Keep the focus on usability and don't be afraid of white space and fewer links, especially on the homepage.

3. Development and Technology

Keep the technology and the website development platform consistent with the website's overall purpose and strategy. Make sure you can control the content on the site and easily make updates from a web browser.

Avoid proprietary CMS software that locks you into one application and doesn't allow you to switch providers. Take the time to understand the basics of the technology platform that you use to build your website.

4. Taglines, Content Headers and Website Content
This includes the written content, images, photos, and other media. After users scan your photos and use the navigation buttons, they'll quickly expect the site's content to deliver value. Do not take taglines for granted because they're key to the site's success.

The homepage tagline may be the most important marketing content on the whole website or possibly in your entire company!

Make sure it's easy to read and understand. Also, keep it *unique* to your company.

AI tools like ChatGPT are excellent resources for writing website taglines and content headers for your key website pages. Ask the AI tool to write website taglines and headers that make the site's pages easy to read and help the website user scan for key points. This will build user engagement.

5. Market Research and User Feedback
The final area involves getting feedback from your target market and watching your website stats. Think about user testing or surveys to get feedback. Do not ask for opinions, but rather ask people to perform a task on the site. You'll always learn something new from this feedback, and it may surprise you.

Ask your target audience to describe *three things* they want from your website and then give them those three things!

Think Like Your Website Visitor
One of the best ways to learn how to manage and lead website design and development teams is by understanding website visitors and how to best meet their needs. This will drive conversions,

traffic, and business growth. It's the most fundamental step toward a successful website, yet most sites are still developed from the perspective of the designer and developer, not the user or customer.

The following chapters break down the key elements of website design and development along with clear instructions on how to meet user needs. Find ways to adapt these to the very specific desires of your target market. The better you can accomplish this, the better your website will convert visitors into business.

Thousands of Research Hours on Hundreds of Websites
The findings you're about to read come from thousands of hours of user testing, user observations and the research and analysis of hundreds of website stats over the past 20 years. This work has identified universal visitor behaviors. We didn't make this up; this is simply what works. As a user of the Internet, you'll relate and might even think of them as common sense. As stated before, common sense is not so common in the world of digital marketing, and many website builders still ignore these findings for improved design.

Website Usability is a Key Marketing Indicator
This book will introduce a new term to you and the digital marketing team that must be a central part of your digital marketing effort: *usability*. This is at the heart of Step Two. How intuitive and easy-to-use is your company website?

Action Items:

- ❑ Review these key website areas with your website designer and developer.
- ❑ Determine if the design you are reviewing is appropriate for your target market.
- ❑ Use a content management system such as WordPress for easy updates.
- ❑ Write a navigation plan and site map before you start your design.

❑ Write an awesome tagline that summarizes your business value in eight to twelve words and is understood by a wide range of website visitors.

❑ Get feedback from site visitors with user testing and surveys.

❑ Set up Google Analytics to track website performance.

What Visitors Want from Your Website

User Intent is King

You may have heard the term "content is king" which is a very valid point; content is very important in digital marketing. However, a better way to think of this is *user intent is king*. Your content is only as good as how it meets the needs of users.

Earlier chapters reviewed the tactical approaches needed to develop a digital marketing strategy and the key elements of website design. Now, we're going to go deeper into understanding your visitors. In fact, we're going to attempt to get inside their heads to better understand their needs and how they will use your website. Let's start with what website visitors want. Results will only be as good as the team's ability to understand what users want to accomplish during their visit.

Understand Your Website Users

A clear understanding of what visitors want from your website is essential when implementing a successful website design or digital marketing strategy. This is easier said than done, and most people don't take the time to figure this out. Rather, they do what they think people want. This "sample-size-of-one" approach can result in a website that doesn't meet user needs. Design your website from the perspective of your target market, and not of your own.

Business leaders who really understand what visitors want will drive growth and marketing results. This is a competitive advantage because most businesses make false assumptions about user needs and consequently minimize their results. We've worked in user testing and website data analysis for more than two decades, and here's what people actually want from websites based on our data, research and analysis.

Get Information and Solve a Problem

They are not looking to read content about how great your company is. They're looking for very specific information that helps them *solve a problem*. Your website must help people find this information and help them solve the problem that initiated their visit. This is the most common intent of the website visitor.

Enhance Their Lives and Convenience

The Internet is vastly popular because it makes life more convenient. Your site must do the same. If the Internet were a challenge to use and hard to understand it would not be popular. Yet, many websites are hard to use and understand. Internet users have no problem using Google to find what they want. For many the struggle begins after they arrive at a destination website.

Your website should be easy to use with a depth of content that meets users' needs. It should help visitors do their jobs better and otherwise enhance the quality of their lives. It is very easy for people to leave your website and search for other options.

Product and Services Information

Information about your products and services can sometimes get buried in a website. It should be front-and-center, and easy to find. The most important factor in driving online conversions and sales is the way users interact with the content about your product and services. A large number of visits to your product and services pages is a good sign. Include links to your products and services in your main navigation menu and make this content attractive to visitors. Go into great detail. Your products and services landing pages can link to volumes of content. Website users will appreciate this content and search engines will rank your website higher in their search results.

Pricing for Products and Services

Pricing is also very important and should be included when possible. This is true for all types of products and services. Cost is one of the biggest issues on your visitors' minds and the Internet has driven transparency in pricing. You can price strategically as needed, but your site must communicate the *value* that comes with your pricing options and explain how your pricing relates to competitors.

Some companies worry that competitors may see pricing and take advantage to hurt your business. For the most part, the upside of visitor engagement with your content is more important than competitors having access to this information.

Business Locations and Contact Information
This is very easy information to display and highly useful to visitors who often come to the site just to look for locations, hours of operation or a phone number. All websites should have a "Contact Us" link in the main navigation (usually in the upper right corner) and in the website footer. Your mobile website should make this a prominent feature that is easy to find in the main navigation.

Delivery and Shipping Information
Shipping and delivery pricing and policies are two of the biggest factors in e-commerce conversion rates. It's important that you clearly explain how this process works and offer fair pricing for shipping. Omitting this information will cost you conversions and sales.

Access to Interactive Information, Search and Research
Users expect your website to function like Google, Amazon, and other top-of-the-line sites that offer a premium web experience. If you offer any functionality on your site, it must be very good because it will be compared to the best online resources. This includes everything from a basic search function to advanced e-commerce features. If you have a search option on your website, users will expect it to work as well as Google. Make sure site functionality is part of your strategy and has a purpose because including it and making it work well can be expensive and time-consuming. It's better to skip extra functionality than to have functions that don't work.

Action Items:

- ❑ Use the above items as a checklist and verify your website has them covered.

- ❑ Check your assumptions about website visitor needs and confirm them with feedback from customers and by reviewing your web stats.

- ❑ Make a list of the top ten reasons people visit your website.

- ❑ Include access to content in each of these areas on your website. If you don't know the top ten reasons, go and ask your target market.

- ❑ Question added functionality on your website and only use it when required by your digital marketing strategy.

- ❑ Make sure products, services and contact pages are on your main navigation.

- ❑ Answer the major question: How does your website enhance people's lives and help them do their jobs better?

How to Understand What Visitors Think About

Think like your customers.

Getting inside the head of your visitor helps you better understand their needs and build an easy-to-use website that gets results. In our research, we've developed a brief list of questions people ask as they visit websites. This comes from thousands of hours spent watching people in user testing sessions and reviewing the data from Google Analytics for hundreds of client websites.

Here are the questions visitors ask as they navigate a website. Answering these questions during the design process will help you build a better website.

What's the website about?

This is the first thought that comes to the website visitor. Ten out of ten people who visit your website should understand what the company does and how it adds value. Every homepage must answer the question, "Am I in the right place?" Not knowing what a site is about in the first five seconds leads to a high bounce rate and low user engagement. People leave websites that they don't understand or are too difficult to use. Online conversions are almost impossible if the visitor doesn't understand the value you provide.

What is of value to me?

After the visitor decides what the site is about, they ask the most important question: How can the website add value to them? This happens quickly and determines if they will stay on the site and dig deeper or leave to find a website that delivers that value. The next step the user will take is to navigate or search the website to find the answers they're looking for.

How do I navigate or search to find what I want?

Most website users will start with the navigation menu. Menus that are easy to use and understand are critical to usability and keeping the visitor on the site. Users will read from left to right on a page, just like they read a book, and scan content and navigation links quickly. They want the links to make intuitive sense before they click to see what's on the next page.

What can I do on this website?

The user will search for functionality to meet their needs and get information. Keep in mind that your website must work well, or the user will quickly leave. They expect the site to function like Google, Amazon and other popular websites. Functionality must lead to a conversion, or it's probably unnecessary.

Is this website safe, and can I trust it?

All aspects of your website must communicate trust, professionalism, and safety. A poorly designed website is less trustworthy than a professional site that's easy to use. People want to know if the site will offer value or if it just wants their money. Design a site that builds trust.

Here are a few additional questions on the minds of your website visitors:

- Where am I?
- Should I be somewhere else?
- Where is the company located?
- How do I contact the company?
- Should I tell others about this website?
- How do I buy online?
- How do I contact sales or customer service?
- If I contact them, will they get back to me in a timely manner?

Meet User Needs by Understanding Usability

User Intent is King

Most people start their website content by answering the question, "What should people know about our company?" This is the wrong question! The right question to ask is, "What is the *intent* of people visiting our website and the individual pages?" User intent is king and drives conversions, or sales funnel movement. Content is only as good as it meets the needs of users.

Think Like Your Website Visitors

It's important to get out of your own way of thinking about usability and think like your users. These concepts are often lost in the design process, and it's the responsibility of the person in charge of the process to make sure they provide leadership and direction in this area. The best digital marketers on the planet live inside the heads of their prospective customers. The worst marketers can't get outside their own heads.

Users Form an Instant Impression

Your website is often the first impression someone gets of your company and your brand. First impressions are important because people have many options and can easily leave a website. A first impression is forever.

The way people use your website is the way they think about your company.

Website Visitors Begin in the Upper Left Corner

People read website content the same way they read books and magazines. They start in the upper left corner of the page, and their eyes move across to the right. The most valuable part of any website page is the upper left corner. This is why the company logo is usually best placed there. Use this space wisely, and as a best practice, place your logo and tagline in this area on all your web pages.

Photos of People Get Attention

Photos catch their eye, especially pictures of *people*. However, many websites make the mistake of using stock photos and clip art. This leaves the user with the impression that you will provide a low level of value, and it's possible to see the same stock photo on multiple websites.

This is not only ineffective; it can lead to serious consequences for copyright infringement. Statutory damages range from $750 to $30,000 *per infringement*, up to $150,000 for *willful* infringement. Photographers and copyright trolls use reverse-image-search apps to discover websites that have copied their work, then send them a letter demanding tens of thousands of dollars or threatening to sue. Even common images often have requirements for attribution that, if ignored, can trigger an infringement claim.

If a picture is worth 1,000 words, think about what each image *says*. What story does it tell? Does that story support your mission, reputation and brand? Use photos of your team with captions to tell the story of your business. Have professional photos taken for the website and avoid stock photography if you can. If you are going to use stock images, use a licensing service like Shutterstock.com and keep a copy of every license. Visitors will decide what a photo's message is, and if you don't clarify its message, they may get it wrong.

Website Users Ignore Advertisements, Graphics and Clutter

People tend to ignore anything that looks like an ad. Users avoid them and stick to content and navigation menus. Users do not know where they will go when they click on an online ad. These types of graphics are seen as advertising and are avoided. This is reported in web stats and user testing sessions. Never use graphics, ads, or banners for your key call-to-action or navigation. Put those links in your navigation menu or use well-designed call-to-action buttons that you can track. Make sure *all* your graphics, colors and fonts are *consistent* with the overall design.

Visitors Ignore Marketing Speak Content

Like advertisements, brochure copy, marketing-speak and large blocks of text are usually ignored. This content is usually interchangeable with other websites and actually says very little about your value.

Here are a few examples of brochure or marketing-speak content:

"Our innovative, state-of-the-art solutions provide our customers with high satisfaction levels."

"Our people make the difference."

"We are committed to the best service and products of any company."

"We provide excellent service, innovative solutions, cutting-edge products and top-notch support."

Almost *any* business can make these claims. Avoid marketing-speak copy and keep your content brief and action-focused.

This content example is more specific to value:

"Leaders in circuit board design for thirty years and one of the most experienced management teams in the industry. Call us today to find out why Apple, Dell and Cisco come to us for solutions."

Here's an even more action-focused approach:

> "A proven productive tool that saves you 30% and improves accounting results. Click here to learn how it works."

Notice a difference? Engage your users in the same way your leading salespeople engage their prospects by talking about the real value your company brings to customers.

The Navigation Menu

It's easy to forget about the navigation menu, but it's one of the most important parts of the website's usability. Keep the navigation menu easy to use. Limit it to fewer than ten main navigation areas and use link titles that your users will understand easily. Keep the navigation consistent on all pages and avoid pull-down menus if possible. Top navigation menus work best, but if you need more room, put the navigation menu on the left side of the page.

Website Users Scan Content and Move Fast

You would be amazed how quickly people scan website content. Designers will develop a site thinking that users will take their time and appreciate the photos and content, when in reality, they *scan* everything in milliseconds looking for something of interest. Use taglines, bullet points and photos with captions to grab attention. Include call-to-action buttons and place all your most important links in the navigation menu.

Many Users Leave Quickly

Bounce rates are a key measurement of user engagement. It's not uncommon to see websites with bounce rates above 60%. This means that 60% of the people who visited the website left immediately without visiting more than one page. Target bounce rates are under 40% for lead-generation websites and under 30% for e-commerce sites. Clear navigation will help you lower your bounce rate and reach these targeted levels.

Users Want Video

Build a robust YouTube channel and regular video content to meet your customer's needs. Videos must help people do their job better. Help them get a better understanding of your products or services and what makes your company unique and special.

Action Items:

- [ ] Design a website that doesn't make visitors think about how to use it.

- [ ] Avoid scrolling banners and text because they're hard to read and people tend to ignore them.

- [ ] Be consistent in your font usage, colors and sizes. This also makes it easier for people to read and follow your content.

- [ ] Make sure there are few clicks and scrolls on each page.

- [ ] Limit the navigation to no more than three levels deep.

- [ ] Make sure your users never get lost.

- [ ] Make sure they never have to leave to another website for content or information.

- [ ] Use photo captions and scannable text.

- [ ] Include easy-to-find contact information and locations.

- [ ] Check your bounce rates and keep them at acceptable levels.

- [ ] Write value-added content and remove marketing-speak.

- [ ] Do not use ads or graphics as navigation or call-to-action links.

- [ ] Put your logo in the upper left corner of all pages and link it to your homepage.

- [ ] Use photos of real people at your company with captions.

❑ If you want to recruit top talent with your website, include a careers section on your homepage and build out a careers page that includes the key benefits of working for your company.

❑ Talk to your website visitors to confirm their needs.

CHAPTER 6:
How AI Helps Meet Customer Needs

The better you know your customers' needs, and the better you meet them where they are, the better results you're going to have. Getting inside the heads of your customers is absolutely critical. AI can help you understand the needs of your prospects and customers.

AI Helps You Identify Your Buyers

A lot of companies randomly look for new customers with shotgun marketing and then try to get as many people as they can to see their brand and buy from them.

The Super Bowl is a great example. You'll see advertisers spending millions rushing to the mass market to make a name for themselves, and that's okay *if* you're a massive brand with a huge market. But most companies don't have that, and they'd be wasting their money doing a Super Bowl ad because they haven't really identified their buyers. AI helps you pinpoint the best customers who are most likely to buy your products.

Get Inside Their Heads

You do that by getting inside their heads. By tapping into this vast amount of knowledge we now have available through AI, you can target your customers, get inside their heads, and understand how they think. Look at *who your best customers are right now*, or who are going to be your best customers *in the future*.

Find Out Where They Research

We've covered building *personas* of your best customers using AI. Once you have those personas built, you can then decide where and how you want to get found in their research. But to do that you have to know *where they're researching.* Not everybody uses Google. Some people research on LinkedIn. Some people research in their email inboxes. Some people research based on referrals or other websites. It's key for you to find out where they research.

You can do this through keyword research for people using Google and by using AI to find where your personas go online to get information.

Once you develop that persona, you can ask AI tools to tell you how to find them. Where do they go to do research online and offline?

Write Content They Want to Read

Then you can follow up with the question, *What content do they want to read?* Because if you know where they're researching, then you can give them the kind of content they're looking for, and that will move them through your sales funnel. Now, keep in mind that a big part of content online today is *video*. And there are many people who *only* take in content via video. It's safe to say that at *least a third* of people who use the Internet *only take in content via video*. Think about that for a second. If they're only going to take in content via video, then we've got to post videos on YouTube and link those videos to your website.

Use AI to Create Video Scripts and Concepts

AI can save time because videos are *based on scripts and concepts*. AI tools can give you those scripts and concepts. Then partner with a local video professional to shoot and edit a script based on that concept.

Go to ChatGPT and enter the prompt, "Prepare a script for a 90-second explainer video about how our company adds value to [persona]." Fill in the blank with your persona profile.

Keep your videos brief. Three to five minutes is the current standard, although TikTok, Instagram and Facebook Shorts are shortening people's attention span.

Don't be afraid of long-form videos, but don't do them at the expense of shorter ones. The video can be as long as you like, so long as it's not *boring*. Use shorter videos to engage people and introduce them to topics. Use longer-form videos to draw people in and give them more information. Videos *should help people do their job better,* or enhance the quality of their lives, and make things more interesting.

Videos are great tools to *showcase the details* of your products and services and to allow people to experience them before they buy. Recently, my garage door opener greeted me with a bang, followed by a loud, scary grinding noise, and then locked up completely. Knowing nothing about garage door openers, I was searching online for "garage door repair service near me" when I stumbled across a video, "How to Rebuild a Sears Craftsman Garage Door Opener." I watched the 11-minute video, and it looked like an easy screwdriver job. The call-to-action was a link to order the parts. Two days and $28 later, the parts kit arrived, and watching the same video again, I was able to replace the broken worm gear in half an hour, saving what would have been a very expensive service call. This is the kind of helpful information your visitor is looking for.

Measure Movement in the Funnel

Videos are also fantastic for driving *movement in the funnel.* All your customers are going through a sales funnel as they do research. AI can help you meet customer needs by creating content in that funnel, by creating *calls to action,* and by helping you *get email addresses* to build your contact database. This is critical because that contact database is going to allow you to nurture relationships and to nurture people in the sales funnel.

Larger companies have larger contact databases, and great digital marketing companies are fantastic at capturing email addresses, which is something AI can help you do by going out, identifying and creating content that people want to read.

Develop a Plan for Gaining Customer Insights

AI can also help you with *market research.* It can help create surveys, create questions to ask in the surveys and then help you analyze the results to put together a plan for content.

The Rule of Three

As you use the AI tool, think about *The Rule of Three*. Information grouped in threes resonates more deeply than other numbers. Cognitive science backs this up. Our short-term memory can juggle about three items at once, making trios easier to process. Remember: Three Blind Mice, Three Little Pigs, Three Wishes, the Three Stooges, the Three Musketeers, the Three Wise Men, etc. Build your messaging around *three benefits*. Not four, or seven, or nine, but *three*. What are the top *three* reasons people *buy* from your company? And what are the three reasons they *remain loyal* to your brand? Your website must communicate those three reasons back to the market.

AI tools help you create a checklist of benefits. Along with confirmation from your customers, you can use AI to identify the key reasons people buy from you. Prompt for, "List the top 10 most valuable benefits of [using your product]." I suggest 10 in the prompt because the AI will often suggest benefits you haven't considered. Then pick the three most valuable. Feature those benefits on the key landing pages and in the content you produce for digital marketing.

It's Better to Be Different than Better

First of all, everyone *claims* to be better, even when they're *not*, so nobody *believes* you, even if you *are*. So, it's better to focus on how you're *different*. Better *still* if you're different in a way that actually *makes* you better, you can safely ignore the rest. Do these things in a way that connects to the personal story of your key customers, and you will be better by being unique.

AI Can Produce a Variety of Content Types

AI will not only tell you what those content types are and *what people want to read* but also produce *first-draft content* for all of those content types, whether it's an eBook, a webinar, a white paper, a research book, a case study, a blog post, a specific article for your market or even a video script.

Your action plan is to get on the AI tools discussed in this book, if you haven't already, and start creating a dialogue around how you could better understand prospects and customers, how you can meet them where they are online and how you can produce content that satisfies their needs and moves them through a buying funnel.

The Use of Story in Digital Marketing

For most of the time humans have been on this planet we have not had the ability to write things down, so the only way we could hand down knowledge from generation to generation was by telling stories. Stories were how we learned what was safe and what was dangerous, how to survive, how to thrive, how to get pleasure and how to avoid pain. All of those things throughout human existence were communicated through story.

Deep in our brains we're hardwired to use stories as a way of remembering emotions, thoughts and feelings. That's why you can remember in great detail a movie that you saw 10 or 20 years ago but then forget what you had for lunch yesterday. What it means for digital marketers is that you have to be in tune with how people remember things.

The confused mind never buys, and most marketing messages are confusing, or worse, irrelevant. Never waste marketing copy on messages that are universal or a given. Most marketing messaging can be summed up in three words: "we, we, we…" "Our people are our most important asset." Yeah, sure. "Safety is our #1 priority." Really? Well, it better be. "In business since 1492." Nobody cares. Effective digital marketing isn't about you. It's about the customer; *their* life, *their* problems, and their *story*.

At Intuitive Websites, we follow the content format suggested in Donald Miller's landmark book, *Building a Story Brand*, and AI can help in all these areas.

I love *Story Brand* because it's a fundamental truth of marketing that *people remember stories*. They forget information and they remember the impact that a guide had on them in their personal story. The role of your company is to be a *guide*, helping the customer who is the hero in their own personal journey to achieve some kind of success, defeat some kind of pain or overcome a villain. And that ends in emotional success.

In *Building a Story Brand*, author Donald Miller argues that customers are wired for stories and offers a framework to simplify your message using *seven universal story beats:* their Hero, their Villain, their Guide (your brand), and the journey to overcome their Flaws and achieve their Desire.

In Joseph Campbell's model, the Hero's Journey, the hero (your customer) is called on an adventure, does battle with a villain, is given advice or special powers by a Guide (that's you) and is transformed. The Hero prevails in the end and returns to tell the story. Think Luke Skywalker and Yoda, who work together to defeat Darth Vader. In digital marketing, the customer is the *hero,* and you are the *guide.* You have the tools and information they need to help them solve a problem or defeat a "monster." As the guide, you have a call to action and a plan to help them succeed, which will end in an emotional success for your customer.

Miller built a consulting business that generates over $10 million a year solely on this book. It really took off because it met a need for marketers to understand how to use story. By aligning your brand with the challenges and problems your customers face, you tap into their emotions, making them invested in your product as the Guide who helps them win. The *Story Brand* approach provides *a step-by-step process* to identify these elements in your brand and craft messaging that resonates, leaving customers eager to become the Hero of their own success story with your brand as their guide.

Miller guides you through seven key steps to structure your message and position your brand as the hero's trusted guide. These seven steps are powerful and provide the strategic insights needed to use the key elements of Story Brand in your marketing.

1. The Hero:
- Identify your ideal customer, the protagonist of your story.
- Understand their desires and aspirations.

2. The Problem:
- Define the internal and external struggles your customer faces.
- Highlight the specific challenges that prevent them from achieving their desires.

3. The Guide:
- Introduce your brand as the wise mentor or helpful friend.
- Position yourself as the solution to the hero's problems.

4. The Plan:
- Clearly outline the steps your customer needs to take to overcome their challenges.
- Show how your product or service acts as a roadmap to success.

5. The Call-to-Action:
- Encourage your customer to take the next step.
- This could be visiting your website, contacting you or making a purchase.

6. Failure Avoids:
- Emphasize the negative consequences of inaction.
- Illustrate what your customer stands to lose if they don't address their problems.

7. Success:
- Paint a vivid picture of the transformed life your customer can achieve with your help.
- Showcase the happy ending that awaits them when they embrace your solution.

By following these steps, you can craft marketing copy that resonates with your audience on an emotional level, making them feel understood and empowered to act. Remember, your *customer* is the hero of their own story, and your brand acts as their *guide* on the path to success.

AI helps you live this message by identifying the benefits people want and the risks they need to avoid, as well as the *guide for change*, the call-to-action, and the plan that your company has to move people to action.

AI is a great story brand support tool. It really does help make things happen. It does this because at the core of making your customer the hero and your company the guide comes an understanding of benefits and risks. AI excels in creating a comprehensive checklist of key benefits and risks for your targeted personas.

East Daley Analytics Connects with Customers

East Daley Analytics is an oil and gas data analytics company helping energy traders and related stakeholders understand these markets. They are thought leaders in this space, and their key digital marketing goal is the growth of their subscriber base. By implementing clear and direct messaging and better aligning their content with the goals of their target market, they increased their subscriber base by 1200%. An added benefit was increased rankings in Google, which drove page views up 91%. They did this using the principles of story and clear, direct and concise messaging.

Become the Hero's Guide

At the core of this book is the concept that you must have a clear company message. If people don't understand what your company does, how you do it, what kind of value you provide, and the benefits you provide, they cannot move forward with you as part of their life story.

First, clarify your company message. We recommend that you do that with very clear taglines and headers on your key landing-page copy. AI can help because you can go to the AI tools and get a sense of your target market and get a sense of taglines that would engage them on the key landing pages, and in particular, your homepage, starting with the tagline in our homepage banner.

Remember, you're not the hero saving the customer. In the mind of the customer, you're the guide. In every story ever told there is a guide who helps the hero through their journey. Your company supports the hero with an offer for *change*, and that offer for change could be a product or service, or it could be information and content, but that offer for change moves them to action because, as a guide, you have a plan. That plan can be several things. It could be as simple as reading helpful content on your website and getting them engaged. It could be giving you an email address, subscribing to a newsletter or submitting a form to schedule an appointment.

But because you're perceived as a Guide, you have a great call to action. A good practice is to include the word "guide" in your tagline. Go to AI and use the prompt, "Let us be your guide to [fill in the gap]." Or prompt for, "How can we be a guide to our target market for [your product or services]?"

This helps you understand story-branded marketing, and when you do this well, the customer defeats their personal villains, avoids the pain and gets what they want.

The story ends in emotional success, and because all buying decisions are based on emotions, buying from you closes the loop of the story. The customer is left feeling like they've made the right decision.

AI and Story Focused Content

AI helps you create content that works for story-branded success because it gives you the benefits and reduces the risks. It helps you understand the benefits that people get when buying from your company and the risks they can avoid, either from no action at all or from making a bad decision and going with one of your competitors. Those benefits and risks are associated with the marketing personas that you've selected. Because you understand the benefits and risks, you're perceived as a *guide* when you communicate them, which causes the persona to feel like you can be part of their personal story and help them achieve what they want to achieve.

AI also helps you *create the first draft and revisions* that will go into your digital content that people will read as they research your business.

It also helps you prepare content for multiple channels so it can be prepared for wherever that persona is looking for in their research. AI can also help create many different types of content or even programming code.

AI can also communicate with you directly about Story Brand in common content. You can have a discussion with the AI tool around what would work well in your business with story-branded content.

Action Items:

❑ Build a list of features, characteristics or benefits that only you can offer.

❑ Include stories about your customers' successes rather than your own.

❑ Position your brand as the helpful guide in their journey.

❑ Simplify your message using the Story Brand framework.

❑ Write clear, direct and engaging headers and taglines.

❑ Focus on three key benefits on your website landing pages.

How Users Get Value from Content

Content is the fuel that drives the Internet, and in many ways, the fuel needed to win at digital marketing. Content is the most important part of your website. It drives conversions, gets you found in search engines, brands your company, and much more. Without it there would be very little reason for people to go online. Content is an important part of both your design work and traffic generation. Yet, having excellent content is one of the biggest challenges.

Content can be defined as anything that's used to communicate with website visitors. Let's dig deeper into website content and how it drives value for your users.

Questions to ask and guidelines to follow when reviewing digital content

Is it clear what your company does?

The first question to ask involves users understanding what your site is about. A clear ten-to-twelve-word tagline should communicate this so everyone understands what your company does. Push your digital marketing team to ensure the site's message is easily understood and test your assumptions with your target market.

Does the website have a clear branding tagline?

Your tagline should also mention your company's unique value and how you are different from competitors. Take time to prepare your tagline and review the upcoming chapter on tagline writing in this book. This tagline is part of the site visitor's first impression of your company and should be featured on the homepage near your logo.

Is the content scannable?

Visitors scan content first, then go deeper to read items of interest. Content should be made up of taglines, headers, sub-heads, bullet points, small blocks of text with links to deeper content pages and other types of easy-to-skim material. Your site can have volumes of content for the user to read, but this content should not be on the homepage or main landing pages. Volumes of content should be deeper in the website. This is also important to Google, as websites with more content rank higher than sites with less.

Keep in mind, it's not easy to read on a computer screen and some content should be easily printable or available in PDF. Archive all your blog posts and include newsletter articles. More to come on blog postings in future chapters.

Is the content organized for usability?

The organization is important, especially as you add more pages across a wide breadth of topics. Make sure your content is easy to find and well-organized in your navigation menus. Only use a search function on the site if it's needed and test it to make sure it produces accurate results. Check your content pages in Google Analytics and set a target average of three to four page visits per user session. This is an indicator of well-organized content. If the average user visits three or four pages, that person has a high level of interest.

Does the content add value?

This is the most difficult part of content because value is defined by your users. Web stats, such as the number of pages visited, an average time on the site of more than three minutes, a low bounce rate and other related stats will show you how engaged they are. This is the measurement of content value and is directly related to online conversions.

Does the user understand the content?

The content must be written in the language that the visitor will understand. Avoid internal company-speak, buzzwords and acronyms. This can also be reviewed in your stats and user testing.

Write your content to about a 7th-Grade reading level, not because your visitors are stupid, but because they're lazy and in a hurry. Use online tools like The *Flesch–Kincaid readability tests,* available from Readable.com and many other sources, to measure how difficult your content is to read. The Flesch-Kincaid reading score for this page comes in at 5.68, or 5th to 6th grade level. Write content that's clear and easy to read, even if your audience is knowledgeable and sophisticated.

You can use AI to simplify dense technical or scientific content. Use the prompt, "Re-write this article to a 7th-Grade reading level," and paste in the text. AI will return a simplified version. "Brevity is the soul of eloquence." ~ William Shakespeare.

Is the content optimized for search engines?

Regularly updated content and author authority drive Google's search results. Google will rank sites higher if they have content appropriate for the search terms and regular content updates from credible authors. We will go into this in greater depth in the chapters on traffic generation and search engine optimization.

Is there a plan in place for content marketing and regular up-dates?

Content will not write itself and won't get done unless there's a specific plan to make it happen, along with the right people to complete the tasks. This is called "content marketing." Content marketing is at the heart of a successful digital marketing strategy. Once again, we will review content marketing in more detail in the coming chapters.

How does content drive conversions?

This is the final word on content: *it drives conversions and sales*. Picture your website content as a sales funnel that pulls people into contact with your company. Following the guidelines in this book will ensure that content delivers conversions.

Action Items:

❑ Include a content marketing plan in your digital marketing strategy.

❑ Assign content updates to a dedicated web author on the marketing team or outsource it to a writer who can articulate your company story.

❑ Track the success of your content in your SEO results.

❑ Develop a content conversion funnel.

❑ Organize content so it's easy to navigate and scan.

❑ Write content from the perspective of the user, not the company.

❑ Layer your content with brief taglines and bullet points on key landing pages, linking to volumes of content for readers who crave more in-depth information.

AI Has Reinvented Digital Content

The Ghost in the Machine

AI generated content is *so* good it feels like there's a person working in the cloud at lightning speed to produce content. This ghost in the machine provides great advantages for digital marketing and content generation. As you start to interact with AI to create content, think about AI in two ways:

First: Your Own Personal Marketing Consultant
AI is like a brain within your brain. It's doing what technology has always done, it improves the human experience and helps you hone your craft. It allows you to prepare actual content you can post for the world to see, and it allows you to have your own personal consultant who helps you do your job even better.

Second: Any content produced by AI is a first draft
Remember that ChatGPT, Gemini and the others are all just large language models. Everything they generate is a *derivative* of the content on which they were trained. They're incapable of creativity, but they are very good at sifting through large volumes of data, and the output is often clearly recognizable as computer-generated. AI can be so eager to respond to your prompt that it will fabricate answers that are simply not true.

Everything that you borrow from AI needs a human to review it before it goes live.

First Drafts Save Time
First-draft content from AI is extremely valuable because most people hate to write. They can edit content but struggle to come up with the first draft. I've been a writer for years and staring at a blank page is a lot worse than getting some first-draft content that you can begin to edit. AI gives you that first-draft content, and in many cases, that first-draft content comes in the form of a story, or a set of bullet points, or a checklist, which means that these are the key areas you need to include in your content.

Another way to apply AI is to take the first draft, edit it, then resubmit it to the prompt for fact-checking. The prompt would be, "Fact check this article" [followed by pasting in your second draft].

You can also prompt the AI to refine and re-write the content in a particular style. Prompt for, "Rewrite this article in the style of [Ernest Hemingway]" (try it for fun). Prompt for, "Using this sample as a baseline, rewrite all of the following articles in the same style as the sample." [insert sample]

Get Clear on Benefits and Value

Another way that AI is reinventing digital content is by giving you content that really matters to your readers, which is focused on benefits and value. The biggest marketing challenge you have as an organization is the communication of benefits and value.

For example, we used AI to help a client write promotional copy for a course they were offering. The offering was a 4-hour seminar on "Lean Startup Strategy in Product Development." The prompt we used was: "What are the benefits for a VP of Product Development or a Product Manager [their client persona] attending a course on lean startup strategy?"

ChatGPT replied,

> In summary, a Lean Startup course can equip Product Managers with practical tools, methodologies and a mindset that can enhance their ability to drive successful, customer-focused and efficient product development processes.

The marketing message became, *"You will learn practical tools, methodologies and a mindset that can enhance your ability to drive successful, customer-focused and efficient product development processes."*

This is much more persuasive than a bullet list of topics in the syllabus, and the course was a huge hit.

Content for Multiple Channels

AI can also provide content for multiple channels. We know from our persona research that people have preferences for how they take in content. You must prepare digital content appropriate for that channel. Content posted on LinkedIn is very different than the content in a blog, a website homepage, an email or an eBook.

AI can help you write content in a style and format for that works best for each channel or platform. It can help you write in the voice you want for that persona, and it can generate these first drafts very quickly.

Your Personal Programmer

AI can also be used to write website code. Now this isn't necessarily a book for coders, but it's important for you to know that if you're building your website in any kind of universal code like PHP or CSS, code can be written in AI and can be pasted into your website. If you're looking to get some movement on your WordPress site or trying to get an interactive tool put together like a calculator, all of that can be done with an AI tool. Those tools create benefits and value for your visitor.

For example, we worked with a roofing company in Atlanta, <u>IBS Roofing,</u> that wanted to show people what the risks were of taking no action on getting roof maintenance done. We used an AI tool to write the code for an ROI calculator explaining the potential return on getting coverage for your roof. That tool was then launched on the website, and to use the tool, they had to provide an email address. Now not only do we have a tool for people to use, but we also have a lead generation device, all created with the help of AI.

Keep in mind, just like in writing first-draft copy, AI-generated code has to be reviewed by a developer and tested before it goes live. But AI can really help because it saves so much time and money, and you don't have to write this code from scratch.

Action Items:

- ❏ Open an account with OpenAI and ChatGPT or with Google's Gemini, and then use that account to help you deal with marketing challenges.

- ❏ When you're reading this book, the first thing to do is take these prompts and put them in and start getting AI to help as your personal marketing consultant.

The Best Digital Marketing Prompts

The more specific you can be when submitting prompts to the AI tools, the better your results will be. It's also important to use complete sentences and correct spelling and grammar.

Instead of "Write a short story about a girl lost in the woods," give the prompt as many specifics as you can.

For example. "Write a 500-word story about a 12-year-old girl who runs away from home and takes refuge in a cabin deep in the woods of northern Michigan. The cabin is owned by a family of bears who have gone out for a walk. Here she finds shelter, food and a place to sleep, that is, until the bears return, and chaos ensues. Written in the style of a cautionary fable."

You get the idea.

The ideal formula for an AI prompt is [Context] + [Specific details] + [Intent] + [Response format]

Context
Start by giving the prompt some background on the information about what you're seeking. For example, an intellectual property attorney is trying to attract new clients. He might start a prompt with, "I'm writing an article for LinkedIn about the importance of protecting intellectual property, particularly patents."

Specific Details
AI works best when you can give it as much detail as possible. "The target audience is business owners of companies with revenue between $5 million and $50 million who regularly develop new products. I want to emphasize the point that you must file for a patent within one year of showing the product in public, offering it for sale or advertising it in any media, or you lose your rights forever."

Intent
Spell out the outcome you're hoping for. "My intent is to attract potential clients into my intellectual property law practice and motivate them to hire me to help them with their IP work."

Response format

Specify how you want the results presented. "Limit the discussion to 500 words, using the format: problem, solution, call-to-action, in a breezy, informal style, suitable for LinkedIn."

Here's what Gemini returned:

Unveiling Your Genius? Don't Let It Become Public Domain!

So, your company's buzzing with a game-changing new product. Funding's secured, the prototype's sleek and visions of market domination dance in your head. But hold on, innovator extraordinaire! Before you shout your invention from the rooftops (or, worse, drop it online for the world to see), consider this: **you only have one year to legally protect your masterpiece.**

Problem: That's right, folks. The patent office plays by the "first-inventor-to-file" rule. Show your invention publicly – think demos, sales, even that *oh-so-tempting* Facebook reveal – before filing, and *poof!* Your exclusivity vanishes faster than a free trial offer.

Solution: Don't panic! This is where your friendly neighborhood patent attorney swoops in, cape and all. We guide you through the filing process, ensuring your invention gets the legal shield it deserves. Think of us as your invention's bodyguards, protecting it from copycats and paving the way for lucrative licensing deals or future acquisitions.

Call to Action: Don't let your million-dollar idea become public domain chump change. Let's chat! I'd love to understand your innovation and craft a rock-solid patent strategy that safeguards your intellectual property and fuels your business growth.

Remember: Time is ticking on that one-year window. So, ditch the social media frenzy and drop me a line. Your future self (and bank account) will thank you.

P.S. Want to impress your network with some patent pro tips? Share this article and tag your fellow innovators! Knowledge is power, and protecting your intellectual property is the ultimate power move.

P.P.S. This post is for informational purposes only and does not constitute legal advice. Please consult with an attorney for specific guidance regarding your unique situation. ⚖

Word count: 498. Whew, made it just under the wire!

Some minor editing, maybe cut the bold bookmark words: *Problem*, *Solution*, and *Call to Action*. Then add your email address and phone number, and Bob's your uncle.

If you don't get a good response on the first attempt, alter your prompt and keep trying. You might re-prompt the example above by entering, "Re-write the article in the more formal, professional style of a lawyer." Or you could try, "Expand this article to 1500 words, suitable for a Law Journal magazine."

Types of Website Content and Usage

Internet content comes in many different forms. But people are notorious for only absorbing content in the forms that are most comfortable for them, so they feel everyone else does that as well.

Not true. People absorb content online in many ways, and if you're a really good marketer, you have to cover all these different ways that people express themselves through digital content.

The beauty of AI is that *it can write for all those different types of content*. This gives people the ability to research and learn through their preferred media, whether it be reading, listening to audio, reviewing a slide presentation or watching a video. Millions of people use each of these content types every day.

Written content is still the most popular form, and it can be supplemented nicely by others to help communicate the value of your business.

A few examples of content types that you can include:

- Written content
- Video and audio
- Blog posts and content articles
- Blog subscription feeds and comments
- Email newsletters
- Podcasts (audio and video)
- Webinars or other training
- Informational articles
- Case studies
- Product reviews and testimonials
- E-books and white papers
- PDF files
- Social media postings and comments
- X or micro-blog postings
- Press releases (internal and external)
- Slide presentations
- Mobile apps
- About Us pages
- Contact Us pages

And more…

This content can be presented to users through multiple channels:

- Business and consumer websites
- Mobile websites
- Website and micro-blogs
- Email newsletters
- Audio and video
- PDF files
- Social media websites and posts
- Press releases and media websites
- Google Docs and other online documents
- Mobile apps
- Branded apps
- Offline marketing

And more...

Each day, millions of people select the online channels and content that's best for them. Don't make the mistake of thinking that one content channel is best or that other people don't use a particular channel because you don't use it. When prompting the AI tools, *specify how you want the content to be generated*, whether it's for a blog, a web page, a video script, an eBook, a white paper, a technical paper or a case study.

You can also use AI to *repurpose* content, say, by compressing a long, technical white paper into a short article for laypeople or a teleprompter script that you'll use to shoot a video. Try different content types and channels and measure the results.

Action Items:

- ❏ Determine what content type is most preferred by your target market and make sure you're providing information they value.

- ❏ Include a content marketing and distribution strategy in your digital marketing plan.

- ❏ Offer content through multiple sources to give website users options.

- ❏ Distribute this content to other platforms visited by your target market.

- ❏ Track and monitor the most popular content and its use.

- ❏ Review your content on mobile devices and track mobile stats.

- ❏ Include visual content with the written word to better communicate value, and always use captions with photos and graphics.

Website Taglines and Content Headers

Website taglines are powerful. In fact, your homepage tagline is *the* most important piece of marketing copy on your website. It's very often the *first thing people see*, and it may be *the* most important piece of marketing content at your company.

People land on a homepage, they see the logo, they see the navigation, they see a banner image and they see a tagline in that banner. If the tagline doesn't persuade them to move forward and to want to know more, then the tagline is not doing its job.

Website taglines are the most direct and clear translation and communication of your digital strategy. Brainstorming tagline ideas and finding ways to simplify your strategy into just *eight to twelve words* is an excellent exercise to clarify and identify your strategy. Keep in mind that first impressions are very important, and website users will only take a few seconds to evaluate the website page they are visiting.

Writing a catchy tagline is the most important content on your homepage

The homepage tagline is the sales hook, the most compelling message on your homepage and often the starting point in your prospect's path to purchase, and wanting to learn more about your company. Not only do taglines summarize the value of your business, they also clearly show users if your website is right for them.

They're important because you only have about two-and-a-half seconds to answer your visitor's question. And they're all asking the *same* question: "Am I in the right place?" If it's not a resounding "YES!" they click away and are gone forever.

What's a Tagline?

They can best be compared to newspaper headlines. Homepage taglines are up to twelve-word phrases that introduce what your company does and a few key benefits. Taglines are critical because people *scan* websites, especially first-time visitors who are just beginning to understand your business.

Slogans Versus Taglines

Many people confuse a tagline with a slogan. They are not the same. Taglines are not slogans or catchy phrases that support the brand, such as Nike's "Just Do It" McDonalds' "I'm lovin' it!" These slogans do not work on their own. They only work when connected to a well-known brand. However, most small- and medium-sized firms don't have a brand that's a household name, so your tagline should clarify what the company is about.

Slogans are brief, often emotional phrases meant to support the brand. There's usually no context for a slogan on its own. Taglines are descriptive and give the reader information about your company. Taglines can stand alone and introduce your company to new website visitors.

Tagline Mistakes

By far the biggest mistake companies make is using a tagline that's generic, cryptic or not understood by the typical visitor. Marketers regularly confuse taglines with slogans. Most users simply overlook meaningless taglines.

Another common mistake is to use internal business-speak that's not understood by your visitors. Many websites do not have a tagline, and instead, use a block of text on their homepage that users are not able to scan. Others put their taglines into animations or image sliders where they disappear and make users work to read them. Some websites may have four or five taglines pulling the visitor in different directions and rotating so that *none* of them are seen by users.

Other websites have no tagline on the homepage at all. They want the design to function as an introduction to the brand on its own. The problem with this approach is that many website users will not know what message your design is attempting to convey unless you use words to tell them.

A tagline is not the same as a slogan. Here are a few examples:

Nike slogan: "Just Do It"
Nike tagline: "Athletic shoes and apparel, no matter what your sport."

Apple slogan: "Think Different"
Apple tagline: "The world's best computing devices, smart phones, laptops, tablets and desktop computers."

United Airlines' slogan has been "Fly the Friendly Skies" for many years.
Their current tagline, "Good Leads the Way," was introduced in 2023 to mark a "new era of travel" and focus on the airline's commitment to its employees, customers and sustainability efforts.

Your tagline is the best opportunity to pull people into your website content. Engaged website users convert at higher levels. Therefore, the taglines on your website should clearly summarize your strategy. Start with a prominent tagline for your homepage.

Examples of Bad Taglines Made Better

We've seen many, many websites that do a couple things wrong: They either have a generic tagline that's replaceable with any other company, or they have no tagline. They just have an image there, and from that they expect the user to figure out what they do, and most people won't. One of my favorite generic taglines is "Innovate Technology Solutions." What kind of technology is not innovative? Solutions to what? Why not put the solutions in the tagline?

Taglines are the starting point for most prospective customers who are new to your brand.

Here are a few examples of actual taglines and slogans. Keep in mind by the time you read this some of these taglines may have changed, hopefully for the better.

TrustAmerica.com

Homepage Tagline: "It's about time. What will you do with yours?"

Many financial services websites use generic taglines that don't usually connect with the visitor or their target market. This company provides services to financial planners that save them time.

A stronger tagline is: "We provide your back-end support, so you save time."

Questions can also work with taglines: "Are you wasting time with administrative headaches?"

These two taglines do a much better job of getting to the heart of the matter for financial planners who will hire TCA for admin and backend office support.

Stone Group Architects
StoneGroupArch.com

Tagline: Positively Impacting People and Place

This is a classic example of a slogan being used as a tagline. What's the positive impact? This is an architectural firm run by veterans who understand veterans' needs and design VA Hospitals in the mid-west.

A more direct and clearer tagline for this website would be: "A Commercial Architectural Firm Run by Veterans, Designing Commercial Buildings for the Veterans Administration and More."

HDI
Thinkhdi.com

Tagline: "HDI; Your Most Trusted Partner"

Their tagline is generic, and thousands of companies could use it. The tagline does not say what they do.

A better tagline for HDI might be: "Training IT professionals to become excellent at service and support."

Does that clear things up? Of course, we are assuming the user knows what IT means.

GEBA
Geba.com

Tagline: "Feds Trusted. Service Driven Solutions"

The word "solutions" is probably the most overused word in taglines on the web. In this case, it's the *only* word in the tagline. In fact, none of the static content on the homepage describes what GEBA actually *does*.

A strong tagline will do just that: "Helping organizations make the right decisions about health insurance and financial security."

PCS
Pcstelcom.com

Tagline: "In Command. In Control"

This company does not need a *slogan* because they're not a national brand. What does that tagline mean? PCS provides telephone systems for prisons and are marketing to large prison systems that will purchase and install their phones.

How about this tagline: "A leader in customized, comprehensive telecommunication products and services for prisons."

That means more to the user than "In Control. In Command."

Aqua-Hot Heating Systems
Aqua-hot.com

Tagline: "Welcome"

Another very popular tagline is the word "welcome." This is a left-over from the early days of the Internet. This company uses a block of text on their homepage that really needs a tagline.

Pretty much everything that's said in that block of text can be summed up in this tagline: "Never run out of hot water in your RV."

Examples of Website Taglines to Avoid

Don't waste the most valuable space on the page talking about things that are universal, given or irrelevant to the visitor.

"In Business Since 1982." Trust me; nobody cares.

"Innovative Technology Solutions." My favorite cryptic tagline that says nothing.

"Our People are Our Most Important Asset." No, they're not. Sell the company, and in a year they'll all be gone.

"Safety is our #1 Concern." Well, yeah, it better be!

"Passionate about Quality." Quality, service, and value are expected of everyone.

"#1 in PCS-PRC coded Software." Says who? And what the hell is PCS-PRC?

"Award-Winning Service." How does this benefit your prospective customers?

You get the idea.

Better to be Different than Better

Everybody *claims* to be better, even if they're *not*. So, nobody *believes* you, even if you *are*. Don't waste valuable copy on things they can get elsewhere. Concentrate your titles and taglines on your *exclusive* features or benefits, things they can only get from your company.

It must also be very clear and direct. AI can help you write taglines that you can put on your website tomorrow that can help you test what works and what doesn't.

AI tools can be used to *write powerful website taglines and headers*. Remember the natural healthcare clinic who used AI to better define their benefits? They can also use AI to write a better tagline that goes in the homepage banner. Their old tagline was: "Not accepting health insurance."

Here are the recommendations from ChatGPT that are so much better:

> "Empowering Your Health, Naturally - Discover a Holistic Path to Wellness"

> "Nature's Healing, Personalized for You - Transform Your Health Journey"

> "Harmonizing Body, Mind and Spirit - Experience Natural Medicine Excellence"

> "Where Nature Meets Nurture - Your Partner in Holistic Health"

> "Revitalize Your Wellbeing - Expert Natural Care Tailored to You"

> "Innovative Healing, Traditional Wisdom - Start Your Natural Health Odyssey"

> "Bridging Nature and Health - Personalized Care for Modern Living"

> "Nourishing Your Health Holistically - Uncover Your Path to Natural Wellness"

"Find Your Balance - Expert Natural Therapies in a Healing Environment"

"Transformative Natural Care - Dedicated to Your Whole Health and Happiness"

There's no need to wait. Replace a poorly performing homepage tagline today and get more people engaged with your website.

Where to Find Great Taglines

Study how newspapers, magazines and photo captions use taglines. They've learned how to capture the eye of the scanning reader and draw them into content. Great marketing companies like Starbucks and Apple also make great use of website taglines and headers.

AI and Great Taglines

AI tools are great for writing website taglines and headers. Ask the tool to write taglines for your key landing pages, including your homepage, and focus on content that engages and moves people through your sales funnel.

Action Items:

- ❏ Follow the instructions in this chapter and prompt AI to write a tagline that sets your company apart and engages visitors.

- ❏ Write new taglines that both describe your company and communicate your competitive advantage.

- ❏ Understand the differences between taglines and slogans and how they're used.

- ❏ Make sure your tagline is understood by your target market.

- ❏ Check your bounce rate. High bounce rates on your website may be a sign of a poor tagline.

- ❏ Connect your tagline with website images and your company logo.

Content Flow to Build Engagement

How to Lay Out a Homepage and Landing Pages

The content flow on your website homepage either stops people in their tracks or encourages and motivates them to read through the page and explore the website navigation. The flow of the content on your website must move people to convert and act.

What is content flow?

It's important to have certain elements on your homepage and key landing pages where visitors go to get information so you can engage with them. That engagement includes *staying* on the website, *reading* the content and taking some form of *action*. Content flow is essential if you want to engage with users and get them to take actions that move toward a sale.

Website Wireframes

The first step in having a great content flow is having a great website content wireframe.

Too many websites go straight to design before they have a wireframe built. A website wireframe is simply what your website looks like with no design elements. The wireframe only contains the blocks of content in each section on the web page.

It's critical when you start developing a website that you start with wireframes. Many companies skip this step. They either do the site internally and start designing immediately, or their agency will even start designing immediately without a wireframe. That's a big mistake. Content is critical to success on any homepage or key landing page, and wireframes drive that content. Prepare a homepage wireframe first before you go to design.

Include the following sections in your wireframe:

Homepage Tagline

Homepage taglines are the most important piece of marketing copy. It's the most important because it's what your customers are going to engage with at the very top of the sales funnel. It will be the first thing they see when they're evaluating your brand. Your homepage tagline should be in the banner of your website. It must be clear and direct. Anyone should be able to read that tagline and know what your company does and it should make sense with the design elements and imagery they're seeing in the banner. Homepage taglines are absolutely critical.

Call-to-Action

In your homepage banner, it's recommended that you have calls to action. We like to see *two levels* of calls to action. One is the bottom-of-funnel call to action to speak to a sales rep. Another call to action gives the visitor the opportunity to get more information by giving you an email address, something like getting an e-book, subscribing to an e-mail newsletter, or attending a webinar.

Benefits and Risks

What comes next in your website flow is a little counterintuitive. Many companies want to start talking about themselves, but what comes next are *key benefits and key risks*. This is where AI can really help you by creating that checklist of benefits and risks that people face when either working with you or selecting another company. This benefit section is critical. It should come after the banner and after your tagline. It tells people what the key benefits are of working with you. Those benefits should be identified by asking your customers, "What are the top reasons that you hire us? What are the top reasons that you continue to purchase from us?" Those are the benefits you want to feature next in the flow.

Featured Products and Services

After the benefits and risk section, we can now have a *featured products and services section*. This is where you put the spotlight on your company a bit and talk about your featured products and services. Now, many companies can't fit all their products and services in this section, so you've got to have the *featured* products and services, the ones that best encapsulate your brand, where people can get more information on those services or products or they can go to key landing pages to see your categories of products or services. This is the area where people can see what the benefits are and look at the products and services.

The Plan and Steps to Action

This next section is an overview of your company's plan. This can also be the steps to getting started. Website users are looking for this type of direction from your company. It is very helpful to feature how to get started on the homepage.

Resources for the Reader

Toward the bottom of the page. This is where you *support your statements*. You support your tagline. You support your benefits and risks by showing people you're a thought leader and having *resources* for them, such as links to blog posts, white papers, webinars and upcoming events.

Testimonials, Client Logos and Case Studies

It's also the place where you put testimonials, client logos, links to case studies and other content about the company that shows, yeah, you provide these benefits, and you can *back it up*.

It's important to put this content *in this order* because if you put testimonials before benefits, there's no connection to what's in it for the reader. But when you *put benefits before testimonials,* then people make the connection.

Main Navigation

Two other things to talk about in your website flow are the *main navigation* at the top of your website and the *footer* navigation. The main navigation is absolutely critical and too many companies don't pay enough attention to this. The main navigation should include four buckets. In fact, all websites should have these four buckets:

1. A link to your services and products.
2. A link to your resources like blogs, videos, articles and more.
3. Your About Us link, which is about your company.
4. The Contact Us link.

These are the four most important navigation pages. In all the data we've reviewed in more than 20 years of doing this work, these are always the pages that are going to be at the top of the navigation system.

Also, because of mobile, you've got to *keep navigation simple*. Having four key areas of navigation, *products and services, resources, about* and *contact,* makes it simple for the user.

Now, that doesn't mean you can't have more expanded navigation because, underneath each of those four areas, you can have dropdowns that connect to lots and lots of content.

Footer Navigation
The *footer navigation* is also critical. Footer navigation should always include links to your social media pages, a subscription option for your email newsletter, should repeat all the navigation from your main navigation and also include any ancillary or supportive navigation, like support, customer service and that sort of thing.

This is important because your navigation should be on *all* your pages. All your web pages should have navigation so users can engage with your website.

AI and Website Pages
AI tools can write a first-draft wireframe and all the individual content that makes up your content flow. What's fantastic about the AI tools we have today is that you can get not only a complete homepage wireframe done but also all these sections written and supported.

In the AI tool, ask this question: "Please write a homepage wireframe for a [fill in the blank with your company or a description of what your company does]."

Remember the natural health medical clinic from earlier in the book? Here is what ChatGPT produced as a content wireframe for a new homepage. For added impact, the focus is on Emily, the targeted persona.

Below is a homepage content wireframe for "Keystone Medicine," focusing on the holistic, natural approach to health care and catering to personas like Emily.

Homepage Wireframe for Keystone Medicine

1. Header
- Logo: Keystone Medicine
- Navigation Bar: Home | About Us | Services | Testimonials | Blog | Contact Us

2. Hero Section
- Headline: "Empowering Your Journey to Natural Well-being"
- Sub-headline: "Discover personalized, holistic healthcare at Keystone Medicine."
- Primary Call-to-Action (CTA): "Schedule Your Consultation"
- Secondary CTA: "Learn More About Our Approach"

3. About Keystone Medicine
- Headline: "Holistic Health, Tailored to You"
- Brief Description: A short paragraph about Keystone Medicine's philosophy, emphasizing the personalized, patient-centered approach and commitment to natural and preventive care.
- CTA: "Our Story"

4. Our Services
- Headline: "Comprehensive Natural Medicine Services"
- Service Highlights (with icons):
  - "Holistic Health Consultations"
  - "Customized Wellness Plans"
  - "Herbal and Natural Remedies"
  - "Dietary and Lifestyle Guidance"
  - "Stress Management & Mental Wellbeing"
- CTA: "Explore Our Services"

5. Why Choose Keystone?
- Headline: "Why Keystone Medicine is Your Partner in Health"
- Bullet Points Highlighting Benefits:
  - "Personalized Care Beyond Symptoms"

- "A Holistic Approach for Long-lasting Wellness"
- "Expertise in Natural and Alternative Therapies"
- "Commitment to Prevention and Lifestyle Enhancement"
- "A Supportive Community of Like-minded Individuals"
- CTA: "Why Keystone?"

6. Success Stories
- Headline: "Hear From Our Patients"
- Testimonials Carousel: Short testimonials from satisfied patients, focusing on various aspects of improvement and satisfaction.
- CTA: "Read More Stories"

7. From Our Blog
- Headline: "Insights for Your Natural Health Journey"
- Featured Blog Posts: A selection of recent articles or posts covering topics like natural remedies, preventive health tips and success stories.
- CTA: "Visit Our Blog"

8. Get in Touch
- Headline: "Start Your Path to Natural Wellness"
- Brief encouragement to contact for a consultation or any inquiries.
- Contact Form: Name, Email, Message
- CTA: "Send Message"

9. Footer
- Navigation Links: Home | About Us | Services | Testimonials | Blog | Contact
- Social Media Icons: Facebook, Instagram, Pinterest, YouTube
- Legal: Privacy Policy | Terms of Service

This wireframe is designed to guide visitors through the key benefits of Keystone Medicine, showcasing its holistic and personalized approach to health, and encouraging them to engage with the clinic for their health needs. This is a great first draft to work with and will improve over time.

When you bring that together, then you have a fantastic digital experience for people who are visiting your website, and you'll see higher conversion rates and higher engagement rates.

Action Items:

- ❑ Learn more about website wireframes using AI tools.

- ❑ Have the AI tool prepare a website wireframe for you based on your industry.

- ❑ Use these wireframes to develop your content sections before they go to design.

- ❑ Get the content in order, develop a website wireframe and build out your navigation site map. Then take it to design, have the design match the needs of your target market and start building out interior pages.

Sample Website Homepage Wireframe

Great wireframes are one of the first steps toward a fantastic website. Not all websites will use this flow, but this is a good template to follow for your next website homepage or key landing page.

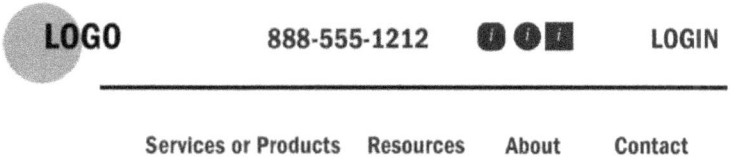

LOGO 888-555-1212 LOGIN

Services or Products   Resources   About   Contact

Banner Image or Video

Clear and Direct Tagline

CTA 1 - Middle of the Funnel
(Learn More)

CTA 2 - Bottom of the Funnel
(Get Started)

BENEFITS SECTION

Three to five clear benefits. How do your services or products add value? How are they better or different from your competitors?

SERVICES AND PRODUCTS SECTION

Three to five featured services or products. Product websites must be visual using product photos and services websites must be descriptive using content and images and/or icons.

THE PLAN OR PROCESS

This section reviews the steps to get started. This is very important for service companies. This section informs people on the steps to get started.

Step One: Discovery
Step Two: Plan Development
Step Three: Build Out and Delivery
Step Four: Follow-up

TESTIMONIALS SECTION

This section includes testimonials, client logos, case studies and examples of completed work. This is where the website user makes the connection between your products and services and the people and companies who buy them.

RESOURCES SECTION

This includes highlights of key resources not a part of products or service information, such as blogs, videos, e-books, webinars and other content.

BOTTOM OF PAGE CTAS

The CTAs from the banner are repeated here at the bottom of the page. In some cases additional CTAs can be placed throughout the web page.

Website Technologies

The previous chapters have focused on understanding usability and visitor needs to improve website design. Step Two, Strategic Communications, also includes website technology and the technical side of how websites are constructed. This is by no means a technical guide but rather a review of what you should know about the technology behind your website and how the development process works.

Technology has become a critical part of business, and the top leadership in any organization should clearly understand the strategic value of technology. You can no longer make the excuse that you don't understand technology fundamentals or pass it on to others for strategic implementation. Technology is simply too important, and today's business leader must be a much more active participant in technical decisions. Poorly informed technology decisions within a company can have huge consequences.

The technical side of digital marketing is one of these areas. You do not need to know every detail of website technology, but you *do* need an understanding of the fundamentals so you can make better business and budget decisions. Here are a few key points business leaders must know about digital marketing technology to better lead their marketing efforts.

Open Source Versus Licensed Software

The original business model for software was based on ownership and the sales of licensed software products. This business model is much less popular as groups of developers collaborate to create free software. This is called open-source software.

Developers then make money by selling *extensions* or *plugins* and offering programming support and development services. They can also take the free software and create an application or website that users pay to access.

Most of the software needed to run a successful digital marketing program will fall under the umbrella of open source. This has changed the industry, and the trend continues as younger generations of computer users make use of open-source software and fewer people pay for licensed software. This has resulted in open-source web development software such as WordPress being used as the development platform for a very high percentage of small business websites. It's important to note why this trend is happening and know it's expected to continue.

Content Management Systems (CMS)

CMS is a term that's used to refer to software programs used for website development. A CMS development platform allows anyone to edit the website from any browser with a simple login. This has put digital marketing more in the hands of sales and marketing professionals and less in the hands of IT staff. The current trend is to use open-source CMS programs such as WordPress.

WordPress is currently the fastest growing and most popular website platform in the world because it's free and easy to use. At this writing, WordPress is used by 43.2% of all websites. Among those created with a known CMS, the market share is even higher, at 62.8%. Most business websites can be built in WordPress at a very affordable cost, and those sites will perform very well.

Plugins and Extensions

These are add-ons that add functionality and performance. All the major CMS website development platforms have hundreds of these plugins available at a relatively small fee. The WordPress Directory currently offers around 60,000 free plugins and 12,000 free themes. Examples include shipping calculators, form generators, calendars, shopping carts, database management tools and more. These plugins must be compatible with the most current CMS version and will need regular updates.

Templates Versus Unique Designs

There are two approaches to website development in a CMS platform such as WordPress. The first is to build a site with a predesigned template, called a *theme*, and the second is to convert a unique design into WordPress. Themes can be purchased at a low cost and can help the development process go quickly. However, you're limited to the scope of the theme, and if it becomes popular, your site may look like other sites using the same theme.

We recommend a unique design for your company based on the strategic vision of your digital marketing plan and the needs of your target market.

Technology and e-Commerce Marketing

There are many e-commerce options available, and it's a highly competitive market space for software. WordPress does not have an e-commerce system as part of its software, but there are many e-commerce plugins and systems that are compatible.

High-level e-commerce websites should use a dedicated online shopping platform. WooCommerce is currently the most popular eCommerce software platform with a 38.74% market share. These platforms also come in CMS, open source and proprietary systems. When deciding if you should sell online, consider this rule of thumb. If your company can sell products and services online, then you *should* implement an e-commerce system to develop new revenue streams. You will be surprised at what will sell on the Internet.

Once you make the leap into e-commerce, you must make the commitment to learn all you can about the technology that powers online sales. This is beyond the scope of this book. However, the Four-Step Process and digital marketing strategies discussed in these pages are the foundation for e-commerce success.

Website Technologies and Multiple Devices

Long gone are the days when the Internet was only available on a desktop. There are now dozens of screen sizes, with tablets, smartphones and other methods for people to find your website. Currently, more than 55% of website traffic comes from mobile devices, and 92.3% of internet users access it using a mobile phone.

You can monitor the ratio of users visiting your website from these varied devices by reviewing Google Analytics data. It is also useful to visit your website on a variety of mobile devices to see what visitors are experiencing.

Responsive design gives your website the ability to *automatically* modify each individual page to the user's screen preferences so content can be viewed on a variety of screen sizes. You may also consider a mobile website or app for smaller screens and tablets. This is definitely an issue, and your site should take advantage of the various approaches that allow you to display and update on a variety of devices from one administrative area.

Digital Marketing Reporting

There's a technical component to selecting, tracking, and setting up effective reporting tools. Whether you're tracking email, social media, content, web leads, web stats or just about any online metric, there's a reporting tool available to track that information. Google continues to be the leader in digital marketing reports with Google Analytics 4, Google Search Console and other Google apps. Visit the resources section of this book for more digital marketing reporting resources.

Action Items:

❑ Make time to learn the fundamentals of digital marketing technology.

❑ Build your website in an open-source CMS platform. Evaluate WordPress as an option for your website development platform.

❑ Do a few Google searches to compare various e-commerce platforms and ensure your IT department brings you the pros and cons of each system.

❑ Set up Google Analytics, Google Search Console and other Google programs as the core of your web reporting.

❑ Make sure your technology is enhancing your digital marketing results and not getting in the way.

❑ Visit BuiltWith.com to see what technologies are used to build any website and for stats on the most popular website development platforms.

STEP 3: INBOUND MARKETING

CHAPTER 7:
Attract People to Your Brand

Your goal is to get found and get heard by the anonymous researcher who's looking for the products and services you offer. Inbound marketing is what gets you found.

Inbound marketing is the process of attracting targeted prospects or personas to your website. Inbound marketing has always been around, but the Internet has become the major force behind its growth and the reason it's a critical part of your marketing efforts.

The Challenges of Inbound Marketing

Inbound marketing can be time consuming. It requires a higher level of marketing expertise and a unique skill set, which may be lacking in your company. There will also be a learning curve to replace old habits, but overcoming these challenges has many positive results and is well worth the time. Also, much of the work done to generate inbound marketing is permanently present on the web and markets your business long after it's first published.

The Company Culture and Inbound Marketing

Inbound marketing is the result of fundamental changes brought about by the Internet. The culture of your company must embrace these approaches before they can take hold. They're not effective on a part-time basis or with limited buy-in from your team. Building the culture starts with inbound marketing education, and is followed by implementation, tracking results and monitoring ROI.

Market Segmentation and Inbound Marketing

When well-executed, strategic inbound marketing results in very specific market segmentation. This leads to better quality visits, more leads, higher sales and more loyal followers. Forget mass-market approaches, segment by online searches and search engine keywords. Inbound marketing makes a small piece of the pie very valuable because customers who come to you are more loyal.

Personas

Use online research methods to identify your market segments and develop "personas" for each of those segments. Personas are brief descriptions of the people in that target market segment. It might include their job title, span of control, age, gender, income or geography and how you can best pull them to your company.

People want to be loyal to a brand because it makes life less complicated. They don't have to repeatedly search through dozens of products and services to get what they need. The better you can segment your target market and reach these personas, the better you can create loyal customers for your brand. Inbound marketing is the approach that pulls them in.

The Death of Cold Calling

Cold calling may not be dead yet, but its effectiveness has dropped substantially because people are inundated with information and want to buy on *their* terms. One way to deal with the decline of cold calling is to convert salespeople to web marketers.

Find salespeople who are inclined to use digital and pull-marketing efforts and put them to work on these new sales techniques. If done properly, their time spent on pull marketing to generate sales leads will have a strong return.

Stay-in-Touch Programs and Marketing Automation

Inbound marketing will generate inquiries and leads, but it's your stay-in-touch programs (also called a continuity program; think airline miles) that work toward long-term sales results. Stay-in-touch programs that nurture your prospects and move them toward a sale must be included in your inbound marketing strategy.

Pull Versus Push Marketing

Many people confuse pull and push marketing. Push marketing is the idea of going out and finding customers through prospecting, cold calling, traditional selling and other techniques that begin with your sales and marketing team "pushing" prospects to you.

Pull marketing involves creating an environment where customers find you and are "pulled" or attracted to your company. Pull marketing is now preferred by most people as they do research online and are very knowledgeable before they make a purchase or even talk to a salesperson. The Internet is the biggest facilitator of pull marketing because it provides easy access to a wealth of information. By the time they call, they may even be more knowledgeable than your salespeople.

Most companies naturally gravitate to push marketing strategies. They're more comfortable with this approach because it's what they know best and what they've done in the past. Many marketers are looking for quick results from push marketing. Pull marketing can complement push marketing efforts and generate higher qualified leads, loyal followers and sales. The best advantage to pull marketing is the fact that most people prefer it to push marketing techniques as it better meets the needs of the online researcher. Pull marketing requires strategic planning, excellent content and solid tracking mechanisms.

Benefits of Pull Marketing

Here are a few of the benefits of effective pull marketing strategies:

- Target visitors to your website and social media
- Build a loyal following and excellent email lists
- Higher online conversion rates
- Cast a wider net for people who otherwise would not have found your site
- Less costly, with better ROI, than many other forms of marketing

Several key strategies must work together in order to gain these benefits. The first step is to make sure inbound marketing is a part of your digital marketing plan. Also, the right team members must be recruited for inbound marketing along with a process for tracking results.

HubSpot and Marketing Automation

A Scalable Solution

Marketing automation is one of the most important changes to digital marketing in the past ten years. It allows *you to stay in touch with contacts,* sending them emails *based on actions* they take online, on your website, your email marketing or your social media content. It offers you an opportunity to nurture prospects and guide them to a sale.

Marketing automation *scales your business.* It allows you to do things that would have taken a team of dozens of salespeople in the past.

Marketing automation has become an essential tool for businesses of all sizes to streamline their marketing efforts and achieve better results. With so many options available, choosing the right platform can be overwhelming.

HubSpot

HubSpot is a market leader for mid-sized and small businesses. HubSpot is our favorite marketing automation toolset because it's easy to use, super robust and affordable. It offers great value, especially for SMBs, because the cost can scale along with the size of your email list, from a free introductory trial to enterprise-level features. You can start small and grow without having to convert to a more sophisticated CRM later on, when switching costs can be prohibitive.

The Ability to Score Contacts

Just like the more complex, more expensive automation tools, HubSpot allows you to *score contacts by what kind of attention they need.* It follows the classic A-B-C approach to scoring your prospects based on their activity. If they visit your website, they get a score. If they visit your social media content, they get a score. If they open your email, they get a score. You can also assign negative scores to people who *unsubscribe*, are *dormant* or who may *open your email but don't click through*. Scoring allows you to send them targeted messages based on their behavior.

Higher-scoring prospects get *different kinds of messages,* and the highest-scoring prospects should get inquiries or phone calls directly from your sales team.

Track and Visualize Your Funnel

HubSpot also allows you to *track and visualize your sales funnel.* You can set and know the different milestones in your funnel and then visualize your results as researchers move through it.

When you can see who is where in the sales funnel, you can then go in and *ask questions* of the sales and marketing team to improve the numbers. People can move to action based on this information and grow sales.

This is an incredibly valuable tool to drive digital marketing success. If you don't already have HubSpot, set up a demo and see for yourself. You can also conduct a free trial, play around with it and then get it up and running.

Here's a Top 10 list of digital marketing automation tools available today, ranked from simple to complex:

Simple:
1. **Mailchimp:** popular and user-friendly, ideal for beginners. It offers basic email marketing automation, landing page creation and analytics.

2. **Constant Contact:** Similar to Mailchimp, Constant Contact provides easy-to-use email marketing tools with additional features like social media scheduling and a website builder.

Medium:
3. **ActiveCampaign:** Offers a wider range of features than Mailchimp and Constant Contact, including marketing automation, CRM and sales tools. It's suitable for a growing business with more complex marketing needs.

4. **Drip:** Specializes in e-commerce marketing automation, helping businesses personalize customer journeys and drive sales.

Moderately Complex:
5. **HubSpot:** An all-in-one platform that combines marketing automation, CRM and website management tools. It's powerful and scalable but can have a steeper learning curve. This is our favorite. Intuitive Websites has been a HubSpot partner for more than a decade.

6. **Pardot by Salesforce:** A marketing automation platform designed for B2B businesses. It offers advanced lead scoring, campaign management and reporting features.

Complex:
7. **Marketo Engage by Adobe:** A comprehensive marketing automation platform with enterprise-level features like account-based marketing (ABM) and marketing resource management (MRM).

8. **Eloqua by Oracle:** Another robust platform for large businesses, offering advanced lead nurturing, campaign orchestration and analytics capabilities.

Highly Complex:
9. **Salesforce Marketing Cloud:** Part of the Salesforce ecosystem, this platform provides sophisticated marketing automation for large enterprises with complex needs.

10. **Microsoft Dynamics 365 Marketing:** Integrates seamlessly with other Microsoft products and offers advanced marketing automation features for large organizations.

This is just a starting point, and the "best" tool for you will depend on your specific needs and budget. Consider factors like your business size, technical expertise and budget when making your decision.

Whatever CRM you choose, it's important that you *work with a specialist* to get it set up and running properly. Depending on the toolset, you should, over time, be able to manage it internally. Eventually you'll probably have an internal specialist at your company who will manage HubSpot for you.

Action Items:

❑ Learn more about inbound marketing and include it in your digital marketing plan.

❑ Assign team members to run an inbound marketing program and look to the sales team to build and support this work as needed.

Answer these questions:

- Who are we trying to reach through inbound marketing?
- Where do they go online?
- How will they find us?
- What will motivate them to contact us?
- Include a strong and consistent content marketing strategy in your inbound marketing plan.
- Gather market research on what works with your current loyal customer base.
- Segment your marketplace into online buyer personas.
- Establish tracking systems and ROI measurement tools to track returns.
- Make inbound marketing a part of your sales and marketing team culture.
- Include a stay-in-touch program as part of your inbound marketing strategy.
- Research your competitors' inbound marketing strategies along with those from other industries that can be applied to your business.

Digital Marketing is Powered by Great Content

At the heart of successful digital marketing is content marketing. Content marketing is the process that draws people to your brand and converts them into customers. It is very strategic and is an essential part of any company's digital marketing efforts. Content marketing is driven by people's need for information before they make a purchasing decision and is behind the growth in pull marketing. It moves people through your sales funnel.

The Content Marketing Process: 10 Steps

More than likely, your marketing department is already doing some form of content marketing. Most companies wing it and do the best they can. However, the lack of a strategic process impedes their results. Content marketing will get much better results with a strategic process that's proven to be successful. Here are ten steps in that process.

1. Write for the Reader

The most common mistake of content marketers is to write from the perspective of their own business instead of using language that's easily understood by their target audience. Each organization has an internal language, a set of terms and methods for communicating that works for their company, but this may not be how prospective customers communicate. The first step in content marketing is to bridge the gap between the company and the reader.

Write content to help your target market do their job better and improve the quality of their lives. Use quality thinking and avoid marketing-speak or brochure content. Write content with value that educates and avoid content that sells or self-promotes.

2. Use Content Marketing to Get Found on Google

The more keyword-rich content on your website, the better you'll rank in searches. Google is paying more attention to websites with blogs and regular content updates.

Here are a few points directly from Google to consider regarding content marketing and search results.

- Generally, the more quality content on your website, the better it will rank in Google searches.
- Google prefers websites with 500 to 1,000 pages.

- Your website gets nine times more traffic when you reach 1,000 pages.
- Adding only fifty pages to your website is equal to 48% more search engine traffic.
- Websites with blogs get five times more traffic than those without blogs.

Also, being at the top of Google search results is important branding for your business. Google searches, or people researching online to find your company, has become a key element in sales prospecting today. Keyword searches and content optimized for Google will bring loyal customers to your website. Your content marketing strategy drives this process, and results are measured in the Google Search Console.

Content Drives Google Rankings and Grows Website Traffic
Larger companies get more website traffic. This happens because they have more content on their website than their smaller competitors. Your goal is to have a content plan for adding pages to your website on a regular schedule. These pages can be blogs, case studies, product and services landing pages, employee bios, articles, video pages and more.

Get started on a content plan so you can look back a year from now and see how much your website traffic has grown as a result.

3. Content as the Voice of the Brand

Many writers may contribute to your content, but it's important to have one consistent voice for your brand. This builds trust and drives simplicity for readers as they learn more about your products and services. Content marketing is used to explain your value, and consistency is critical to communicating a clear brand message. This content provides a personality to your brand and the consistency leads to better marketing results.

4. Translate What You Do Well Into Digital Content

Write about what your company does well. Get very specific on product and service content that's unique to your company. Website visitors will appreciate this because it's what they're looking for. What you do well is loaded with benefits, and content should be used to explain this, including videos, photos, graphics, audio and other media. Tell the story of what you do and how you do it. Also, remember that marketing verbiage and ads are not usually perceived as valuable content.

5. Make Content a Competitive Advantage

Giving content away has become a competitive advantage. Many companies resist this because they believe they're giving away their secrets. However, those secrets are not as important as you think. If you don't give them away, others will. The upside beats the downside; you're only hiding value if you don't distribute excellent content. Your digital marketing and lead generation strategy determines how much to give away. Anyone can compete with content, and if you don't, others will, which will take away market share, and you may not even see it happening!

6. Write Great Headers and Taglines

Headers, taglines, and photo captions are the most read content online. This content should be direct, simple and catchy for visitors who will scan your website for areas of value. When website visitors see the benefit in headers and taglines, they will pursue deeper content for more information. Excellent headers and taglines save people time and create value.

7. Communicate in Layers

Website visitors scan content quickly. You can meet their needs by using taglines, headers and short blocks of text on key landing pages as scannable content. The website reader should be able to go deeper into your site and find volumes of content and information as needed, but they will only find this content if they can first scan and search.

Set up your content in layers. In addition to an intuitive navigation menu, taglines and brief bullet points with links to more information are the best ways to accomplish this goal. Keep your content on the key landing pages brief. Most website content can be cut by half and still communicate the same message.

Websites provide an opportunity for almost limitless amounts of content to meet visitor needs. Organize this content in layers so users can first scan, and then dig deeper to find more details. Improved search results are an added benefit.

8. Always Use Captions with Photos and Graphics

Photos are by far the most looked-at content on the Internet. Photos without captions tell different stories to each person who sees that photo. Always write clear and direct captions for all your photography so everyone can easily understand the photo's message and purpose. As I discussed earlier, avoid clip art and stock photography, which can be seen as clutter. You can find the same stock photo on many different websites, creating brand confusion. Use real photos of real people and things at your company, along with a caption on each photo. This will likely get the most attention.

9. Watch the ROI

Overall, content marketing is cheaper than traditional advertising and many other forms of marketing. Still, you should set up tracking methods to monitor conversions and track the ROI from content marketing and, for that matter, all digital marketing efforts. Content marketing should have excellent and measurable ROI. Content marketing is also more permanent than most forms of sales and marketing because content placed online will be there for a long time.

10. Create a Company Culture for Content Marketing

It's especially important for sales and marketing staff and top leadership to embrace content marketing. Writing and preparing content is hard work, and support must come from the top. The transition to content marketing from traditional push marketing can be difficult and requires leadership. Start by using content around the office that can be rewritten for the web. Improved marketing results will help drive the culture needed to implement a winning content marketing strategy.

DIY (Do It Yourself) vs. DFY (Done For You)

Most people don't like to write content. They didn't like to write content in school and don't like to write content at work. Most people procrastinate on content and put it off. We're late to meet deadlines, and it's just the way things are when it comes to writing. To top this off, the most frequent lament we hear from other website developers is, "We can't get the client to supply (revise or approve) the content."

You need experts who can write digital marketing content. Either you contract writers who know what they're doing, or you can work with an agency, but be careful. Most subject matter experts, and even thought leaders, are not necessarily good writers. Have someone skilled at grammar and writing mechanics review and proofread *everything* before it's published.

Also, make sure to proof content coming from an agency. A bestselling author on the topic of sales engaged an agency to generate content on a regular cadence. One of the articles they published was titled, "Five Reasons Sales is Better than Sex." They published the content without submitting it to the client for review. Well, you can imagine the blowback. The article went viral, and our friend's email blew up with negative comments. He fired the agency and demanded they retract the article, publish an apology and refund the fees. They refused, and the damage was done.

The biggest advantage of working with an agency for content is the comprehensive approach to content for all channels, including the three major channels of your website, social media and email marketing. An agency can help you prepare campaigns and write content that works for all those channels. Hundreds of the websites we've worked with over the years have seen success from this approach.

One of our clients, Wiggam Law, has seen tremendous results from their content marketing efforts. Wiggam Law is a multimillion-dollar law firm based in Atlanta that provides tax resolution services for small- and medium-sized businesses. Wiggam hired Intuitive Websites to build a new WordPress website, generate content, get visitors to the site, and convert those visitors to inquiries. We used content to deploy effective SEO, launched and managed a winning Google Ads campaign, implemented HubSpot automation and posted regular social media content. Following our Four-Step

Process and using these content marketing strategies have increased Wiggam's inquiries and leads by more than 100%.

Barriers to Effective Content Marketing

There are many barriers to content marketing and most people avoid it as much as possible. Many people in sales and marketing have not developed the necessary writing skills to be effective in content marketing.

Here are a few of the common barriers you will need to overcome.

- Don't have the time or the people.
- The team will have to work too hard.
- Giving away free content will not work for the company.
- The wrong skill set in the marketing or sales staff.
- Many people hate to write.
- Unable to relate to the customer or understand online prospecting.

Don't let these barriers to content marketing get in the way of your success. Find the right people, including a great writer, and build a team to implement content marketing strategies.

AI – The Critical Tool for Content

We've talked quite a bit about the importance of content meeting user needs, moving them through the funnel, push and pull marketing, inbound marketing and all those fantastic and useful things.

AI is having the biggest impact on digital content of *any* application that's been around in recent years since the Internet itself.

The two biggest barriers we have in writing content are finding a content writer or finding the time to do it ourselves. AI solves both of those problems. It's a tool for writing first-draft content, and it saves time because it produces the content immediately.

AI has changed the face of digital marketing because websites that offer more content get more traffic and grow faster. This is supported by Google and by what we've seen in the last 20 years of doing digital marketing.

AI Generated Content Will Get You Found

AI-generated content will get you found in Google searches and social media posts, and get your emails opened because AI can help you write benefit-focused content that moves people to action.

AI and Search Engines

AI could also write content that can be pasted on your website and indexed by Google and other search engines. In fact, at the time of this writing, there was some concern that AI-generated content might be excluded from searches or even be banned by Google, but this hasn't happened. But your *readers* can tell. They may even use AI tools to detect AI-generated content.

Here are three tools that detect and flag AI-generated content:

Copyleaks: This popular plagiarism detection tool offers an AI detection feature that analyzes text for patterns common in machine-generated writing. It provides a score indicating the likelihood of AI authorship, making it ideal for various uses like content verification and academic integrity.

Crossplag AI Content Detector: This tool integrates seamlessly with the Crossplag plagiarism checker, specifically looking for AI-generated content. It uses an AI Index (0-100) to indicate the probability of human or AI authorship, offering nuanced results.

Grammarly: While primarily a grammar and plagiarism checker, Grammarly's premium plans include AI detection. It analyzes writing for specific features common in AI-generated text, providing helpful insights alongside regular proofreading features.

Just to be safe, submit your *edited* AI content to these tools to see if you've done a good job of humanizing the text.

You should also use AI to fact-check any AI-generated content before publishing. Early AI tools have demonstrated a tendency to "hallucinate," sometimes fabricating facts and stories out of thin air. Start with the prompt, "Fact-check the following article and correct any factual errors," and paste in the human-edited version.

AI and Google

Currently ChatGPT is the standard for AI tools to prepare content. Google has a tool called Gemini and has strategic business issues with AI because AI may pose a threat to its Google Ads program. And here's why. Whereas Microsoft has figured out how to monetize ChatGPT and license it to other software applications and other companies for many uses, Google has not found a way to monetize AI the way they monetize Google Ads. In fact, there's a threat to Google Ads in that people may stop using Google when they have AI at their fingertips.

This book can get you ready for a future in which fewer people are researching on Google and more people are using AI tools to research where to buy products and services.

AI is going to change search. We know this is going to happen. And we must be in front of it and on top of it when it does. Given how websites are coded and set up for SEO, the principles of SEO that we use in Google now will transfer to AI. We've already seen it with some results in ChatGPT.

Using AI to get found in searches to come.

There will be a time soon when we converse with AI on our smart phone or other device and rely less on Google and social media for research. To be ready for this evolution, make sure your website and digital content follow the principles of EEAT. You want your content writers and your AI tools to write content that expresses your *experience*, *expertise*, *authority* and *trustworthiness*.

- **Experience**
  Content to show experience in your field and marketplace. Experience is built over time and by showcasing the volume of work you have in your field.

- **Expertise**
  Content that expresses your thought leadership and knowledge in your space. Not only do you have experience, but you also have the expertise to do the work well.

- **Authority**
  Content that expresses your authority in your marketplace is critical because the visitor wants to know that you're a thought leader and a key resource.

- **Trust**
  Content that can be trusted by readers and that builds trust for your brand. This includes an updated copyright date on your website, easy-to-find locations and contact information, a privacy policy, intuitive navigation, one key domain name for your company, regular website updates and ease of use.

AI is Your Trusted Source for Thought-Leadership

You do that by writing *content that is thought leadership.* In fact, AI can help you *identify where your thought leadership should be.* For example, content that shows your experience is content that talks about how long you've been in business, the kinds of customers you've worked with and the kinds of problems you've solved, which then ties into blog posts that help people do their jobs better. That shows your experience because you're writing content that helps people solve problems or gain something.

Expertise is where your thought leadership really shines because this is where you write content and produce videos that show people *how to use your products and services to do their jobs better.*

You provide content in your key areas of thought leadership that talks about *where your company is a leader* in its market space.

This will then also *build authority* for you. Authority comes from links coming into your website, associations that you belong to, trade shows you attend, logos of companies you work with, case studies and customer testimonials; all these things build authority.

Content that is trusted by readers dovetails into this as well. This is because the personas you're targeting want to know that you understand them, that you're empathetic to their needs, that you understand what their pain points are and that you are working to build trust with them. For example, content that talks about *your mission* as a company and the *values* that you bring to the marketplace *builds trust* in readers.

One surefire way to build trust is by *positioning yourself as a thought leader*. So think about thought leadership this way: In your industry, there are places where you excel and know how to meet customer needs better than anyone else. Most companies go about doing that day-to-day and they don't think about it very much. But digital marketing requires you to *tell those stories,* talk about how you are the best in your space and translate those differentiators into meaningful content for the user so they can take it home and act on it.

Your action item in understanding your thought leadership is to *find seven different areas where you are a leader in your market space*.

Use those seven areas as the key topics for blog posts, website content, eBooks, webinars, white papers or technical papers, and then express your thought leadership with content. The principles of EEAT will not only get you found in Google searches today but also in the future as the online researcher moves more and more to AI tools to find solutions.

Action Items:

- ❑ Include an EEAT content marketing strategy in your digital marketing plan.
- ❑ Meet with your key sales and marketing staff and develop a process for content marketing as a regular part of your digital marketing efforts.
- ❑ Assign the content marketing work to people who show initiative and want to write. Some of these people may be outside contractors.

❑ Understand and segment the audience for each form of content.

❑ Determine your content outlets, types, and topics.

❑ Assign a team member to schedule content placement in various channels.

❑ Make sure all content is optimized for search.

❑ Develop a schedule for regular content placement and updates.

❑ Track results and conversion rates to determine your ROI.

Using Digital Content to Get Found

Understand Your Prospect

Your digital content is only as good as how it matches and meets the intent of the reader. Let's take a closer look at what it takes to make this digital content effective and impactful and how content drives results. Blogs are an excellent starting point.

How Website Blogs and Content Drive Website Traffic

Blogs are at the core of a successful content marketing program and just about every website should have a blog. Here are a few key points business leaders need to know about developing a blog.

Blogs Drive Website Traffic

Google loves websites with blogs and regular content posts. Websites with blogs get five times more traffic than similar sites without blogs. This is reason enough to have a blog. However, it becomes more compelling given the fact that website visitors like to read blog content as part of their research. Also, one of Google's major missions is to prevent spam websites from getting listed in their search results. Websites with regular blog posts and excellent content are not generally considered spam by Google.

Tell Your Company Story

Think of your company blog as an online content channel that tells your company's story on a regular cadence. It becomes an ongoing discussion about what it means to do business with your company and your market in general. This is very helpful in defining and building your brand in the eyes of the world. Here are a few key blog approaches used to get content marketing results.

- Place your blog on your main URL and do not use a separate website address or domain for the blog.
- Set a goal to write a new blog post every week, bi-weekly, or even daily, if possible.
- Keep blog posts brief and use headers to break up the text and for SEO.
- Each blog post should be optimized around a *single keyword phrase*.
- Track visits to the blog in Google Analytics and monitor how your blog not only drives traffic but also leads to conversions.
- As a rule of thumb, target about 400-600 words for each blog post. It's fine to have some posts that are short and others that are much longer. The key is consistency and relevancy for your readers and Google.
- Include share buttons to social media so readers can easily share your blog content with others.
- Include a link to your blog on your main navigation bar. This link may include other content resources such as articles, white papers, videos and more.
- Analyze your top-performing posts for length and audience engagement.
- Research what your competitors are ranking for in terms of content length and target those ranges.

Begin with Blog Categories
Start your company blog by developing blog categories or a blog table of contents. This goes a long way in defining the purpose of your blog and how it will meet the needs of your readers. Here are a few ideas to help with developing blog categories.

- Tell stories that happen at your business.
- Discuss industry issues.
- Write about your competitive advantages.

- Write about influential people or companies as they relate to your company.
- Discuss common problems and how to solve them for your target market.
- Include comparisons of products and services that matter to your target market.
- Review price issues in your blog.
- Conduct reviews of products and services.
- Write about the best of the past year.
- Include awards and company or industry news in your blog.
- Review competitor blog categories for ideas.

Keep an archive of previous blog posts on your website. Blog categories should include an archive and the ability for the reader to search for blog posts and organize them by date. Include at least four blog categories. It's fine to have a generic category for miscellaneous postings.

Distribute and Share Blog Content
Blogs and social media content should be interchangeable. All blog posts should be posted on social media and distributed to subscribers through RSS feeds. RSS is a technology that easily allows people to subscribe to your blog posts from your website and automatically receive blog content as it's posted. This is an excellent way to distribute content that can be shared among your target market. The quality and value of this content will determine how it's shared and distributed.

The About Us Page and Blog Content
Even though blog postings describe your company in great detail, there's still a need for an *About Us* page, and it should be part of your main navigation. This could be one of the most important pages on your website and will probably be in the top ten most-visited pages. Take the *About Us* page seriously because this page can drive conversions.

Here are a few key issues to address in your *About Us* pages:

- Use the About Us page to build trust and credibility.
- Think of it as the company resume.
- Include a link to this page in the main navigation menu.
- Keep the page current.
- Measure the stats and visits to this page.
- Include a conversion point and call-to-action on the About Us page.

Here are a few suggestions for the types of content to include on your About Us page:

- Company history
- Biographies and photos of team members
- Client lists, case studies and testimonials
- Location photos
- Videos and photos to describe your company
- Business approaches and philosophy of the company
- Other descriptive content about the company

Get Back What You Put In
Blogs take time and energy to be effective, and the potential return is equal to the effort you put into them. Just like many forms of digital marketing discussed in this book, there's no quick fix; however, blog posts will get indexed within Google search results and will be read by your target market for years to come. This is true of any content posted to your website and a major benefit to a value-added content marketing strategy.

How Blog Content Can Land Six-Figure Deals
Wiggam Law was looking for blog content topics that could have a real impact for their client base. One area of tax law they were sure would rise in popularity in the Fall of 2023 was information about the Employee Retention Credit (ERC) business audits. ERC payments were made by the federal government to companies who experience business losses because of COVID. The intent of the ERC program was to help companies keep workers. Wiggam knew that Google searches were sure to increase as companies that were being

audited by the IRS over their use of ERC funds went to Google to research their options.

Wiggam knew the IRS was going to start cracking down on companies that took large ERC credit payments but did not meet the IRS guidelines. Sure enough, the IRS announced a program to audit and fine companies accused of bad ERC practices, and people flocked to Google for more information. Wiggam ranked high on those searches because they were ahead of this trend and had already written blog posts for their website like this: https://wiggam-law.com/blog/irs-issues-moratorium-erc-claim-processing/

More ERC blog posts were added to the website over time and their foothold in Google continued to grow.

They also added an SEO-focused landing page you can see here:

https://wiggamlaw.com/tax-services/employment-taxes/employee-retention-tax-credit/

Wiggam was ahead of the curve on ERC and how they can help companies when going through an IRS audit. Their key content pages and blog posts ranked high in Google searches because they were there first, and Wiggam closed over $100,000 in new client revenue.

Social Media Strategies

Many millions of words and thousands of books have been published on social media. Not a day goes by that major media outlets are not discussing social media issues and it has had a tremendous impact on society and our everyday lives. Understanding how social media impacts your company is important so you can provide the right direction to your sales and marketing teams.

No Quick Fix with Social Media
If you're looking for a quick fix or fast return, you'll be disappointed in social media. It takes time to build interest and followers. Without a loyal following, social media delivers very poor results. Social media can be a very effective content channel to

communicate your business strategy, but it cannot stand on its own. It must be a part of a comprehensive digital marketing plan, content strategy and traffic generation program.

Welcome to the "Internets"

George W. Bush's famous line during his debate with John Kerry about the "Internets" has some truth to it. Social media websites like Facebook and LinkedIn have so many users these websites can easily be considered Internets within the Internet!

Your company's presence on a social media website starts with your company page, which is really another website for your company within the social media platform. Facebook lets users create six different types of pages:

- Local business or place
- Company, organization or institution
- Brand or Product
- Artist, band or public figure
- Entertainment
- Cause or Community

Your Facebook profile can appear in up to three of these categories.

These social media pages should follow the same strategy as your company website. The design and content should complement your current website.

Social Media and Content Marketing

For most companies, the primary use of social media is content distribution to attract attention and drive traffic. Make sure all your blog posts are distributed through the major social media channels. At a minimum, have a presence and post content on these social media websites:

- YouTube
- Facebook
- LinkedIn
- Google My Business

- X (formerly Twitter)
- Instagram
- TikTok

There are many more social media sites, but these are currently the most important for content to reach the right readers and for SEO purposes. Also, stay on top of the news so you're not caught by surprise when a social media website takes off or disappears.

Google and Social Media

Google appreciates and rewards content activity in social media, especially the big three: Facebook, LinkedIn, and Instagram. Google is rewarding companies that establish themselves as content authorities on various subjects with higher placement in search results. This happens over time as you place content online and collect readers on social and through your blog.

Also, links to your website from popular social media sites are useful and can improve placement in Google search results.

How Much Time Should You Spend Marketing on Social Media?

Think of social media as a content and sales tool bringing a return based on the effort you put into it. The amount of social media content your company needs depends upon your digital marketing goals, sales targets and how you're using other digital marketing tools. Your digital marketing plan should estimate the amount of social media needed based on marketing priorities and your expected return. For most companies, weekly activity and content postings are enough to stay visible and drive traffic. It's important to make sure your company website is in alignment with your digital marketing strategy before you spend considerable time on social media.

A Complement to Marketing and Sales Efforts

The best use of social media is as a *complement* to your current sales and marketing efforts. Don't expect too much but stay active enough to have a presence. Your presence in social media over time will assist in driving traffic to your website, provide content to a wide range of readers and support your brand. Find ways to use social media as a support to what you already do well in sales and marketing.

Social Media and Selling
Social media websites are very effective prospecting tools, especially LinkedIn. The key is to take part in the conversation, join groups, meet people and network. All the rules of effective selling apply to interactions in social media but with a much larger prospective audience. Results come when your target market gravitates to the value you provide and become followers, readers and distributors of your content. Your sales team can reach out to these prospects as sales leads.

Remember, your content is very transparent on social media. If you're just looking to sell and promote your company, your results will be poor. If you're looking to add value and help others, you can expect a great return.

Social Media and Customer Service Support
For larger companies, social media has also become a support to customer service. Businesses are watching conversions on social media to help them better service their target market. There are many online tools to help track this content. There are not usually enough conversations happening on the social media sites of small- and medium-sized companies, so their challenge is to start the conversation and attract attention. This happens when you post valuable content. Don't get too caught up on the negative content on social media. Focus on adding value and providing a great service or product and look for positive feedback as a result.

Social Media is Top of Funnel
Prospect engagement with social media comes early in the sales funnel. Many of these people are new to your brand or have been watching you but not buying. Social media can be used to pull them into your website, click on mid-funnel content like eBooks and webinars, or send them to an event or webinar. These things help move a social media follower down the funnel and closer to becoming a customer.

Results are Difficult to Measure

Social media results are difficult to measure because most people only read social media posts and do not interact. They may also find out about your company on social, then search for your website on Google. This is why social media stats can be misleading, and social media marketing must be seen as a support to SEO efforts and content marketing. You can measure direct traffic from social media in Google Analytics, and social media sites like Facebook and LinkedIn offer the ability to place ads on their sites and review basic stats activity from visitors.

Action Items:

- ❑ Include social media in your digital marketing and content marketing plan.

- ❑ Develop a company homepage for LinkedIn, Facebook, Google+ and other social media sites as needed for your business.

- ❑ Track referrals from social media sites to your company website and the number of likes and followers.

- ❑ Post weekly content to social media sites and link it back to your website.

- ❑ Post your website blog posts to major social media sites.

- ❑ Use various forms of content, such as video, photography and other media.

- ❑ Determine your areas of content expertise and work toward being an online content authority on those subjects. Use social media as an outlet for that content.

- ❑ As a business leader, regularly visit your company's social media sites to monitor activity and stay relevant to your content marketing themes.

- ❑ Keep track of major changes in social media and how the most popular social media sites are used by your target market.

Website Partnerships and Links to Drive Traffic

Google was one of the first search engines to use website popularity as a key indicator of a website's relevance. The Google founders believed websites with more *incoming links* from other websites should rank higher in search results. The more popular the sites linking to your site, the better the search results in Google. This, along with a very simple and easy-to-use homepage, contributed to Google's fast growth and eventual dominance in web searches. In fact, Google still remains one of the easiest search engines to use, which has contributed greatly to very high usage and market dominance.

Inbound links are no longer the primary driver of SEO results in Google. In fact, they've created a huge spam problem for Google, as websites with irrelevant links rank high up in search results. However, links to your site continue to be a significant part of how Google ranks websites, especially if those links are from popular and highly visible sites. Let's review a few of the key issues when you're working to increase your search results from inbound links.

Build a Relationship to Get Links

There are several ways to get inbound links. One of the best is to develop an alliance or partnership with websites in your industry visited by your target market and to request a link exchange. Contact the company directly and make a business case for the link. Explain how the link will help both companies.

It is also important to establish links from directory and general resource websites.

Here are a few suggestions of the types of websites that can provide strong inbound links:

- Industry-related websites
- Association websites
- Industry resource sites such as ThomasNet.com
- Local Yellow Pages websites (YP.com)
- Online directory websites such as Yahoo

- All the major social media sites
- For an additional list of directory sites and to get inbound links, visit Yext.com, which can also provide industry-specific sites and local options.

Avoid Spamming

Collecting inbound links that have no relation to your website is not recommended by Google and may be considered spamming. This approach to inbound links may result in Google penalties. Many SEO companies offer link-building services, which may produce results; however, make sure you build links of value and relevance to your website so your site complies with Google's anti-spamming rules. If you are doing something just to trick Google and drive more traffic, you're running the risk of Google blacklisting your website. Also, avoid posting too many blog posts, hoping to get inbound links. Google considers this spamming.

Multiple Domains and Duplicate Content

Occasionally, web marketers will buy dozens of domain names and build dozens of similar websites, all linking back to the mothership website. They're looking for more traffic and inbound links. This is a very thin strategy and is frowned upon by Google. Building multiple websites solely for the purpose of search engine rankings may bring a penalty from Google, as they may see duplicate content as spam. Multiple websites from the same company with unique domains should only be used for unique market segments to meet user needs, not to trick Google into higher search engine rankings.

Track Results in Google Analytics 4 (Google Analytics)

Links to your site are called *referrers* in Google Analytics, and this is a key metric worth watching. Keep a close eye on the conversions coming from these links. You may find that traffic coming from targeted referring websites through inbound links could have some of the highest conversion rates. This is in addition to the improved search rankings.

Action Items:

❏ Include an inbound link strategy in your digital marketing plan.

❏ Task your marketing team to develop a list of the most popular websites visited by your target market. Reach out to these companies for a link exchange.

❏ Develop a list of association and directory websites in your marketplace.

❏ Track inbound links through Google Analytics and Google Search Console.

❏ Get a link from your website development or ad agency provider to your site.

You can also type into the browser, site:[your domain name] to see a list of all of the pages on your website that have been indexed by Google.

Simplicity Drives Results

The Rules of Simplicity

1. Simplicity takes direction from the market. Ask your customers why they do business with your company and repeat that back to prospects in your key messaging.
2. Focus on *three key messages* and take a stand. Summarize your key benefits in three easy to follow statements on your key website landing pages.
3. Simplicity drives conversions and sales. People buy when you make it easy and uncomplicated for them to buy.

You can go to the AI tool and ask it to simplify content. In fact, you could take a 2,000-word technical article and ask AI to "Summarize this for a lay person, in 300 words, in an informal, breezy style," and it will. This is a great way to summarize content and get to a header or tagline as well.

Simplicity is key to digital marketing. Simplicity allows people to move through the funnel. People want to buy from companies that are easy to research and easy to buy from. One of the ways to keep it simple is to go to your customers and ask them to share *the three reasons why they buy from you.* Their answers will help you formulate your three key messages that will be on your homepage. You can then go to the AI tool and ask it to expand on those reasons and generate content around them.

Here's an example.

Response time is often an important criterion for customers, particularly in the Age of Amazon. They hate being told that they can expect a delivery "Sometime between 7:00 AM and 4:00 PM," particularly if the issue is urgent, like a broken water pipe.

I prompted Gemini with, "Customers of a mobile plumbing services company say the #1 reason they call is that they are prompt to respond. Expand the sub-benefits of prompt response from the customer point of view."

The AI generated the following:

Reduced Stress and Anxiety:

- **Peace of mind:** Knowing that help is on the way quickly alleviates the stress of a plumbing emergency.

- **Proactive action:** Immediate response allows the technician to tackle the issue before it worsens, preventing potential water damage and further stress.

- **Minimized disruption:** Avoiding delays means less disruption to daily routines and schedules.

Increased Confidence and Trust:

- **Reliability:** Punctuality demonstrates the company's professionalism and commitment to customer service.

- **Respectful treatment:** Feeling valued through a prompt response fosters trust and confidence in the company.

- **Positive experience:** Timely service sets the stage for a more positive overall experience with the company.

Financial Advantages:

- **Reduced damage:** Faster response minimizes the potential for water damage, saving money on repairs and restoration.

- **Lower repair costs:** Addressing issues early can prevent them from escalating into more complex and expensive repairs.

- **Time saved:** Less waiting means less lost productivity or inconvenience, potentially saving customers money or time off work.

Convenience and Ease:

- **Flexibility:** Quick response times accommodate busy schedules and unexpected emergencies.

- **Reduced wait times:** No need to spend hours waiting for a plumber, minimizing disruption and inconvenience.

- **Streamlined process:** Efficient service keeps things moving smoothly, making the experience less stressful.

Additional benefits:

- **Safety:** Prompt response can be crucial in addressing gas leaks or other safety hazards quickly.

- **Transparency:** Clear communication about arrival times builds trust and avoids unnecessary worry.

- **Positive online reputation:** Timely service contributes to positive online reviews and word-of-mouth recommendations.

By highlighting these sub-benefits, you effectively demonstrate **the true value proposition** of your prompt response time, going beyond mere speed to showcase its impact on the customer experience, finances, and overall satisfaction.

That took 11 seconds.

By speaking directly to their motivations, you turn your website into a customer magnet. I would also guess, with high confidence, that *you wouldn't have thought of all of those benefits on your own.* Now you can take one of these sub-benefits, like the Financial Advantages, and address it in a blog or an article. Or go deeper in your discussions with customers and ask them to rank-order the benefits that have the most impact on their choices. Winnow and articulate these values in your website and your content within the Rule of Three.

The Mobile Researcher

Why Screen Size Matters

The lesson here is simple. People research on the go and are highly mobile. The area of concern for digital marketers is knowing what screen size people are using and how digital content is displayed on various screen sizes. Build your website in a responsive theme that adapts to various screen sizes and maintains a positive user experience. Test your website and digital content on a variety of devices and look at your data to know what visitors are using to experience your brand.

The use of mobile devices and various screen sizes to access the Internet is growing fast and will make up a significant portion of visits to your website. At this writing, 81% of retail shoppers use their mobile phone to research, and 57 to 70% of B2B buyers use mobile. Those numbers have been steady for a few years now. That's incredibly important for both B2B and B2C.

More than 55% of website traffic comes from mobile devices, and 92.3% of internet users access the Internet using a mobile phone. There are approximately *4.32 billion* active mobile internet users. In this chapter we will review what you need to know about mobile devices on the Internet and how to position your company to reap marketing benefits from this rapid growth.

Many factors are driving the growth of the mobile Internet, and there is much to consider in understanding this trend. Also, the growth of the mobile web is here to stay and bound to change and adapt to more efficient mobile devices such as tablets.

Apple Products Lead the Way

Apple and Samsung currently dominate the smartphone industry. Currently, Apple accounts for 59% of smartphones sold in the US, while Samsung accounts for 24%. In fact, these two smartphone manufacturers have been leading the market since 2013. These devices have changed how people perceive the Internet from a static interface to something they can take with them anywhere. Yet, there's a lot to consider in understanding how to market through mobile devices.

Mobile Usage Limits User Options

Users perform very few tasks on their mobile devices and rarely read in-depth online content. They're mostly looking for brief content, an address, a phone number or photos with captions. Keep this in mind when designing a mobile website.

What are the three most common things your targeted users are doing on your mobile website? How can they easily use their mobile device to contact your company? What content is most important, and can it be read on the mobile web? Limited user options on mobile devices force web marketers to focus their website's navigation, content and contact information. It has also forced web pages to be longer as users scroll mobile devices for content.

Everything is Smaller

Younger people are more likely to use mobile devices because they have better vision and are not tied to an office or desk. They're more patient with sites not optimized for mobile but are less likely to buy. This is key to understanding that the over-fifty demographic will need reading glasses to view content on a mobile phone. Make it easier on their eyes with larger fonts, graphics, and menu items. This demographic has more money to spend online and will appreciate a mobile website that's easy to use.

Mobile Devices Drive Sales

The mobile visit will generally be an opportunity for the user to gather information that will lead to a purchase. Spend time helping these users buy on mobile and take time to make it easy for them to scan products and services and get in touch. Summarize product and service information so it can be read on a smartphone or even smaller screens.

Users Want Information Now

The Internet has created an environment where people can get answers to any question immediately. This means it's not OK not to know! Based on how users navigate mobile websites, it's better for them to contact your company directly for answers. The majority of mobile users only visit one or two web pages. You can meet their need to get an answer with an easy-to-find email address link or phone number.

The Death of the Traditional Office

Mobile devices enable people to work from any location in their home or workplace. COVID accelerated this trend as well. This is leading to fewer offices away from home. This trend will continue and drive the need for mobile devices with larger screens. Where are your targeted mobile users likely to be when researching your company? Are they likely to read your emails or website on a mobile device? Look to Google Analytics for answers to these questions.

Responsive Design

Responsive design is currently the most effective website development process for mobile devices in a variety of screen sizes. The second-best option is to build a website with a unique design specifically for mobile. Responsive design is preferred because the design elements remain the same as the website automatically adapts to various screen sizes and browsers.

Responsive design is an advancement in website technology because the issue in the future will not be whether or not your website can adapt to mobile devices but whether it can effectively display on a large *variety* of screen sizes and types. These screen sizes can be anything from a small screen inside a pair of glasses or an Apple Watch to large projection displays and 70+ inch smart TVs.

What is Unique to Your Target Market?

Determine what's unique to your target market in the way they use the mobile Internet and meet those needs on your mobile website. Also, gain an understanding of the types and sizes of screens most likely used by your target market to surf the web.

Action Items:

❑ Identify the top three functions mobile users want from your website.

❑ Make sure your navigation is simple and use large fonts on your mobile site.

❑ Conduct market research to get answers about mobile website usage.

❑ Think about a mobile app as a solution for smartphone users.

❑ Check out your competitors' websites on a smartphone or other mobile device.

❑ Consider responsive design as an option for your website so the site is able to modify itself for each individual user's screen size.

❑ Track mobile visits to your website in Google Analytics. If your mobile traffic is approaching 15-20% of your overall visits, it's time to invest in a mobile website or a responsive design website.

Influencer and Referral Based Digital Marketing

This is a critical part of digital marketing and has changed over time. Ten years ago, we were concerned about getting inbound links. That's all changed. Google doesn't put as much emphasis on inbound links, but what's really taken off in the last ten years is *the growth of influencers.*

These are people who have the attention of your target market, and it doesn't matter what space you're in. It could be a very niche B2B business or it could be a huge consumer brand in B2C. Influencers have the ear of your target market and they can refer customers to you who come at you mid-funnel or the bottom of the funnel. You must have a plan for influencers. It's a key method to drive traffic to your website.

You can use AI to develop *influencer programs and sales plans.* You don't use AI to find the influencers because it'll make them up; do that through Google search and through other influencer tools.

You can *use AI to build personas of influencers* and then use content to attract them, but for the most part, your influencer strategy will be based on the *relationships you form with these influencers.*

Segment your database in HubSpot, or whichever marketing automation system you use, to separate influencers from the rest of your contacts, because you're going to build a relationship with those influencers, and you're going to talk to them directly about sharing content you produce and sending people to your website.

If you want to have a great influencer strategy, *you need to know what influencers want,* and for most influencers, the number one thing they want is to *get more followers* or *provide content to their followers* that keeps them around. They need content and resources from you. Partner with these folks and ask what kind of content they would like, then prepare that content for them.

Now, some influencers want to make money from their database, and many influencers have agents. Some of the influencers out there are making millions of dollars through agents and through sponsorships from big brands.

For most of you reading this book, you want to find those niche influencers who have the ear of your target market. You want to get them to share your content or have you as a guest on their podcasts. This is another way to build awareness and get more people to your brand.

Think of your *influencer strategy* as a sales strategy that's heavily influenced by digital.

CHAPTER 8:
Grow Website Visits

If you build it they will come. Well, maybe.

Website traffic generation, a part of Step Three of the Four-Step Process, is by far the most popular of the Four Steps and certainly gets the most attention. Every company wants as much traffic as possible. Many digital marketing agencies make traffic generation and getting results in Google their key selling points.

We've found that it's the combination of the Four Steps driven by an excellent strategy that drives results. Just getting traffic is not a complete solution. It can be expensive and takes time.

Traffic generation is important but does not stand alone as the key ingredient to success in digital marketing. That's why it is Step Three in the process. Get the strategy and content right first.

Website Traffic Generation Requires Hard Work

Drawing visitors to your website has become more challenging than ever. New websites struggle to capture the number of visitors that go to older, more well-established websites. It takes time to build traffic. It takes content targeted for the key persona who want to read it.

The amount of traffic you get is, in many ways, equal to the amount of work you put into it. The hard work you put into building traffic should create excellent ROI. This book will help you develop a traffic generation strategy to drive business growth.

Search Engines and Traffic Generation

Traffic from Google searches and direct traffic are the two most likely sources of visitors for most websites. Many people use Google instead of their browser to find a website, even if they know the company name or domain name.

Search engines such as Google require you to pay attention to many factors so you can be found in their search results. Although direct traffic is great, business growth will come from people experiencing your brand for the first time through a Google search. But there's more to traffic generation than search engines.

A Comprehensive Approach

Just as digital marketing in general needs a comprehensive approach, so does traffic generation. As you move into the upcoming chapters on website visitor growth, keep in mind all these efforts work together to grow traffic from a variety of sources.

You must understand the fundamentals of website traffic generation and what drives traffic to your company website. The good news is that traffic generation to your website can be easily summarized for a few key traffic sources. Remember to drive traffic to your website *after* the strategy is in order and the design is great. Driving traffic costs money and time, so it's not a good idea to drive traffic to a website that's not already optimized for success.

Website traffic sources can be broken down into three major areas.

Google Analytics breaks down the sources of website traffic into three major areas: *direct* traffic, *search* engine traffic, and *referral* traffic.

Direct Traffic

This is traffic that comes to your website by typing your website URL or domain name into their browser, or from a bookmarked page within the visitor's browser. Direct traffic is an indicator of your brand's popularity on the Internet and will usually have the highest conversion rates. Much of this traffic is generated by word of mouth and from offline marketing.

It's always best to have a domain name that matches your company name. For example, if your company name is ABC Widgets, your website should be ABCWidgets.com. This will make it much easier for direct traffic to find you. Otherwise, you may end up sending direct traffic to a competitor's website.

Search Engine Traffic

This is traffic that comes to your website from a major search engine. It can be from organic results in free listings, social media or paid advertisements. Much of your traffic will come from searches on your company name, which makes this traffic similar to direct traffic.

Search engines should drive at least 50% of your overall traffic, and you should work hard to be found in searches using the keyword terms most appropriate for your company. As of this writing, Google's current market share for search is dominant, sitting at around 92%.

Referral Traffic

The third form of traffic is referral traffic. This traffic comes from another website through a link. At one time this was an important factor in search engine rankings, but it's now an indicator of your site's online reach and your ability to build a partnership with websites that attract your target market.

Six Traffic Generation Areas of Focus

You can go one step further and break down your traffic generation efforts into six key areas of focus for the digital marketing team. These areas will be discussed in more detail in the coming chapters, but here's an overview for now.

1. Offline Sales and Marketing

For most companies, the most valuable traffic comes from those who know your brand, are current customers or have been referred to your website. This traffic will be listed as "direct traffic" in Google Analytics, or they will use your company name to find your site in a search engine. Make it easy for people to find your website by including your URL on all your company materials and on any items that are seen by your target market. Do not get so caught up in your digital marketing work that you ignore offline marketing efforts that drive highly qualified traffic to your site.

2. Search Engines

Search engine traffic is one of the best sources for new customers and can be broken into two areas. The first is *organic* traffic coming from your SEO efforts. This is the traffic displayed in the free search results. The second form of search engine traffic is from *pay-per-click* (PPC) ad programs, such as Google Ads. Traffic from search engines consists of brand-name searches and new targeted searches based on keyword research and SEO. Many people use Google to find your website by searching your company name. You will learn more about SEO in upcoming chapters.

3. Content Marketing

Content marketing is not only a key part of search results but also a traffic generation strategy. Users will come to your website for valuable content, which can be used to pull targeted traffic from a variety of sources. The key is to have a content marketing plan to drive these results. Email marketing, your online content, blogs and other content types are examples.

4. Social Media

Social media is one of the best interactive channels for content distribution and traffic generation. It is also important for SEO and branding. Social media websites such as Facebook and LinkedIn have become so large that they can be considered their own version of the Internet. There's also a lot of hype associated with social media, so it's important to set the right expectations and goals for results. It is also one of the fastest-changing parts of digital marketing. Look at the changes happening at X, formally known as Twitter.

5. Email Marketing

People use their email inboxes to research options. When they need your products or services, they're likely to open your email and click on the link that sends them to your website. This is why regular emails are so important. You want to capture people's attention with value-added emails.

6. Partnerships and Links from Relevant Websites

It's important to see links coming to your site as partnerships with other websites and not as link exchanges or search engine bait. There should be a reason to have links to your website, and you should reach out to appropriate websites to request a link. Google continues to rank websites with inbound links higher in search results, although this is not as critical as it was in the past.

Action Items:

❑ Include a traffic generation plan for each of these six areas in your overall digital marketing plan. Remember to include offline marketing in these efforts.

❑ Make sure each area is coordinated with the digital marketing strategy.

❑ Check assumptions with your website data in each area through your Google Analytics reports and stats.

❑ Learn more about content marketing and develop a plan for content to drive website traffic.

❑ Identify the social networks frequented by your target market and develop a strategy to reach them with content posts.

❑ Learn how to research keywords and the fundamentals of SEO.

❑ Develop a value-added monthly email newsletter that people want to read, share and save.

❑ Make sure people can give you their email addresses for eBooks, webinars, events and more.

❑ Develop a list of websites that should link to your website and pursue a linking strategy with those companies.

What You Need to Know About SEO and Google

Before we dive deeper into digital marketing strategy, let's first review Google. At the time of writing, Google is the single best resource for digital marketing. At least half of the online searchers looking for you will find your website through a Google search.

You should have a fundamental understanding of how Google works and what it's doing on the web, as it has a significant impact on your business.

Get to Know Google

Google became popular because their homepage is so easy to use. They emerged at a time when search engines were cluttered, and homepages were focused on displaying ads rather than the search. Google quickly took advantage of this growth in traffic by introducing online ads through a pay-per-click program, now called Google Ads. This was not a new idea and was already happening at a search engine called GoTo.com, which changed its name to Overture, was purchased by Yahoo and is now owned by Microsoft.

Google surpassed and dominated competitors by providing a very easy-to-use homepage that produced excellent results based on a website's popularity. Google also offered many free tools, including Google Analytics for measuring website stats, the Google Search Console, YouTube, Gmail, Google My Business, Google Maps and more.

Google's policy of simplicity and giving away free services to grow their user base worked very well. Today, more than ever, Google is looking to monetize these services and products into increased revenue from multiple sources, but most of their revenue comes from Google Ads.

What Does Google Want?

A great question to ask is, "What does Google want?" The better you understand Google's mission, the better you can take advantage of what it offers. It's important to know that Google has very ambitious goals to be just about everything Internet, and more.

Here are a few key things to know about Google:

- Google makes it a priority to prevent spam in web searches.
- Google wants to reward websites with great content that's updated regularly.
- Local search and mobile advertising are a key part of Google.
- Google sees Microsoft, Facebook, LinkedIn and Apple as competitors.
- They also have ambitious plans for the future of technology that has nothing to do with search engines.
- Google is building a significant customer support presence to help people use their many products and build Google Ads campaigns.
- Google wants to grow Google Ads significantly, as most companies are not using Google Ads.
- Google gives away many services and products (like Gmail) for free, and this is likely to change over time as they attempt to recruit new paying customers for Google Ads and other services.
- The best web data and statistics collection on the Internet belongs to Google, and they're using this wisely to market online.
- Everything Google gives away for free is used to gather marketing data to better sell other services and get more clicks on ads.

Google is Branding

Google is an important part of your branding and digital marketing strategy. Google is *so* important to your brand that a top search result in Google is, in itself, branding for your business.

Getting found at the top of Google results for your targeted search terms is not just about getting found but also about defining your company, services and products. The definition of branding is the impression left in the minds of your target market when exposed to your company. Part of that branding strategy is how your website appears in Google search results.

Sales Prospecting is Now Google Searches

Google has managed to flip the sales process on its head as prospecting is replaced by Google searches. This has driven the growth of inbound marketing, which we will discuss in more detail in coming chapters.

Inbound marketing is the process of bringing people to your website and online content. This pulls them into your company and leads to an interaction that starts the sales process, as opposed to your sales team prospecting or cold calling them for business.

Here are a few questions to ask about how Google is changing your sales process:

- How has Google changed the way your sales team prospects for business?
- Is your sales team finding prospecting more difficult?
- Are you getting found in Google searches for targeted search terms?
- Is your sales team using Google searches to drive sales and leads?
- How does your target market use Google to find your products or services?

Google Ads

The Google Ads program is the driving force behind their success. In 2023, of the $305.63 billion in revenue the company brought in, a whopping $227.86 billion came from search ads. If done right, the ads work. Google Ads has helped thousands of companies grow their sales online. We're waiting to see what impact AI will have on Google Ad revenue.

Most companies are not taking advantage of this digital marketing opportunity because they don't have the knowledge to run the ads properly, or they've tried Google Ads in the past and didn't see results. Google Ads are used to drive traffic to your website. As you have now learned, if your entire digital marketing process is ineffective, then driving more traffic to your site will not bring a return on your time and money.

Google and AI

Google uses excellent AI technology to improve search results and get targeted results from Google Ads. The issues are how will Google compete with ChatGPT and how they will monetize AI to generate revenue. When you combine this with the potential for AI to power search, the future seems uncertain for Google and their ads. One area they may pursue is competing with Amazon for product sales and retail. They certainly have enough website traffic to make this happen if they choose.

Google's Popularity

Just about all your customers and prospects use Google.

Here are the numbers:

- Google accounts for 91.54% of the global search engine market
- There are 5.9 million Google searches per *minute*.
- Top-ranking Google search results see a 22.4% click-through rate.
- In the U.S., 63% of Google searches occur on mobile.
- Of all web traffic referrals, 66% come from Google.
- Most Google search terms are three to four words long.
- Featured snippets appear twice as often on desktop as on mobile.
- 46% of Google searches have *local* intent.
- 50% of the U.S. population uses voice-enabled search.

As of writing, there are 192,888,216 *active* websites on the Internet, and more than 5x that number are inactive. Every day sees the creation of 252,000 *new* sites. It's the world's largest haystack. Your goal is to get found when your target market is doing research through Google! A basic understanding of how Google works, and what it wants, is critical to making this happen.

What's Up with Google?

Google is a digital marketing powerhouse, and we are subject to its needs, desires, whims and never-ending appetite to make money. Understanding Google and what it wants helps you be a stronger digital marketer. A clear understanding of Google will help you improve SEO results and be successful with Google Ads.

Let's take a look at some of the motivations driving Google and tips to help you benefit.

The Google Monopoly

Google has an effective monopoly for search engine ads. There are no significant competitive options for displaying ads in search. This lack of options hurts advertisers because Google can charge whatever it wants. In fact, they can tweak their Google Ads algorithm as needed to meet their revenue targets.

Google is being challenged by the feds, but our government does not know how to manage this monopoly and does not have the ability to work together to break Google Ads into several competing companies.

As of this writing, Google's monopoly has grown, and ads are more expensive than ever. Their customer service is at an all-time low (think call centers in India), and it could be years before anything changes.

A Monopoly does not have to compete with other companies, so marketers don't have options to go elsewhere, and no new search engine is coming along any time soon. People should have options, as a free market helps buyers motivate companies to make decisions in their customer's best interests. This drives the quality of advertising results and value for customers, which is not currently happening at Google.

A Constant Drive for Increased Profits

Google's leadership wants to make money. In fact, they want to make more money every year and find ways to increase profits. The CEO of Google makes more than $200 million a year!

Much of Google's bad behavior comes from a constant desire to increase profits at a time when ad revenue may be dropping and as online researchers look to other digital channels for their buying research.

What's sad about this is Google is not adding additional value but still taking their profits. Here is what one Google advertiser, Uri Thatcher, the CEO of TouchUpDirect reported:

> "Over the years Google has continually raised our cost of advertising. We have the same impression share, as well as basically the same competitors, we've always had. We know and understand our competitors, and we know and understand our own business. The competitive landscape is a healthy one.

> "The issue is that the competitive landscape is NOT what's driving our advertising costs. For instance, in Q124 our ad costs with Google alone have risen 48%. Our paid ad revenue has risen 30%. Our impression share has remained flat. Our organic revenue has *declined* by 7%.

> "This begs the question, why are our ad costs increasing so dramatically? Ostensibly, all the cost is driven by competition in the bid cost for each relevant search term or keyword. Except that we have the *same* competition as always... soooooo, how can that be? How can it be that when one of our competitors falls out of the bid auction, our costs do not decline? These are questions Google never answers."

The squeeze on advertisers is happening to thousands of small businesses and Google needs to know people are taking notice.

Maybe Google needs extra cash to pay their ongoing legal fees?

Here is a summary from a leading Google Ads specialist at Intuitive Websites:

> "Since 2019, I've watched the push for more and more practices that make money for Google and are not in the

best interests of the client. They started to push actions that waste clicks and they've stopped showing all the search terms that convert. Google does not seem to want advertisers to have the information they need to be more targeted."

When a company pushes profits at all costs, the specialists who know how to actually run the business and understand customers best tend to be pushed out of key decision-making roles. They're usually replaced by number-crunchers looking to cut costs and raise prices. Google is not aligned with customer needs and is looking to maximize corporate returns and make money at all costs.

Zero Click Search

It gets worse. Google does not want people to click on organic search links. Why would they? They want you to stay on the search results page until an ad gets your attention. This is called "zero-click" marketing. To best market your company you must craft an SEO strategy for the actual search results page. This is positive for your company because your brand can be seen by thousands, or even millions, of Google searches even if people don't click to visit your website.

This makes title tags and meta descriptions more important than ever, along with local search for Google My Business and Google Maps. Make sure your Google My Business listing is accurate and updated. Check your Google Maps listing and write title tags and meta descriptions for each web page that will attract people to your brand. Use AI tools like ChatGPT to help draft meta descriptions and write effective title tags.

Google's Greatest Fear

Google is scared to death. They're afraid that one day people will stop using Google. No one has a contract to use Google, and people don't pay for many of their services. If people don't use Google, they don't click on ads.

The amount of money Google can make from giving away free services like Gmail and Google Docs and then using our personal data is limited. Google makes money when people click on ads.

Google's homepage is very easy to use and hasn't changed in 20 years. Google also works hard to remove spam websites and make sure their search results are relevant to the user's intent. Google's AI is a big part of driving quality search results. They do these things to keep users going back to Google. Make sure to keep your website fresh with regular content updates that your users want to read and never, ever spam Google!

Focus on quality website content your users will want to read and that positions you as a thought leader. Build a well-structured and well-designed website using AI content for first drafts, outlines and content ideas, and do not post 100% AI-generated content on your website.

Running Google Ads

If you plan to run Google Ads, focus on quality and measuring your direct return from the ads in the form of leads or sales. Cut costs from Google Ads as much as possible. Start small in local areas where your customers can be found on Google.

And, of course, a monopoly does not have to provide refunds for mistakes in your ad campaigns. Don't go it alone with Google. *Work with experts on your Google Ads campaigns or get ready to be taken to the cleaners by Google.*

Use AI Tools to Deal with Google

AI is a huge threat to the Google Ads cash cow. Why will people need the Google search engine when they can use a personal AI assistant to research products and services?

Ironically for Google, AI is the key to dealing with Google and driving results for your website and your brand.

Action Items:

Here are action items you can start doing today to leverage AI and market effectively on Google.

- ❏ Use AI to create marketing personas for your product and services and write content they want to read.
- ❏ Get targeted benefits for these personas from ChatGPT and build your SEO strategy around those key benefits.
- ❏ Get on the Google Search Console and Google Analytics 4 and learn how they work.
- ❏ Know your sales funnel and what drives conversions in the funnel.
- ❏ Develop web pages that move people to action
- ❏ Follow the principles of EEAT and be a content thought leader.

Talk to Google on the Phone and with Google Search Console

It has historically been very difficult to communicate with Google. It was impossible to reach someone on the phone and hard to know when Google indexes your site and includes it in search results. Google also has account representatives to help with Google Ads setup and questions. The direct phone number for Google Ads is 877-906-7955. More to come in later chapters on both Google Ads and the Goggle Search Console, two must-have Google products to effectively market online.

Google Forces Measurable Value with Google Analytics

Google has replaced the lack of measurable value in marketing or advertising with real-world, real-time data. If your marketing efforts fail to show a measurable return, chances are you will stop funding them. Google has driven this by making everything they do extremely measurable. This is a fundamental shift in marketing, advertising and sales that's still in progress.

Google's major tool for driving ROI is Google Analytics, a leading website data program run and managed by Google. They give away

Google Analytics for free so *you can see for yourself* the return and power of digital marketing and closely track your Google Ads budgets and returns. Google Ads is also a very solid tracking and monitoring program for website data and online conversions.

The Google Search Console

The Google Search Console is one of the most important top-of-funnel reporting tools. It's amazing how many companies are not taking full advantage of this tool. It's still provided by Google for *free*, and it allows you to see all the searches that are done that get your website ranked. You see the *keywords,* you see *the position* of your website and you see *how many people click through*. This is an incredibly valuable tool for moving people into your sales funnel.

It gives you an opportunity to see *where you might be missing keywords*. These are keywords that people search for and would otherwise land on your website. It also gives you an opportunity to see which keywords you're ranking for but are *ranking low*. For example, you might have an excellent keyword that you want to get found for, but you might be positioned in 50th place in Google.

No one's going to find you at position 50. You *want to be in the top 10,* so have your SEO team focus on improving that position. The Google Search Console also helps you see where *outdated content* might be falling in the rankings, which might tell you to get this content updated so you don't lose your position.

All marketers and business leaders should have access to the Google Search Console for their websites. In conjunction with Google Analytics, it makes up *the core reporting tools* that you need to find out how successful your website is in Google searches.

Google and Privacy

A key area to watch in the coming years is how Google responds to privacy issues. Currently, Google knows more about its users than any other online platform. If Google continues to offer a free email service in Gmail and index the world's websites, it will never be synonymous with online privacy. What you must be aware of is how Google uses Cookies to track website visitors for Google Analytics. Over time, more of your visitors will not be tracked unless they give your website permission to track them. This means it is more important than ever to acquire emails and grow your list of loyal followers by gaining permission to market to them. This will allow you to see your website traffic coming from your target market and nurture them with tools like HubSpot, email marketing and social media content.

More Google Tools and Resources

Google is the starting point for the most essential digital marketing tools and resources. Google has a variety of tools that are standards in digital marketing and statistics. Most of these tools are free and can be found by searching Google and developing an account with Google under one username and password. Here are a few of the most important Google tools:

- **Google Analytics** — used to measure your website stats in great detail.
- **Google Keyword Tool** — for researching keywords used to find websites.
- **Google Search Console** — to track how Google has indexed your website in their search engine results and see what search terms are being used to find your site.
- **Google Ads** — the Google online advertising program.
- **Google Alerts** — Google will track and email content to you as it's posted on the web, based on requested search terms. For example, if you set up an alert for your company name, then any time your company is mentioned on the web, Google will send you an email with a link to that new content.
- **Google Trends** — a report showing trends in search by keywords.
- **Think with Google** — a newsletter with the latest findings in digital marketing and a variety of topics.

In addition to these tools, Google also owns YouTube, Google My Business, and Google Maps.

Stay informed about what is happening at Google. Knowing what motivates and drives the world's most popular search engine will improve your digital marketing skills, and AI is a part of this. AI is causing disruptions, and how people research will change over time. The best marketers are thinking about their future customers and how they will be researching products and services online in the years to come.

We will see how Google's role changes and if it can avoid the fate of AOL, Lycos, Yahoo and others who ignored the needs of their target market and lost out to Google. What goes around comes around!

Everything You Need to Know about Pay-per-Click

In the early days of the Internet, a search engine called GoTo.com began running ads alongside their organic search results. These ads were sold through an automated auction and bidding system, and advertisers were only charged if they received clicks on their ads, which linked to the advertiser's website. The top placement in search results went to the highest bidder. Bidding started at a penny per click. This became known as pay-per-click (PPC) advertising because the advertiser's account was only charged when someone clicked on the ad and visited the advertiser's website.

GoTo.com changed its name to Overture.com, and was eventually bought by Yahoo. Their software still powers the Yahoo paid search, which is now run by the Bing search engine from Microsoft.

While the concept of PPC ads and auction bidding was started by GoTo.com and expanded by Yahoo, it was actually Google that took this to an entirely new level with Google Ads. Millions of advertisers began using AdWords, and Google's revenues exploded. AdWords is what makes Google one of the most valuable companies on the planet. Google leveraged the popularity of their search engine to sell new AdWords accounts and drive incredible growth. AdWords allowed any website to attract large numbers of visitors as long as they could afford the click charges.

Google Ads continues to be a viable online marketing resource with excellent ROI when pursuing specific target markets and keyword niches. The most successful Google Ads campaigns are highly targeted and carefully matched to the keyword searches most likely to result in sales.

How to Get Started with Google Ads

The first step is to set up a Google Ads account. It's free, and you can use the same login for Google Ads as you do for any other Google app, such as Google Analytics or Gmail. In fact, it works best when *all* your Google apps are set up under one account. This starts by securing a Gmail account for your company, and this email address can be used for all your Google logins.

Following the Google Ads account signup, you will need to set up your campaigns and segments for each campaign, called Ad-Groups. These segments are very important because of how you select keywords and prepare ads. It also forces you to segment your online marketplace, which brings value to all your marketing efforts. The final steps are to select keywords and write ads.

Here are a few recommendations from our many years of Google Ads experience:

- Keep your ads very simple and very direct.
- Set up unique website landing pages for your ads.
- Include a call to action in your ads.
- Test three or four ads per AdGroup.
- It is better to have more AdGroups than ads.
- Use keyword research to segment and establish AdGroups.
- Include negative keywords to avoid unwanted clicks.
- Some keywords can dominate results and must be segmented.
- Your ads will display based on your bids and Google's relevancy.
- Link Google Ads to your Google Analytics account and track conversions.

There are many tools and reports associated with Google Ads and a very good help section with videos. Take time to review this information and watch the Google Ads videos on the Google Ads website.

Target to Get Results

There are three principal methods for targeting qualified traffic in Google Ads: *keyword* selections, *ads* and user *location*. When done correctly, this is where the genius of AdWords can produce results for just about any website. Use keywords and ads to specifically target exactly what will bring results for your website. Also, Google Ads gets results by complementing an organic search and gives your website the opportunity to be seen at the top of the scroll in Google search results. Targeting by location provides an opportunity to target any location in the world and better control your budget. In many cases, this is the key to excellent ROI from Google Ads.

Use Google Ads for Market Research

The data that comes from a live Google Ads campaign is incredibly insightful. Even if you don't produce many leads or sales, the data alone is worth the investment. You will see an exact number of searches for each keyword and the popularity of your ads in those search results.

Google Ads should convert 1 to 2% of impressions from searches, and high-performing ads can have a click-through rate as high as 10%.

This data will provide feedback to many other parts of your sales and marketing programs. In fact, Google Analytics may start providing less information for free and instead rely on marketers to set up Google Ads accounts to get search data. In fact it's already happening!

Google throws a very broad net, so make sure to target your keyword settings and include negative keywords to avoid paying for the wrong type of traffic.

What's the Cost of Google Ads?

The total budget you'll allocate to Google Ads is based on your expected return. Whether it's the benefits of market research or direct sales, Google Ads should result in solid ROI. Your ROI results are driven by how well you implement your Google Ads strategy and how well you monitor and measure conversions. Your budget can be as low as $500 per month to get value for Google Ads.

Perform a Google search in your industry and see if competitors are using Google Ads. More than likely, their ads can be found running in Google Ads because they're getting results with an acceptable ROI. They get those results because the advertiser has total control over their Google Ads budget. This is true whether you spend thousands of dollars or just a few hundred. This almost-guaranteed ROI from a well-run Google Ads program is the best reason to test Google Ads as part of your digital marketing plan.

Google Ads and AI

Google is currently using advanced AI to target people with digital ads. This has helped the Google Ads program reach high success rates and drive conversions.

AI can also help every part of the Google Ads set-up process, from planning Google Ad strategies to writing the ads, testing keywords and analyzing the data.

While it's important to understand the fundamentals of Google Ads, it's best to work with a professional who is a Google Partner.

Another thing that AI can do to support your Google Ads strategy is help you *write content for landing pages.* Google Ads must go to *specific landing pages that match user intent.* Every visitor to your website is asking a question, and it's always the *same* question, "Am I in the right place?" When they click on that ad, the next thing they need to see is a landing page that 100% matches that intent. Whatever they're looking for, they need to see an *exact* match. If you're renting cabins in the woods in Knoxville, Tennessee, and someone searches on an ad and says, "I want to rent a cabin in the woods in Knoxville, Tennessee," *that landing page better be about cabins in the woods near Knoxville.* I can't tell you how often websites don't do that. Ads often go to generic pages that aren't specific, and their conversion rates are horrible. Use AI to match user intent with Google Ads, then you'll see conversion rates as high as 5% to 10% and that drives a nice ROI on your ad spend.

Action Items:

- ❑ Set aside a test budget and establish a targeted Google Ads campaign.

- ❑ Search in Google to find your competitors in Google Ads and determine their strategy. They may have a few good ideas you can copy.

- ❑ Focus on targeted keywords and simple direct ads with a solid call to action.

- ❑ Link your Google Ads to Google Analytics and track your results.

- ❑ Don't worry, competitors can't drain your Google Ads budget by repeatedly clicking on your ads. Google has set up tracking methods to prevent this.

- ❑ Contact Google directly for help with Google Ads at 877-906-7955.

CHAPTER 9:
Digital Marketing and
the Sales Funnel

INBOUND
MARKETING

RESEARCHERS
SEO, Blogs, Websites, Offline Marketing, Social Media, Digital Ads, Influencers

MIDDLE OF FUNNEL
CALL-TO-ACTIONS (CTA)

LEADS
Website Landing Pages, Email Newsletters, eBooks,
Webinars, White Papers, Podcasts

BOTTOM OF
FUNNEL (CTAS)

MARKETING QUALIFIED LEADS
Phone Calls, Chat, Email, Contact Forms, Online Calendars

SALES & MARKETING
ALIGNMENT

SALES QUALIFIED LEADS
Sales Follow-Up, Marketing Automation, HubSpot
Optimization, Email Campaigns, Sales Meetings

CUSTOMERS

Growth can only happen through an improved funnel. Either you get more people in your digital sales funnel, or you improve the quality of prospective buyers to increase conversion rates. Whatever path you take, the growth of your company comes from an improved sales funnel.

In my book with Karl Becker, *Sales and Marketing Alignment*, we go into detail on the sales funnel and its role in growing your business. Understanding how your digital funnel drives sales is key to growth, so let's take a deeper dive into how this works, and how AI can help you get movement in the funnel.

Offline and Digital Marketing Work Together

Unless you're strictly an online business, which most companies are not, one of the biggest contributors to digital marketing success is what you do offline. Your company's brand and reputation will drive the most qualified traffic to a website that will convert at the highest levels.

Ultimately, your website supports your overall sales and marketing strategy and must be in alignment with what you do offline to maximize results. Yes, offline marketing helps you win at digital marketing! Here are a few things to consider when aligning your online and offline marketing efforts. *Digital marketing should support what you do offline* with your traditional sales and marketing efforts, like print ads, TV, or trade shows.

Pay Attention to Digital Marketing

The company website is easy to ignore because it's not usually a part of the daily routine of the business owner or leader. You can make it a part of your regular sales and marketing work by regularly reviewing web stats and scheduling a digital marketing meeting at least once a month. Use these meetings and web stats to ask questions about web strategy and how it impacts the company's overall marketing plan. Your web stats must be seen as a key business indicator to be reviewed regularly.

Website Domain Name

Most people will look for your domain name as the first step to visiting your website. They expect the domain name to match the company name. This should be an exact match! This is very important because you can send web traffic to your competitors by using a domain name that does not match your company name. We've consulted with many companies where this was the case, and a poorly chosen domain name was sending traffic to their competitors.

For example, if your company name is Standard Manufacturing, but your domain name is StandardInc.com, you'll be sending traffic to StandardManufacturing.com.

If a competitor has that domain name, then they will get your web traffic regardless of their actual company name. In fact, much of *their* web traffic will come from *your* offline marketing and referrals.

This is so important that you should seriously *consider changing your company name to match an available domain*. Also, it's better to have a long domain name that is your full company name rather than a shorter domain name that's cryptic and hard to remember. This makes it easier for people to refer others to your company.

Put Your Domain on Everything

Anything that's printed or visible to prospective customers should include your domain name. This includes invoices, packaging, vehicles, buildings and other parts of your business that are seen by prospective customers. This will drive qualified website traffic.

Coordinate Digital Marketing with the Sales Team

Your sales team has a unique understanding of your visitors. You'll find some salespeople are excellent web marketers. They offer website design options, prepare online content, run social media programs and more. They should at least have input into digital marketing efforts and regularly attend meetings. As prospecting becomes more difficult, more sales professionals will depend on digital marketing for lead generation.

The Website is an Extension of the Sales Process

The sales team talks to prospects and customers every day. They're in the best position to understand what motivates users to become paying customers, and how to develop a conversion process that seamlessly transitions the lead into their sales funnel.

For many companies, the Internet is their biggest source of leads, while prospecting has transitioned to content marketing to drive inquiries and leads. Get the sales team involved in the process to drive results and improve ROI.

What Works Offline Works Online

Look at what has driven the success of your company offline and translate those tactics to your website. Tactics that work offline should be translated to digital and closely monitored. This can include promotions, special pricing, advertising campaigns, media resources and more. This is set in motion with excellent website content that users can easily find on the web.

Action Items:

- ❑ Make sure your domain name exactly matches your company name.
- ❑ Put your website domain name on all your printed materials.
- ❑ Coordinate digital marketing efforts with your sales team.
- ❑ See your website as an extension of your formal sales process.
- ❑ Find what works best offline and translate it to the Internet.
- ❑ Develop a digital marketing plan and strategy for inbound marketing for lead generation.
- ❑ Pay attention to your digital marketing efforts and how they're coordinated with offline efforts. Have web stats sent to you once per week.

Traffic Growth at the Top of Your Sales Funnel

Let's dive deeper into the differences between pull and push marketing and how they impact website traffic and your overall digital marketing efforts.

Pull and Push Marketing Defined

As we learned in the previous chapters, push marketing involves tactics such as finding customers through prospecting, cold calling, traditional selling and other techniques. It's the process of the sales and marketing team pushing prospects to the company. Pull marketing is a strategy that involves creating an environment where customers find you and are pulled or attracted to your company. Pull marketing is now preferred by most people as they do their research anonymously online, and they're very knowledgeable before they purchase, or even talk to a salesperson. These preferences have changed the traditional sales funnel and how companies should understand the new prospective customer.

People Prefer Pull Marketing Approaches

Prospective customers prefer pull marketing techniques. They want to research and find you rather than getting a cold call, and the data supports pull marketing. Take a look at these findings from ThinkWithGoogle, a Google research study.

- 82% of B2C consumers research before buying.
- 57% of B2B buyers research before making contact.
- Four out of five consumers use multiple devices to research.
- Mobile devices are expected to account for 44% of ecommerce by 2025.

These numbers are conservative estimates and are increasing over time.

Your goal is to get found during their research on multiple devices, platforms, and websites. This is the essence of pull marketing and the biggest differentiator from push marketing. Also, pull marketing requires that you know your prospective customers very well.

Understanding the New Prospect

The Internet has influenced buying habits in many ways, and out of this has come a new, educated buyer with many options. Here are a few key points to remember about the new consumer and your prospective customer in B2C and B2B markets:

- They scan content for value and will read on portable screens.
- They want quick, concrete, relevant and timely advice.
- While most just read, some want to comment or ask a question.
- They look for organized websites that they can trust.
- People are more important than companies or brands.

- They are very skeptical of what they don't know.
- They can see through the sizzle and marketing hype.
- They look for transparency to build trust.

The New Digital Marketing Sales Funnel

The new sales prospect and the growth in pull marketing have resulted in a new sales funnel. The sales funnel is a visual representation of the actual steps in your company's sales process and selling cycle. It's large at the top because more time is spent on those action items, and more people enter the funnel at the top than come out the bottom as buyers. The change toward an emphasis on pull marketing has led to a new sales funnel, as seen below.

The New Funnel

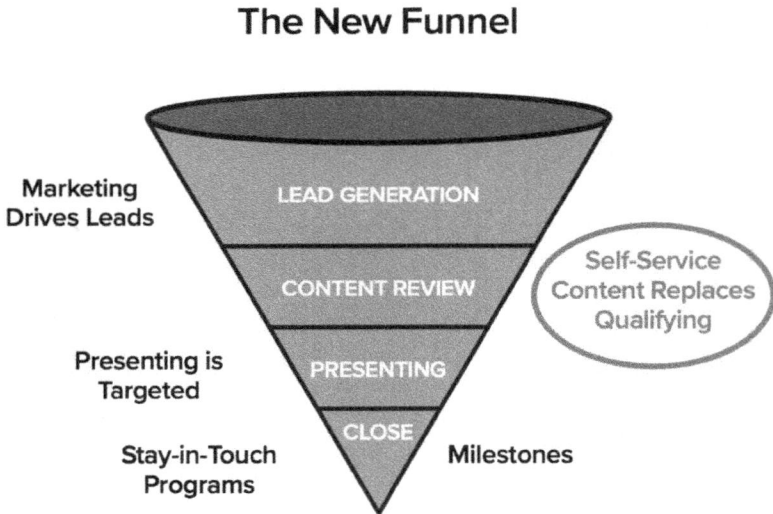

Marketing Drives Leads — LEAD GENERATION
Self-Service Content Replaces Qualifying
CONTENT REVIEW
Presenting is Targeted — PRESENTING
CLOSE
Stay-in-Touch Programs — Milestones

Marketing Drives Leads

The old sales funnel was all about prospecting and qualifying customers, getting them into a sales discussion and then hoping you can close. That's like the old Zig Ziglar sales model: prospect, qualify, and close, close, close. This has completely changed over the last 10 years.

The new sales funnel is about using content and continuity campaigns to drive leads, presenting content that is *highly targeted* based on the unique needs of that individual user, and lead generation as opposed to prospecting.

Presenting is Targeted

In the New Sales Funnel, you've got to use all these inbound tactics to bring people to your brand because people want to research anonymously, find your brand themselves and see that you're a good fit. They read your content, experience your website and *reach out when they're ready.*

What's happened is this self-service content has created *a really smart consumer.* These smart consumers *may know more than your sales team,* and that's okay. You want your sales team to be able to service them, to be a guide, to *facilitate* their needs. You don't need to have salespeople who are 100% product or industry experts. They need to serve as guides and resources, and then the new sales funnel is supported by your marketing automation, the stay-in-touch programs you put in place and the *ability to close* someone in a meeting on the phone or a Zoom call.

How People Consume Digital Content

Self-Service Content Replaces Qualifying Questions

Salespeople today are *much more focused on closing* than on any other kind of selling, so you must be a facilitator and a guide to make that happen. This is the new sales funnel.

Sales Funnel Milestones and Conversion Rate Optimization

In this new sales funnel, prospecting is replaced by pull marketing, which generates qualified leads from online marketing. These prospects have been educated about your products and services by reading your content and then contacting you once they establish value. Your content should be *plentiful, relevant and available* on the web.

Qualifying your target market is much more focused and based on self-service research efforts by your target customers. This is driven by *content marketing.* Your presentations are very targeted and customized to the prospect's needs. Any prospects who fall out of the funnel at any time should become part of your stay-in-touch program. Closing takes less effort. It becomes a natural part of the process and isn't forced. This is a new approach to sales milestones, and the sales process is brought on by pull marketing. Share this information with your sales team and use it to coordinate efforts between sales and marketing.

Seven Key Digital Marketing Funnel Milestones

1. Website Visit
2. Social Media Interaction
3. Email Acquisition and Subscriber Growth
4. eBook or other Gated Content
5. Webinar or Event Registration
6. Website Form Submission
7. Scheduled Call with a Knowledge Expert or Salesperson

The companies that do these things well are growing faster than those that don't.

Metric number one is *website visits*. These are key to the growth of your company. Bigger companies get more traffic. Growth in visitors means that your company is growing. Declining website visitors means they're going somewhere else. Traffic is a leading indicator, so a decline means that your sales are probably going to drop as well.

Number two is *social media interactions*. How many followers do you have on your social media accounts, and how are people on social interacting with your brand? Larger companies get more activity on their social media. You can be purposeful about social by finding your personas on social media platforms, attracting them to the brand, and growing your contact database.

Number three, *acquiring email* addresses and growing your database is key to your growth as a company. Larger companies have larger databases and your website must have an email subscribe button and be focused on acquiring email addresses. One of the ways to do that is in the next two items, which we call *middle of funnel CTA's.* Once someone decides to download your e-book or access other gated content, they will be willing to give you their email address and not be anonymous anymore because they value your content.

Two great middle-of-funnel tactics are #4, *e-books,* and #5, *webinars.* During the time of COVID, webinar registrations went through the roof. I saw this at the VISTAGE organization, where I'm a speaker. Before COVID, we would offer a webinar through VISTAGE, and if we got 100 people to register, we were celebrating. If we got 200 people, that was fantastic. After COVID, we were getting close to 1,000 people attending webinars because they didn't have to sit in their cars in traffic. They were working from home and had the time to get the training they needed to do their job better. Webinars and eBooks all rely on thought leadership, and of course your content must be both *relevant and valuable.* If you have great content people will give you their emails so they can stay in touch.

Capturing email addresses is more important than ever because of the new privacy rules and because of Google's stance toward privacy. But once someone gives you their email address, now you can use marketing automation tools to stay in touch. You can score them as a lead and hopefully move them toward a close as a new customer.

At the bottom of the funnel are *website form submissions.* These are form submissions, phone calls, or emails that originate from your website. I like forms because they're easy to track and you can control what you're getting from the customer. Shorter forms have higher conversion rates, while longer forms qualify more but have lower conversion rates. I really encourage everyone on a website to have a simple submission form so someone can get in touch with you quickly and easily without having to give you a lot of their information.

You've got to have forms on your website because often people won't have easy access to their email on the device that they're holding at the moment. Today, 63% of Google's organic search traffic originates from mobile devices.

And then #7, and this is bottom of funnel, which is to actually *schedule a call* with a knowledge expert or salesperson. They should be able to do this online. There are apps like Calendly.com or Acuity.com you can link to, or you can offer a form that connects directly to your CRM, like HubSpot, to schedule time with a salesperson.

These are the seven key metrics that most companies want to watch. Improve these metrics and you'll grow your business.

Salespeople as Content Experts

Salespeople should become digital marketing content experts. Whether they're writing blog posts, networking on social media or performing various content marketing tasks, their customer and company knowledge is essential to pull-marketing success. Not all salespeople will excel at this, and many will have nothing to do with writing content. However, you may find hidden gems in your sales team who love online marketing and can make your pull marketing very successful. Finding a salesperson who loves to write is key to this strategy.

Action Items:

- ❏ Educate your sales and marketing teams about pull and push marketing strategies.
- ❏ Develop your sales funnel with key milestones based on pull marketing approaches and strategies.
- ❏ Set targets and goals for each step in the process.
- ❏ Include this in your content marketing and digital marketing plans.
- ❏ Share this information with your sales team and recruit their help with implementation.
- ❏ Visit competitor websites and evaluate how they're using pull marketing techniques.
- ❏ Research your "new" prospective customers to understand how they will research your company online and what will motivate them to contact your company.

The Importance of Email Marketing

Email marketing has been through a lot. We used to embrace email marketing, and people did a ton of it, but recently, people are much more skeptical of email and more protective about what lands in their in-box. The email response rate varies from industry to industry and campaign to campaign. If you have a response rate of *less than 10%,* you should be working on your email marketing strategies to boost your open and response rates.

Email marketing is still very important, so if you send emails to your database and you get a 20 to 30% open rate, those are great numbers. You want to market to that database because 20% to 30% of people *will* open emails and *will* engage with you.

- Email marketing generates $42 for every $1 spent.
- Mobile devices account for about 60% of email opens.
- 64% of small businesses use email marketing to reach customers.
- 89% of marketers use email as the primary channel for generating leads.
- 82% of marketers worldwide use email marketing.
- 99% of email users are checking their email daily.
- Professional marketers have found a 760% increase in revenue from building email lists and using email campaigns.
- Half the world's population has an email address, resulting in 4.3B accounts globally.
- 4 out of 5 marketers said they'd rather give up social media than email marketing.[1]

We're going to find the other 60 or 70 % who don't open emails. We'll find them through Google searches, LinkedIn and other ways. But capturing an email address and putting it into an automated CRM tool like HubSpot is still critical.

---

[1] https://www.luisazhou.com/blog/email-marketing-roi-statistics/

About one in three small businesses don't use email to market their products and services. They're missing out on what may be the most cost-effective form of online marketing available. It's common for business leaders to see email marketing as spam, but the reality is that loyal customers and targeted prospects are looking for valuable content that can improve the quality of their lives or make their job easier.

Email allows you to meet those needs and reach thousands of targeted subscribers in a way that's unmatched by other forms of direct marketing.

Here are the steps to get started with email marketing.

Build a Great Email List

The very best email lists include people who voluntarily sign up (opt in) for your email marketing program. Another good source is email addresses collected from online sources such as your website and social media. Email marketing success will always be based on the strength of your list and the value subscribers get from your content. Purchased email lists do not usually deliver enough value in building a great list of loyal followers. In addition, using a purchased list is likely to upset people who feel they're being spammed. We don't recommend using your email list to prospect for new business by including people who have no connection to your company.

Make it easy for website visitors to sign up for your email content on your website. Your list should be comprised of loyal followers, current customers, referral sources, prospective customers and others who know your company. Start with those who know your company best and build a great email list. Some people will obviously ask to be removed from your list or unsubscribe. Don't dwell on these people, as they will usually be a small percentage overall.

Email Signup Box

Place an easy-to-find email signup box on your website in the upper left corner of the homepage. This allows easy access from your most loyal followers and those most likely to subscribe. Email subscribes can be tracked in Google Analytics and should be seen as a key conversion point.

Prepare Excellent Email Content

Emails with poor content are deleted or flagged as spam. Emails with excellent content will be read, distributed around the web and drive visits and online conversions. Write desirable content that helps people do their jobs or improves the quality of their lives. It should also include a strong call to action and/or promotion.

The graphic design of your email blast should be appropriate for your target market. Many email marketers make the mistake of overdesigning their email blasts, which leads to low response rates as most people prefer content over graphics. Interesting photos and valuable content will draw email subscribers to your company.

Monthly Email Marketing

The frequency of your marketing emails depends upon your online strategy; however, once per month is a good target for most email newsletters. This is enough frequency to stay top-of-mind with subscribers, but not so often that they become annoying.

Coordinate email with social media, blogs and other content

Email newsletter campaigns work best when coordinated with online articles, blogs and social media. Content and special promotions sent in your marketing emails should also be included in social media. Also, ensure you archive all your email newsletters on your website and code them for SEO. Allow website visitors to *subscribe* to your blog posts and your email newsletters and announcements.

Track and Measure Email Results

There are dozens of very good email marketing providers with excellent tracking capabilities. Programs like MailChimp, Constant Contact, iContact and others are easy to use and have excellent reporting tools that often link to Google Analytics. These tools will cover the bases needed to ensure your email campaigns follow the rules and drive success. These software tools have excellent pricing and are easy to set up to deal with subscribing and unsubscribing issues.

Action Items:

- ❏ Set up an account with an email marketing service such as MailChimp.

- ❏ Add an email signup box to your website.

- ❏ Use AI to generate headlines and content ideas that fit the interests of your personas.

- ❏ Make a list of email topics that help your target market do their job better or improve the quality of their lives.

- ❏ Make a list of email promotions and calls to action that have worked in the past (offline or online).

- ❏ Assign a content writer to prepare brief, informative emails.

- ❏ Make use of excellent photography with captions in email blasts.

- ❏ Make sure subscribers can easily opt out of your email lists.

- ❏ Plan a monthly marketing email and track results in your web stats.

AI and the Sales Funnel

As your personal sales and marketing consultant and second brain, AI tools support you as you set the strategy for your sales funnel, determine the key funnel milestones, grow top-of-funnel awareness and move people through to a close.

Most companies struggle in the middle of the funnel, and this is where AI shines. It can provide topic ideas for middle-of-funnel content and write the first draft for eBooks, white papers, webinars and videos. These are the things people review when making buying decisions. People are also willing to give you an email address for access to this content.

AI can help with suggestions on how to move people through the funnel based on the persona you are targeting, and then it can prepare the first draft of content that engages the buyer.

Ask ChatGPT or Gemini these questions and get your sales funnel conversion started:

- What marketing tactics move people through the sales funnel to buy [your product]?
- How can we build awareness at the top of the sales funnel for [your product]?
- What are a few middle-of-sales-funnel resources and topics people want in this market?
- Write an eBook or White paper on [this topic.]

Make sure to connect these middle-of-funnel strategies, tactics and content with your personas. Wiggam Law was able to optimize this and hit a home run.

They were looking for resources for the online researcher to better understand tax resolution for businesses and how Wiggam could help. The solution was a highly targeted blog that not only met the needs of the online researcher but also got Wiggam found in Google searches. You can see the blog here: https://wiggamlaw.com/blog/ Notice the blog topics and how they're targeted for both SEO and highly informative for website visitors.

The blog drove more than 150,000 views to the website, more than 60,000 visitors from Google, and more than 700 inquiries. Now that's movement in the funnel!

About 10 % of inquiries become clients of Wiggam, with an average order of about $6,500. That's almost $500K in new revenue, not including big corporate accounts and reoccurring revenue.

This is how a blog and SEO can optimize your funnel and drive sales growth.

STEP 4: CONVERSIONS AND ROI

CHAPTER 10:
Project Management and Action Items

In Part One, we introduced you to the Four-Step Process. In Part Two, we went into detail on each of the Four Steps. In Part Three, we'll pull all the steps together with instructions on how to successfully *implement* the action plans needed to exceed your digital marketing goals, drive conversions and get ROI from your time and money.

Project Management Makes Things Happen

Digital marketing and website design and development projects are where the best-made plans can go haywire, and poor project management can lead to major problems and delays. This is an area that needs attention to drive ROI from digital marketing.

Many of these issues come from the nature of the work and the complexities of digital marketing in general. As you'll read in the coming chapters, problems also come from conflicts between the varied skills needed to market online. Project management can become a major obstacle to results if it's not done well, as it's a key ingredient in rising above the digital noise.

The most common results of poor project management are a delayed launch, sub-par performance or low conversion rates. Poorly executed project management has resulted in the failure of many digital marketing projects, and it's a major reason why many websites are hard to use or don't make sense. The good news is there's a way around these headaches.

Growth-Driven Design (GDD)

GDD is a process for planning and managing digital marketing projects based on the principles of agile and lean project management. It works great for planning digital marketing efforts because it's based on incremental improvements and continuous updates to get results. When combined with the Four Steps, GDD will vastly improve your website and digital marketing results by improving how projects are managed.

Growth-Driven Design

At Intuitive Websites, we follow GDD, and it has transformed our agency. To make websites successful, we take off bites of work, we call those *sprints,* and during the sprint, we do as much as possible, and then re-measure to create the next digital marketing sprint.

This is how it works. You look at your website and realize we've got to make some changes. Let's figure out what we want to get done in our next sprint. And let's say our sprint is going to be six weeks or three weeks or three months; whatever the window may be, it doesn't matter.

But what matters is that it has an **end** because, at the end of that sprint, we will then look at what's been accomplished. We'll look at the results and then set up a *new* sprint, make a new set of changes and we'll take those live. Then we'll measure those and see how well they're doing, and then we repeat this process.

Using Growth-Driven Design (GDD)

Of all the concepts we've talked about in this book, GDD may be the most important. Lacking an organized program structure around getting digital marketing done can lead to a chaotic approach, costly mistakes and ineffective digital marketing.

Many companies struggle with this. The reason people don't touch their website for two or three years is because it becomes such a pain that they don't want to deal with it. In fact, if you think about the traditional website design process, you've got to think about it as a broken process. It's not working. The idea that a website developer is going to gather content from a company, put together a website, and launch it so that it's effective, that approach just doesn't work. It takes a very specific approach to get digital marketing to work.

GDD is a great approach to do this. It's a HubSpot process for fixing that traditional, broken website process. You get things done in incremental steps and work toward constant improvement, as opposed to finishing a project.

Here's why that's important. Your website is never finished. It's constantly evolving and changing. A lot of folks have an idea that their website is like a brochure. Once it goes to the printer, it's done. That's not the case. It's not even the case with books today.

Books are printed on demand and can be updated as needed, and so is your website. That means if you look at your current website and you see something you can improve, there's no reason to wait. Make those changes immediately because then your users will experience a better website. That's important because every single user is deciding whether to move forward and engage or leave and go elsewhere. If they have an improved experience, they're more likely to stay and dive deeper into your website and eventually reach out to your company and perhaps even become a customer.

The other reason this is important is these visits generate data about what people do. If you make a change to your website and start collecting new information, you'll know more about what they're doing. If you leave it as it is, then there's no change in the data, so you can't make decisions on it.

This is an incredibly important point in growth-driven design. Make changes, track the data, and let the data suggest what needs to happen next.

This starts to relieve the pain from website design. You don't have to keep working at this thing 'till it's perfect before going live. Instead, the website is in the state it's in right now and can always be improved. There's always more you can do on the website to better meet user needs. Growth-driven design is a process for continuous improvement. It's ongoing and it should be broken into *sprints*.

A website sprint is a span of time that you can use to get things done. At Intuitive Websites, we like to set three-month sprints because most of the work we do is very strategic. It involves work on the website content and all the different factors involved. We set very specific goals for our sprint window, and then we look to get those things done within the sprint.

Then, when the sprint is completed, we can go back and look and see what's working, what's not working, what gave us wins and what didn't, and then we can set the next sprint based on analysis of the data.

This process is extremely valuable and was built on the principles of Agile Project Management, which completely revolutionized software development. It's the reason we have all the fantastic software we have today. Developers learned the concepts of incremental improvements and ongoing updates, and that it's better to launch and get data than to wait until the website's perfect.

Use growth-driven design to really supercharge your digital marketing and your websites.

AI and Growth-Driven Design

AI can be your personal growth-driven design consulting expert. You can have a dialogue with AI around any of the challenges you have in project management for your website, digital marketing or putting sprints together.

The AI tool can help write the sprint. If you ask the question and explain your challenges to the AI tools, you will get a fantastic sprint back and the AI tool can follow growth-driven design principles.

In the Wiggam Law example mentioned earlier, all their successes were built on the principles of growth-driven design over a series of sprints. We're still running sprints today. Jason Wiggam, the CEO, recently told us that his leads have doubled since following growth-driven design. You too can see results like that if you put these principles into practice.

When you do this, you get all kinds of benefits:
- It drives results faster based on the data you see from your changes.
- You move away from the ongoing pain of website design where people are waiting for a site to launch and waiting on everybody's opinion.
- You implement a process for continuous improvement that your website visitors will love because every website visitor hitting your site gets the best version of your site that's available.

Think about how great that is. Every time a new visitor uses your website, they're getting the best you have for them. They're not seeing a website that's been out there for three years, waiting for a new one to come on board.

Anyone not using AI to supercharge this process is also using a broken system because AI can now give you *content* immediately, give you a very clear list of *benefits* for your website, help you write *taglines* and headers and can even help you with *design ideas, graphics* and *images*. Now even if you're using AI to design this website, you must also have a human there with the creative touches that really make the website look great. I encourage you to continue being creative with your website design and make it unique to you. Even if you're using a website template, make that template unique to you with *graphics that only you have.*

AI to Support Project Management in Digital Marketing

Earlier, I mentioned how important AI is for creating benefit checklists. AI can also create action items for project managers. You can be as specific as you like when you go to the tool and start asking about action items.

Action items and processes must come from a Project Manager. This is usually someone on your team who is going to be managing projects, schedules, people, action items and deadlines. Project managers do not have to be digital marketing pros. They must be project managers, and if you're using an agency, we recommend that a project manager work closely with a coordinator within your firm.

Project managers can use AI to help them with all these things. Use the following prompts to better manage digital marketing and website projects.

- Create a checklist for the design and development of my new website.
- Develop a project plan for SEO on my website.
- Create a checklist for a successful email marketing program.
- Write an action plan to get results from social media and develop an outline for a social content calendar.
- Prepare a task list for website content writers.
- Develop a list of action items for each member of the digital marketing team.

A project manager without AI is like a writer without a notebook. AI is an essential tool. They must have it. We will talk in more detail about the kinds of things project managers can use the AI tool for in digital marketing.

Discipline and Focus

Digital marketing project management takes discipline and focus: discipline to track the overall goals of the project and focus to keep in mind the needs of your website users. There are many options and various methods for being successful online, but the key is to stay true to your goals of increased sales and better marketing results. A guidepost to help in this area is to focus on decisions that will attract your target market to your digital marketing channels and meet user needs. This is easier said than done, but the results are well worth the effort.

Variety of Skills

It takes a project manager with a unique personality to bring together the variety of skills necessary to implement a digital marketing project. Marketing, technology, design and other dissimilar skill sets must come together effectively to get results from digital marketing. Project management is the glue that holds it all together.

Many project management challenges appear when one area dominates the others. It's very common for technology staff or designers to set strategic direction for your efforts. However, this is not the best approach. Strategic direction should come from the company's leadership.

The Four Steps and Project Management

Each of the Four Steps requires different levels of project management. Design, development and traffic generation are much more time-intensive and include many more action items. This is where the project manager will spend most of the time. Step Four is almost entirely composed of project management and setting priorities. The Four Steps help bring purpose and efficiency to the challenges of managing digital marketing projects.

Action Plans and Worksheets

In the Appendix you'll find action plans and worksheets that help you track your online marketing activities and ensure priorities are set and tasks are completed. The key will be the development of a process and hiring the right person to manage the work. The project manager doesn't have to be skilled in technology, programming, design or other areas of digital marketing. In fact, it's preferable if the project manager does not have a specific background in *any* of these areas so they don't bring bias into this work.

Action Items:

❑ Implement growth-driven design. Make sure that you have sprints in your design process so that you have a time frame for what you want to get done.

❑ Make sure you have a system for measuring the changes you made on your website. For example, you change a call to action, and you change it from "contact us" to "speak to a professional." Watch for movement in your stats.

❑ Let's make sure that you measure that return and that you measure the traffic on the website with Google Analytics, and that you keep improving.

Digital Marketing Project Management

This is one of the first people to add to the digital marketing team and will be key to excellent results. The Project Manager is the glue that holds all the action items and team members together to realize the digital marketing strategy. Don't take this position lightly. This should be an internal position in the company, and you must give them the tools and responsibility to manage the project's priorities properly.

Digital Marketing Team Selection

It takes time to find the right people and build your digital marketing team. Digital marketers are in high demand and their skill sets and experience can vary greatly. The Project Manager plays an important role in this area. He or she should be tasked with implementing the legwork and developing a process to find, interview and recruit team members. This includes employees, agencies and contractors.

Because digital marketing work is easily measured and results are clearly transparent, develop a test project for new team members to assess their work ethic, skills and performance before they're hired. The project manager should also make recommendations regarding replacing poorly performing team members.

Digital Marketing Meetings

A key job function for the project manager is the scheduling and organizing of meetings. He or she should help prepare the agenda, determine who needs to attend and track the action items coming out of each meeting. Over time, the project manager may even run the meeting and keep team members on track. One of the most important outcomes of digital marketing meetings will be assigning action items and due dates. These are managed and tracked by the project manager.

Reviewing Priorities and Measuring Results

The project manager may not have the final say on priorities and action plans but should be involved in reviewing those areas and understanding how to measure results. This includes organizing and following up on action plans. Not all the action items are of equal importance, and the team can't do everything at once.

This is where the project manager prioritizes the action items by their impact on goals and implementing the digital marketing strategy. It's important to keep the project manager aware of the big picture and the ROI of these efforts.

Oversight of the Digital Marketing Team

The project manager is the taskmaster for communication between each of the digital marketing team members. This includes communications with contracted team members and other subcontractors, as well as employees. The Project Manager looks for inconsistencies in team member action items, and because they have access to all the action items, they're in a unique position to make sure things stay on track. This includes feedback on the performance of each team member.

Website Updates and Content Reviews

The project manager should also spot-check the work of the team. This includes checking the website for broken links and other technical and design glitches, along with other things, such as grammar and spelling errors. The project manager should also work with the team to organize the timing of website content and placement of content on the website and social media.

CHAPTER 11:
Conversions to Leads to Sales

Measure Your Website and Digital Marketing ROI

The return you get from this work is seen in a variety of ways. A solid digital marketing foundation leads to a strong brand and company identity. This is not easily measured, but companies with strong brands thrive.

Other parts of digital marketing have a very clear and direct return on time and money because you can measure and identify the source of your sales and which digital channel makes people aware of your services and products. In Step Four of the Four-Step Process, we will review ROI and track the results of your digital marketing efforts.

At the core of Step Four is website *conversions*. How you design and develop your website will impact its ability to generate inquiries and sales. Let's take a closer look at online conversions as they impact your design and development process.

ROI Success Starts with Goals
You must know where you are going to best determine the return from your digital marketing journey. Your marketing goals are your guideposts, and your digital data guides the way.

The marketing goal of every website should be to convert visitors into customers. This is also the great challenge, as many websites are online brochures that focus more on describing the company than converting users. It starts by developing a *conversion strategy,* which must be included in your Digital Marketing Plan.

This conversion strategy is the *real* measure of a website's effectiveness and its ability to convert visitors into sales. This is not an easy task, and there are no quick fixes. It starts with learning about online conversion, and what makes it work. Converting even a small percentage of your visitors into sales can drive a very high ROI.

Most small companies are notorious for not tracking the ROI behind sales and marketing functions. They tend to wing it and rely too much on anecdotal information. Digital marketing is data-driven and removes the blind guesses that often result from the lack of quantifiable sales data. The first step in determining ROI is establishing the necessary analytics and processes to track it.

Here are the most important digital stats to watch and review with your team as they drive the conversion process and sales funnel:

- Total website visitors
- Number of web pages per visit
- Time on the website and web page
- Bounce rate
- Most popular pages
- Entry pages and exit pages
- Traffic sources, referrers and search keywords
- Conversions and sales tracking in Google Analytics
- Shopping cart abandonment rates
- Sales funnels and user paths
- Social media impressions and engagement
- Email open and conversion rates
- User location, country, state and city
- Mobile versus desktop
- Google and social impressions

There are many more statistics available, but these are a starting point and the most important for monitoring strategic results and Key Performance Indicators or KPIs.

The data reported in your digital stats should be matched against other KPIs in the business. From this comparison, important KPI trends will emerge. One of the most common trends will be the relationship between website visitors and gross revenues. Another trend to review is website engagement and its impact on conversion rates, which also drives gross sales.

As you begin to monitor these stats, you will see many comparisons with business KPIs, and you can begin to ask questions about how the trends impact each other. The process will also help you find the unique web stats for your business that become KPIs.

Measuring Strategic Results

Stats and Key Performance Indicators (KPIs)

Most business leaders do not regularly track their digital stats. This means they're missing out on very important trends that help track overall success. It also means you can gain a competitive advantage by watching your website stats and acting on what these stats communicate. Your digital marketing efforts are important enough that these stats are KPIs measuring business success. Don't be blind to this. Understand how increasing or decreasing website visits and other trends impact your company and include that data as a key measurement tool for business success.

Get Access to the Data

For most business leaders, the first step is getting access to your website data and reports. Google Analytics 4 is currently the best website statistics program available. This program is more than adequate for most business websites. All websites should take advantage of this free service. If you haven't done so already, set up Google Analytics. Ask someone on your team to send you the reports *weekly* if possible. Also, schedule a *monthly* digital marketing meeting to review these statistics in detail and ask questions.

The Google Search Console is also highly useful, and a must-have reporting tool. It is the only tool available that shows you the keywords people use to find your website and where your site ranks on those keywords. Today's popular SEO tools use the Google Search Console as their source of data.

There are other providers of web stats that take Google's data and combine with other platforms such as SEMRush or HubSpot. One such tool is Agency Analytics.

How to Set Digital Marketing Goals

Google Analytics reports on hundreds of web statistics and variations. It can feel overwhelming at first. Yet, understanding which statistics are most important and how to interpret those stats are the first steps in setting digital marketing goals. Let's start with an overview of the most important web stats to track and a review of how to set goals in each key area.

Website Visitors

This can be measured by total visits, unique visits, new visitors and repeat visits. Your site should target about 75% of total visits from new visitors. Critical mass for websites is usually reached when traffic volumes approach a minimum of 1,500 to 2,000 visits per month. This is the most important web stat to follow closely, and it's a key business indicator for your company. Review website visits weekly, if possible.

Pages per Visit and Time on Site

This is an indication of interest and website engagement. Target four to five pages per visit and three minutes on the site as goals. This will drive a healthy conversion rate.

Engagement, Events and Bounce Rates

Google Analytics 4 is optimized to measure engagement rates with your website. It will tell you how long people stay on a web page and what they do while they're there. The bounce rate is a measurement of visitors leaving immediately, or bouncing off your website, versus going deeper and visiting more than one page. A bounce rate of 25% means that 25% of your website visitors leave after visiting just one page. Target a bounce rate below 40% for lead generation websites and 30% or below for e-commerce sites.

Traffic Sources

There are three basic sources of website traffic:

1. Search engine traffic (organic and paid)
2. Links from other websites
3. Direct traffic

Set a goal of 50% of your traffic coming from organic search engine results and 25% or more coming from links from other websites. Direct traffic is good but doesn't usually represent business growth from new site visitors. Most direct traffic comes from people who already know your company.

Top Pages Visited

These are your visitors voting with their clicks on what interests them the most about your website. People are impatient and want information fast. Your key website landing pages must be thorough and include benefit-focused content that meets visitor needs or they will leave your website. Getting people to click on more than one page of your website is rare, but when they do, it shows a high level of engagement. Knowing your most popular pages helps identify user intent and makes the website research less anonymous.

Online Conversions

Online conversions are inquiries or sales generated from your website. Target 1 to 2% conversion rates for lead generation efforts and 2 to 5% conversion rates for e-commerce websites. Any action taken by your website visitor can be considered a conversion, which is also movement in your sales funnel.

Sales Conversion and Average Order Amount

How good is your sales team at closing sales? What percentage of sales leads does the team convert into sales? What is your average order amount for closed sales? These two numbers are important parts of the ROI equation and will drive your return from digital marketing investments.

There are many more stats and data points in Google Analytics. However, these are the most important. Set benchmarks and targets in each area and review them in your monthly digital marketing meetings.

- Establish a Google Analytics and Google Search Console account for tracking data on your website.
- Set goals for your Google Analytics stats and calculate ROI from those goals.
- Schedule monthly digital marketing meetings to review this data.
- Assign action items to team members and review outcomes in the monthly meetings. Update and review all action items during the meetings.
- Determine your sales team's closing ratios and your average order amount.
- Review the conversion and ROI worksheets in the later chapters of this book in more detail.

What You Need to Know About Google Analytics

Google Analytics is the Internet's leading website statistic monitoring program. It's provided free by Google so web marketers can use the data to measure results from Google Ads, and so Google can monitor web data from millions of websites. This has worked very well for Google, now one of the world's most successful and valuable companies, currently valued at $1.954 *trillion* dollars.

In return, Google Analytics has become a valuable resource and a key business and marketing indicator. Google believes that once web marketers see the data, they will work to get more traffic to their website through AdWords, which provides ever more revenues for Google.

Google Analytics as a Key Performance Indicator (KPI)

The Google Analytics data from your website is a key business indicator and will help you understand market share, how your brand is interpreted, the composition of your target market segments and much more. Business leaders should review this data regularly and compare it to other key indicators. Just reviewing the data and asking questions is extremely valuable.

If your website traffic is dropping, lower sales may be on the horizon. The same is true for increasing traffic. Companies with higher website traffic are generally larger and grow faster than those with fewer visits.

Google Analytics 4 can help you see trends in your business before they impact your bottom line. Google Analytics is a great tool for monitoring market share based on website visits and conversions. Because of the growth of pull marketing, where prospective customers research in anonymity on the Internet before making contact, it's possible for companies to experience market share losses and not know it's happening until it impacts revenue. Watching your web stats allows you to see these trends and modify your marketing strategy as needed.

The best and most straightforward way to view the data from Google Analytics is to think about visitor *trends*. In most cases, traffic increases to your website indicate that sales are growing, while traffic declines indicate a loss of potential customers. (Of course, seasonal variations and one-time events can impact these trends.)

Google Analytics is a leading indicator in many areas, including the content preferences of your target market, use of mobile devices, links from other websites and much more. A well-informed and strategic business leader will include website data in key indicator reports.

Conversion Monitoring is for Marketing, not IT

As I mentioned earlier, set goals for each of these key stats. Don't make the mistake of turning these reports over to your IT department or others on your team to analyze without reviewing and understanding the data yourself. This information will help you make better decisions and drive marketing results, as the reports are the guideposts for the success of the digital marketing strategy. You can bet your competitors are watching this data on their website.

The Google Search Console

Google Search Console is an essential part of your SEO work and should be linked to Google Analytics as a key tracking tool. The focus of Google Search Console is *getting found*. Google Search Console is important in Google's goal of preventing spam websites from being offered up in search results. It's important for web marketers so they can see the keyword phrases used to pull up their website in search. As of writing, much of this keyword data is being blocked in Google Analytics. It appears that Google does not want to provide the information for free and would rather have web marketers use their Google Ads program to see search impressions and gather keyword data.

Google Search Console allows you to see the communications between your website and the Google search engine. Google Search Console and Google Analytics are two of the most important online tools needed to drive results from digital marketing.

Action Items:

- ❑ Review Google Analytics 4 data from your website weekly or monthly.
- ❑ If needed, have these reports emailed to you or printed and on your desk.
- ❑ If possible, attend regular digital marketing meetings with your sales and marketing staff and ask questions about Google Analytics stats.
- ❑ Link Google Analytics to Google Search Console and AdWords.
- ❑ Develop Google Analytics into a leading indicator for your business.
- ❑ Ask questions about trends in your web data and use the information to make better strategic marketing decisions for your company.

Digital Marketing Stats and Benchmarks

We've reviewed the importance of monitoring web stats and their impact on sales revenues and ROI. Setting realistic benchmarks and targets to help accurately measure results is critical to online marketing success. The best web stat of all is an online order or a lead for your sales team.

You should now have an idea of the number of conversions you can expect from your website, given the volume of traffic. This is where a conversion strategy can make a big difference in your results. Start the process of setting your goals and benchmarks by clearly defining your conversion strategy using the following steps:

- Set up Google Analytics and Google Search Console.
- Establish a conversion strategy in your digital marketing plan, defining how online conversions happen and what will motivate a website visitor to convert.
- Make a list of all the various types of online conversions within this strategic approach.
- Include effective calls to action and conversion points in the strategy.
- Schedule digital marketing meetings to develop action plans based on website data and reports.

After these foundational items are in place, you can begin thinking about setting targets for your digital marketing goals and benchmarks, as revealed in the data from Google Analytics and Google Search Console.

Digital Marketing Targets

The targets will vary based on the size of your company and current web strategy

Here are the most important digital marketing targets and benchmarks to establish and monitor:

Unique Visitors – Target a minimum of 1,500 unique visitors per month with growth of about 20% per year. Website data becomes more useful as you increase website visits. A target of 2,000 or more website visitors per month is ideal.

Page Views per Visitor – Each visitor should view at least four to five pages on average. This is a measurement of engagement with the site's content, and sites with fewer page views per visitor have fewer conversions.

Time on Website – This is also a measurement of the visitor's engagement and should average at least three minutes.

Bounce Rate – The bounce rate should be below 40% for content-based lead generation websites and below 30% for e-commerce websites.

Traffic Sources – Traffic sources comprise three key areas. The first is *search engine traffic*, which should be more than 50% of your site's total visits. The second is *direct traffic* or visitors who know your website domain name and go directly to your site. The third is web *traffic from other websites* that link to your site.

Blog Postings – Post content to your blog at least weekly. The blog should be one of the top 10 most visited sections on the site.

Social Media Postings – Social media content should be posted weekly and visits to social media sites should also be tracked, along with interactions from social media to your website.

Lead Conversion Rate – Target a conversion rate of 1% to 3% of total visits becoming sales leads for a lead generation, content-based website.

Online Sales Conversion Rate – Target a conversion rate of 3% to 5% for e-commerce websites selling products online.

Shopping Cart Abandonment – Set a target of less than 50% for e-commerce shopping cart abandonment rates. This means less than half of the people who complete a shopping cart should drop out of the process before they purchase. Your CRM can automate a follow-up with abandoned shopping carts, perhaps by offering the items at a lower price. This can be a very effective way to harvest sales that would otherwise be lost.

Average Order – This applies to e-commerce websites and should be over $100 per order if possible. This stat should also be tracked for lead generation sites, as it will impact ROI calculations.

Extend Website Targets into the Sales Process

These targets should be reviewed and compared with your sales team's benchmarks. All these targets work together to measure sales and marketing effectiveness and drive revenues. A key conversion point for the sales team is the ratio of web leads that turn into customers. Another key factor in this conversion rate is the length of time customers stay with the company. Both of those benchmarks are related to your digital marketing efforts and the quality of your leads. The quality of your website visitors is a result of your digital marketing strategy.

Website Heat Mapping

Heat mapping provides you with a visual overview of what people do and where people click on individual pages. This is a great reporting tool for understanding how people engage with your content, what motivates them to dig deeper and their intent. Tools like CrazyEgg and HotJar are excellent for heat mapping your website to better understand your visitors.

Digital Metrics are Leading Indicators

Companies that track digital marketing data are getting leading indicators for how their business is going to perform, and companies that track data are going to grow faster than those that don't. This has been proven, as HubSpot monitors tens of thousands of website instances and folks who have accounts with them, and they can see in the data that the companies that look at their data are growing much faster than those that are not.

Companies that are aware of what's happening with their data grow faster than those that don't, but only about 85% of companies have a good website, know how to do digital marketing or are doing any marketing at all. About half of them do it well.

If your website traffic is increasing, it generally means you're getting more leads and your company's growing. If your website traffic is decreasing, it usually means that you're losing market share. For example, during the time of COVID, websites that dealt in hospitality or travel saw their traffic fall off a cliff. No one went to those websites. The website traffic was totally in line with their sales. As COVID dissipated and we got back to normal, their website traffic grew again. And that's true across all sectors. It's a leading indicator for your market share and how your company is going to perform.

There are aggregate tools are becoming available. These aggregate tools will take data from sources like Google Analytics, HubSpot or SEMrush, and put them together in one nice package. We recommend that you use an aggregate provider. We use a product called AgencyAnalytics, which pulls all this data together and gives you nice reports that have summaries and dashboards. You can put your goals in there, you can customize reports, and you can see the data points you want to see. That's really the state of where things are today.

What we've found in real life is that you need an agency to help with this. It's hard to have the skill set on your team to make this happen.

Now, if you can get a really good digital marketing person on your team, they can set this up. But this is a great use of your agency. The agency can be responsible for providing you with this data and offering insights on how to improve.

Screenshots from AgencyAnalytics:

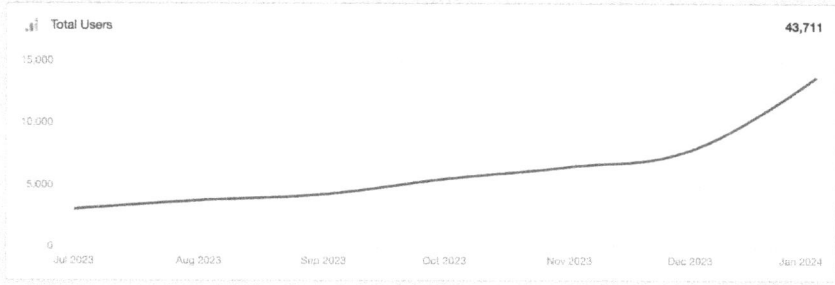

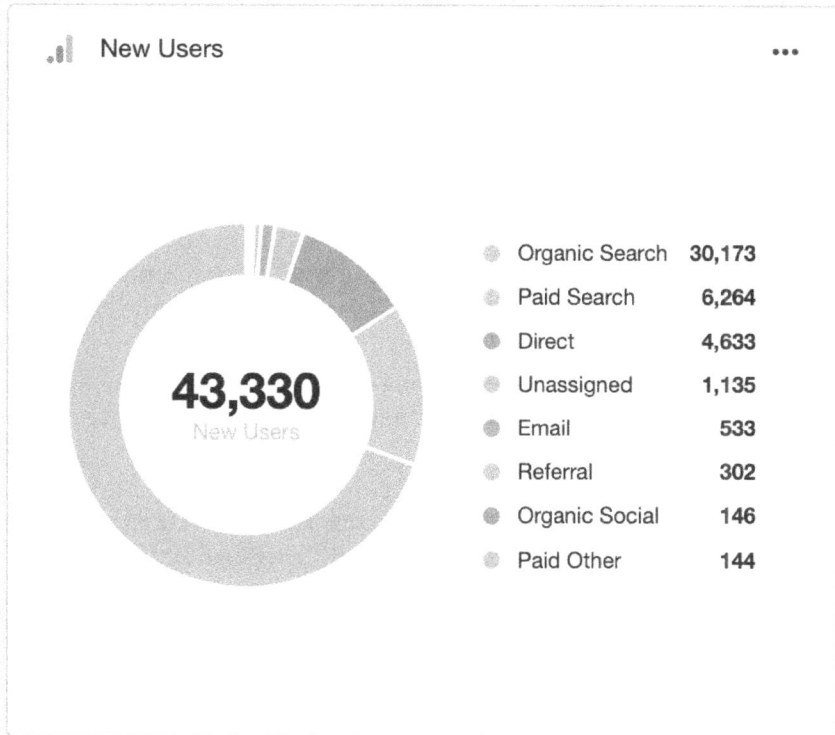

Sessions	Total Users	Views	Conversions
50,879	**43,711**	**95,522**	**2,206**

.ıl Total Users   43,711

15,000

10,000

5,000

0
Jul 2023   Aug 2023   Sep 2023   Oct 2023   Nov 2023   Dec 2023   Jan 2024

.ıl New Users   •••

43,330
New Users

●	Organic Search	**30,173**
●	Paid Search	**6,264**
●	Direct	**4,633**
●	Unassigned	**1,135**
●	Email	**533**
●	Referral	**302**
●	Organic Social	**146**
●	Paid Other	**144**

Conversions are the milestones you must measure to achieve digital marketing success and movement toward a closed sale. The key is to track and measure digital conversions and to make sure your website has one or more of these conversion strategies in place with call-to-action areas throughout each page.

Conversions are the beginning of a relationship and should place leads into a sales process that results in an ongoing relationship that develops into a customer. These are the strategies that should be defined in your internet marketing plan. They should be measured to set a target conversion rate, determine overall marketing ROI and to exceed sales goals.

Test assumptions by asking for feedback from web visitors and performing user testing.

Get creative and be realistic about results. When you've maximized your conversion rates, then work on getting more traffic. Keep monitoring and improving your website to get better conversion results. Remember, your website is a constant salesperson for your company, and it's always under construction!

AI and Digital Metrics

AI tools can help you better understand results by generating a dialog with you around your website data and recommending areas for improvement. If you see low engagement rates, go to ChatGPT and ask how to increase engagement rates on your website in your market. If you're seeing low conversion rates, ask ChatGPT what type of content is needed in your market to increase conversions from your targeted personas.

The tactics and strategies you use in the first four steps all work together to optimize conversion rates, which in turn provide ROI.

Develop a Conversion Strategy

It's important to identify how conversions happen by getting inside the heads of your website users and understanding their needs, hot buttons, and intent. The better you understand how to meet user needs, the higher your conversion rate. Website users are very focused on getting what they want, and website data is a key indicator of that intent. This can be tracked in your web stats, as an online sales funnel, e-commerce data, or goal completion. Survey the target market and conduct user testing to better understand user goals, and then use that information to develop your strategy.

The website should clearly communicate the value and benefits of doing business with your company. Highlight what your business *does well* and use that to drive a conversion strategy.

Define Your Digital Conversions

Websites exist for conversions. Yet most websites do not fully take advantage of the variety of conversion options available. You should measure many types of visitor interactions that are considered conversions. Start the conversion process by clearly identifying the conversion behaviors most appropriate for your digital marketing strategy.

Google Analytics 4 can monitor a variety of conversions and predefined user goals and it has become the foundation for defining and tracking conversions. A very effective strategy is to allow for multiple online conversion points because users convert through different means.

Online Conversion Tactics

The most important website KPI is online conversion. Measuring conversions and how they happen is *the* key. There are many ways a visitor can become a customer, and many of these paths start with an interaction on your website. All of this data is available in your web stats reports. Determine those conversion points and track them. These are obvious KPIs that have a direct impact on revenue.

Here are examples of digital marketing conversions to track:

- Phone calls or emails
- Website submission forms
- Website chat functions
- Email signups
- Blog postings
- Social media following and likes
- Online sales

- Content downloads
- Driving to your store or location

Conversion Examples

Any visit that results in some form of interaction with the website is a conversion. There are many ways to measure a conversion on a website.

Here are a few examples:

- Direct website visits and targeted page visits
- Visits to the *Contact Us* page
- Email newsletter subscriptions
- Viewing or reprinting driving directions
- PDF download or application submission
- Webinar or event registrations
- RSS subscription to podcasts and blogs
- Sending content to a friend or coworker
- A phone call to a dedicated website phone number
- Inquiries via email, phone or web-based forms
- Submitting a form to receive something free
- Printing a coupon from the website
- An email to the company from the website
- Sending a link to a friend or referring a friend
- Viewing multimedia on the website
- Making an online donation or pledge
- A direct sale via the website
- Driving to your store or office

This is not a complete list and conversions are only limited by one's imagination, business needs and user intentions.

Conversion Types and Stay-in-Touch Programs

Getting an online conversion is a big accomplishment. It says a lot about your website's content, usability and branding and your digital marketing in general. People don't convert unless there's real intent, and even the best websites only convert a small fraction of visitors. However, getting the conversion is only the starting point.

More has to happen in order for online conversions to grow sales over the long term. The key objective is for an online conversion to be the first step toward a sale or an ongoing customer relationship through a well-established stay-in-touch program.

Stay-in-touch programs are the methods used by your company to remain in contact with your target market, sales prospects, loyal followers and customers. These programs come in many forms and will be reviewed in more detail later in this chapter.

Let's start with a more detailed review of the various types of online conversions and a few strategies for an effective stay-in-touch program. We will begin by gaining a better understanding of your site's visitors.

Get Inside the Head of Your Visitors
It's a big step for visitors to move from the anonymity of reviewing a website to contacting your company. Website users are moved to action when the content on a website motivates them to get more information or buy. This usually happens after several websites are visited and researched and your website content wins them over. If your website does its job, it will be easy for web leads to understand why you are better than your competitors. Website visitors have done their homework and want to be taken seriously. Because of this, a web lead is a very important lead.

The better you understand the intentions of the website visitor, the better your site will convert new customers. Don't guess at this or wing it—get real data from your web stats and through market research. You will find in your research that website users like options and have various preferences for making contact.

Visitors Prefer Different Conversion Options

It's important to note that web users don't care if you know how they contacted your company, and they prefer a variety of contact methods. The boundary of how people convert can be very blurry at times, especially if they call your office or don't reach out to you online.

This can make tracking conversions difficult. Therefore, a variety of conversion points can help drive leads and sales. This ensures your site is meeting the needs of all your visitors.

Here is a summary of several online conversion points preferred by a variety of users:

- Direct Online Sale
- Telephone sale or inquiry
- Call to support or customer service
- Email inquiry
- Contact form submission
- Blog RSS subscription
- Email newsletter subscription
- Social media follow or like
- Refer a friend
- App download (with no purchase)
- Podcast subscription
- Webinar or seminar registration
- PDF or other download
- Security, privacy and return policy statements
- Testimonials, case studies and reviews
- Shipping information
- Usability of the Contact Us page and checkout process

Multiple conversion points help grow your stay-in-touch program and better market your website and company by meeting user needs. Find those that work best for your website and track the results.

The Conversion Process

The online conversion process can be broken down into a seven-point process. Each of these seven areas must be addressed in your digital marketing plan and included in your website design process. These are the ingredients of a successful online conversion process to drive sales growth.

Online Content – The content preferred by your target market is the most common entry point for your website and the conversion process. The content will attract visitors to your company and motivate them to contact you.

The Offer – This is the specific piece of content that drives interest from website visitors and moves them to a call to action or contact with your company.

Call-to-Action (CTA) – Your call to action is the conversion point where the user takes action. This could be filling out an online form, providing an email address, getting a phone number or some other conversion point. A complete list of conversion points is included above.

Landing Page – This is the page where the user reads *more* about the call to action and completes a form or gets a phone number. There's an art and science to landing pages that drive conversions. Keep it simple and test various offers.

The Submission Form – Short submission forms that ask for basic information get higher conversion rates. Longer forms qualify better but have lower completion rates. All websites must have submission forms on the Contact page and throughout the website.

Contact with the Sales Team – The sales team receives the contact information, follows up and adds it to the stay-in-touch program and CRM system. Respond promptly.

Stay-in-Touch Program – The sales team should remain in contact with all leads and add those leads to the company's stay-in-touch program.

Conversions and the Stay-in-Touch Program
The success of online conversion programs is only as good as your stay-in-touch program. Develop a strategy for keeping in touch and allow for multiple channels.

Here are a few ways to keep in touch with your target market after the initial connection is made with the prospective customer:

- Email marketing
- Webinars
- Social media content postings
- Blogs and RSS feeds
- Podcasts
- Website content updates
- Direct mail
- Phone calls and CRM systems
- Calls to action and incentives
- Face-to-face meetings

The key to successful stay-in-touch programs is strong content and a solid distribution strategy to make sure you remain in touch. These programs are very powerful and should be very cost effective with an excellent ROI.

Ecommerce Versus Lead Generation

Most digital conversions fall into two broad categories: either direct online purchases or lead generation. Most readers of this book will be primarily looking to generate leads from their online marketing efforts. All websites should make it *easy and intuitive* to make contact. Keep in mind that the Internet has replaced the phone book, and many people will go to your website just to find a phone number and office hours.

In lead generation, the content becomes the strategy. How you present and organize your online content will determine how well your site converts. Target a conversion rate of 1% to 2%.

Follow-up and stay-in-touch programs will be critical to actually closing the lead. Without them, your web leads will not produce a return. More on stay-in-touch programs in later chapters. Use web content to develop a sales funnel and drive inquiries.

For e-commerce websites, the products become the strategy. Merchandising, that is, how products are presented, is critical. Just follow best practices; there's no need to start from scratch. Understand seasonality and other online shopping trends and target a conversion rate of 2% to 4% for e-commerce sales. If you can sell directly online, then you should.

Website Usability Generates Conversions

Many websites are difficult to use and are actually barriers to conversions. The easier your site is to use, the higher the conversion rate. User testing is a highly valuable form of market research that provides data for accomplishing this goal. Ask people to visit your website. Ask them what they're trying to find and give them tasks you can observe.

The solution is to be brave and keep it simple! Focus on two or three conversion points and include them on *all* web pages and especially in navigation menus. Avoid heavy graphics, write in the language of the user and conduct user testing to verify your assumptions. Remember this formula: Easy-to-use websites convert at higher rates.

Get Qualified Website Traffic to Increase Conversions

This should be obvious but it's not, as most websites have bounce rates above 50%. It's *better to have less traffic than the wrong traffic*. Great content and a solid traffic generation strategy will achieve this goal. Review your stats to make sure the *right* traffic is coming in and realize that low conversion rates may mean poor-quality traffic. Make sure your company *value, benefits* and *focus* are clear throughout the site and that search engine strategies match conversion goals.

It's common for digital marketers to want more traffic when what they *really* need is a better *conversion rate*. Set a goal of 3% to 5% of your website traffic converting. If this traffic is coming to you because they already know your brand, then set a conversion goal of 5% to 10%.

Call-to-Actions (CTAs)

All websites must have clear call-to-action points located near key content areas and in the main navigation. Thumbnails are a great design approach for combining content areas with call-to-action buttons or conversion links. Include a *Contact Us* or *Buy Now* button on every page or in every thumbnail.

Calls to action can be in taglines, captions, content, navigation systems and more. Follow best practices and meet the comfort level of your target market. Bigger is not always better, so avoid large ads or graphics. The best call to action is your navigation menu and written content. Include online submission forms on key content pages that are simple and easy to complete.

Forms and Content Sign-Ups

Should website visitors have to sign up before you send them information? It depends, but it's usually not a good idea because users don't like it. Test variations and see what happens. Giving away loads of free content is usually the best conversion tactic.

Follow this rule of thumb with submission forms: shorter forms have higher conversion rates, while longer forms qualify the user more accurately but have lower conversion rates. Determine which is best for your business strategy.

Measure Conversions

Set up an account with Google Analytics 4 and track conversions by type of visitor. Develop an ROI method to calculate your sales revenue from web-based conversions. Google is very good at measuring conversions and setting up conversion paths, especially if you're running paid ads. Train marketing staff to look for these conversions and ask people how they heard about you and what motivated them to make contact.

Measure and track *all* conversion points, including your e-commerce sales data. The bottom line with conversions is ROI, and all conversions can be measured against ROI in great detail. We have an ROI tool on our website that can help you run the numbers on your website to determine ROI.

Try it out: https://intuitivewebsites.com/website-roi-calculator/

AI is an amazing tool for understanding KPIs.

In fact, you can use ChatGPT or Google's Gemini and ask the question, "Hey, my website's not performing well. I'm only getting [this much] traffic from [these sources.] What can I do to increase my traffic?" You'll get amazing responses about how to get more traffic for your website, and you can ask those questions based on the market space you're in.

You can also put your analytics right into ChatGPT and ask it to analyze the data for you and show trends, observations and ways to improve. Put a summary of your current website data into the ChatGPT prompt and ask it for suggestions on how to improve results. You can also ask about conversion points and improving conversion points.

ChatGPT is like having your personal data analyst consultant right at your side to help you figure out what's going on. Use the prompt to have a conversation with the AI tool and you will get great insights that will only improve over time.

Design a Website for Conversions and Growth

The goal of this book, and the objective of your digital marketing action plans, is increased sales revenues for your company. The sales process starts with an online conversion, most often coming from your company website.

Sales growth is driven by various forms of website conversions and your digital marketing strategies must be tied to a *path to purchase*. In part, website conversions are defined as *any contact or interaction from a website visitor* to your company generated from your digital marketing efforts.

There are many ways to track and monitor conversions. This includes the process of moving your visitors toward contact with your company. This is the *online sales funnel*, and Google Analytics can be used to monitor the steps users take along this path. The user path along the online sales funnel may not be a direct contact but should be a step in the right direction toward contact with your company.

Website Conversion Funnel

It's important to structure your website navigation and content as if it were a sales funnel. This is the natural progression the average web visitor takes as they move toward a conversion. For example, a website visitor will first start at the homepage and determine what your company is about and where they can find value. From there, they will gravitate to more information about the company, your products or your services. At this point, some users will dig deeper for more detailed content as they do research. Others will gravitate toward their preferred conversion method following this content review. Tracking the sales funnel in Google Analytics will provide insights into how to increase conversion rates. The online sales funnel often begins with various content pages and usually ends at your website's Contact Us page.

The Contact Page

The Contact page is one of the most important pages on your website. Its goal is to drive visitor contacts and should be included in your main navigation menu. The Contact page must include various contact methods because website visitors have different preferences for getting in touch with your company.

Include the following contact methods and information on your Contact page:

- Dedicated website phone number
- Address and locations
- Driving instructions
- Map to your location
- Office hours
- Web submission form
- Email address

Communicate clearly that you want to hear from them, and let visitors know how long it usually takes to get a response. Website visitors appreciate a quick turnaround, and quick responses lead to higher close rates. Also, include contact information in the footer or header of every page.

Calls-to-Action (CTA)

Website CTAs lead people toward a conversion point. Be creative, as there are no limitations on the types of conversions you can establish and track online. The better you understand how website visitors prefer to contact you and what motivates them, the better your conversion rates.

Be generous with your content. You will see results and more conversions. If you don't provide this content, your competitors will.

In addition to the contact methods found on your website's Contact page, include these key conversion points on your website and in social media:

- Email newsletter sign-up
- Blog and content RSS feeds
- Share buttons for social media and email
- Free downloads of specialty content or white papers
- Call to action buttons for special offers
- Likes and follows on social media

Website Submission Forms

Always include a website submission form on your site. Keep in mind that shorter forms get more conversions, and longer forms get fewer conversions but tend to better qualify the lead. Visitors often prefer forms because they may not be able to easily email you from their computer or mobile device, and they may be researching your business after hours when no one is available to take a phone call. Also, forms are easily tracked in Google Analytics and are generally excellent online conversion points. Respond quickly to form requests to maximize your conversion rate and close more sales.

Here are a few ideas for generating more conversions from your website:

- Website visitors are impulsive, so keep content scannable and links simple.
- Set the right message and call to action in your content.
- Place calls to action near popular content and on every page.
- Allow for more depth of content for analytical people.
- The shopping cart must be first-rate, easy to use and intuitive.
- Use color photos with captions.
- Avoid objects that look like ads or large graphics. Online advertising is a turn-off.
- Customize landing pages for unique web search terms.
- Content and knowledge drives conversions, not flash and graphics.
- Product photos on all pages and detailed descriptions are very important
- If possible, offer a money back guarantee.
- Call your website the "Official website for XYZ Company".
- Use a dedicated web phone numbers on every page.
- Test special offers and incentives, especially free shipping.
- Is the motive of the website to sell stuff or help people? Make the site's purpose to help people.
- Draw qualified traffic from the search engines.
- Have a professional, high-quality design.
- Use consistent branding and messaging on the site.
- Be very well-organized in navigation and usability, as this builds credibility.
- Load the website with content and media that excites visitors.
- Use a compelling offer that moves people to action.

Action Items:
- ❑ Make sure there is a link to your Contact Us page in your main navigation and that it's present on all web pages.

❑ Include various call to action buttons on your web pages and understand your site visitors' preference for conversions.

❑ Set up conversion tracking in Google Analytics and in Google Ads to track ROI.

❑ Establish a conversion rate goal of 1% or more of total website traffic.

❑ Monitor which type of website traffic converts and build on that data to refine your digital marketing strategies.

❑ Review your competitors' conversion points and make use of best practices.

❑ Test several conversion options to determine what types of conversions work best.

❑ Include spam prevention methods on your contact forms and email addresses.

❑ Develop comprehensive marketing analytics based on the marketing funnel and conversion tracking.

❑ Use consistent branding and messaging across all touch points.

❑ Being very well-organized in navigation and usability builds credibility.

❑ Load the website with content and media that excites visitors.

❑ Make compelling offers that move people to action.

❑ Have a "Sign up now!" button for free content and newsletters.

❑ Be generous with your content. You will see results and more conversions.

❑ Research the conversion methods preferred by your target market.

❑ Outline your conversion strategy from the seven items listed in this chapter.

- [ ] Write a strategic stay-in-touch program and marketing automation plan as part of your digital marketing plan.
- [ ] Include a budget (time or money) and ROI analysis for your stay-in-touch program.
- [ ] Select the stay-in-touch channels that work for your target market.
- [ ] Develop content and call-to-action themes to build your email list. Post all stay-in-touch content to your website and code it for SEO.
- [ ] Talk to your target market for feedback on how they want you to stay in touch.

Bosca Leather Products Grows Web Sales 700%

Bosca is a 103-year-old manufacturing company specializing in men's wallets and briefcases with a large and very loyal customer base. However, these loyal fans were *not buying* from the company website or even *finding* it. Keyword research showed people were looking for the company in much greater numbers than were visiting the website or buying through the online store.

The company's primary strategy was to achieve a higher online conversion rate with an easy-to-use website that featured the products loved by Bento's loyal buyers. The new website was a success and became a key sales channel, attracting not only current customers but also new buyers who expanded Bento's base of loyal fans.

Bosca pursued their loyal customer base and people searching for the brand. This worked to identify missed opportunities in their current digital marketing strategy and immediately increased sales from the website.

Bosca designed and developed an easy-to-use e-commerce website targeting the demographic representing their most loyal customers. They highlighted the bestselling products with excellent content and photography and a focus on up-selling new product categories.

They built an SEO strategy for the brand name so their website was highly visible in any search for their company name or related searches, driving sales from the website to record levels. Bosca supplemented those searches with paid ads through Google Ads.

The surge in sales resulted in a new digital marketing focus for the company. Ongoing digital marketing meetings and action items are now a major part of the Bento marketing agenda. This is needed to sustain and grow web sales. The team tracks the ROI of every dollar spent on digital marketing against online sales.

In the first year following the implementation of the Four-Step Process, Bosca reported a 700% increase in web sales. Direct website sales are now a key channel for the company.

Digital Marketing Meetings

The best place to review website stats, conversions, KPIs and ROI is in regularly scheduled digital marketing meetings. These meetings become the core of your digital strategy implementation as they drive the action plans, build accountability and set project completion dates. These meetings are the engine that drives solid KPIs and digital marketing ROI.

Here is a typical agenda for a digital marketing meeting:

1. Digital marketing goals and sales targets
2. Review of web stats and data
3. Website design and development updates
4. Traffic generation strategies
5. Website content updates
6. Social media updates
7. Email marketing results and schedule
8. Competitive website review
9. Monthly digital marketing action plan

Regularly scheduled digital marketing meetings provide the fuel and accountability to drive digital marketing ROI. At a minimum, schedule a monthly meeting to review website data and action plans. These meetings force the team to review data and develop action items that drive attention to digital marketing efforts and measuring ROI. The team should focus on reaching website goals as seen in Google Analytics data. It's the day-in and day-out work on improving these stats that drives growth.

The simple act of setting a meeting and reviewing this data will help drive ROI and train you and the team to be more effective web digital marketers.

How to Run a Digital Marketing Meeting

This book has made strong arguments for the importance of effective digital marketing, the use of inbound and content marketing and the necessity of measuring ROI. Yet, most companies fail to give digital marketing the proper attention by reviewing their web stats or developing ongoing action plans to improve results. One of the best things an organization can do to break this pattern is to schedule monthly digital marketing meetings.

Holding monthly meetings keeps people accountable regarding completing digital marketing action items and reviewing web stats and data. Each action item and website statistic can be reviewed for its impact on digital marketing targets and ROI. It also forces the team to learn more about the meaning behind the web stats.

Who Should Attend?

The digital marketing team should be made up of a variety of individuals with a variety of skills. This includes designers, technology staff, photographers, content writers, SEO specialists and more. For the most part, these meetings should be attended by the key decision-makers involved in running digital marketing programs. This would include the digital marketing director, traffic generation staff and project managers.

Design and technology team members can be brought into these meetings on occasion, but they're not necessarily the focal point of the meetings, nor should they lead the meeting. Many business leaders make the mistake of spending too much time on technology and design issues because the meetings are generally driven by designers and developers. Develop action plans in the meetings to provide direction for graphic designers and IT and use the meeting time to review strategy and major action items.

Action Items and Accountability

Each meeting should include a review of your online marketing goals and targets. This includes a review of web stats from Google Analytics, Google Search Console, SEO reports and other data. The stats review should highlight the areas where online marketing efforts are excelling and where there is room for improvement as measured in your digital marketing targets and goals.

Digital Marketing Meeting Topics

Here are common topics to include in a typical agenda for an effective digital marketing meeting.

Digital Data and Stats Review – This is an analysis of Google Analytics, Google Search Console, AdWords reports and other SEO and digital marketing reports. Work with monthly data and compare year-to-date stats against the prior year and monthly goals.

Goals, Targets and ROI – If you don't already have goals, set them before your first meeting and review your targets as they relate to your web strategy.

Competitive Website Reviews – Many competitor websites and online marketing strategies have excellent best practices you can learn from. Review competitors' websites in your meetings and find best practices that can work for you.

Usability and Conversion Analysis – This is a review of what works on the site to drive conversions. Website usability impacts conversions and the meeting is a good time to discuss the site's usability and user testing. There could be an issue in usability if your website conversion goals are not meeting targets.

Design and Development Updates – This should be discussed in each meeting as it can improve branding, usability, and overall conversions. Include feedback from users in these discussions. Design is never completed and can always be improved. Web stats shed light on the effectiveness of your design.

Website Traffic Generation – This discussion is mostly about increasing visitor traffic through SEO, new content, social media and links from referring websites. This is an ongoing process that's never complete and is measured very closely in your web stats.

Content Marketing Updates – Content drives both traffic and conversions, and the digital marketing meeting is a good place to review online content results. Use the meeting to determine which content is most popular and develop action plans to add new pages and posts to the site and other content that can help attract visitors and motivate them to contact your company.

AI Review - How is the team using AI to accomplish their action items? This is a key point for discussion in your digital marketing meetings.

Monthly Action Items – Action items, team member accountability and due dates are critical to digital marketing success. Assign a project manager to see action items are completed. This final agenda item is the reason for the meeting; without it, meetings can be a waste of time.

Action Items:

- ❏ Schedule monthly digital marketing meetings for the next twelve months.
- ❏ Use the agenda in this chapter and ask team members to come prepared to review each area.
- ❏ Budget about sixty to ninety minutes for the meeting and close with a review of action items with assigned team members and due dates. Your first meetings will take more time but will become more streamlined over time.
- ❏ Set criteria and targets for action items.
- ❏ Be prepared to answer questions about digital marketing data in each meeting.
- ❏ Leave each meeting with a clear action plan to improve digital marketing results.

How the Sales Team Should Handle a Lead

Extend Website KPIs into the Sales Team Process
Website data and conversions should be tracked as they flow into your sales process, and those leads should begin discussions with your sales team. Make sure your sales team is responding to web inquiries and tracking their conversions. This will determine your return on digital marketing efforts. The better your sales team can convert a web lead, the better the ROI.

The first contact with a web lead will often be from your sales team. It's important that the team understands how to deal with leads, knows when to continue selling and when to place the lead in the stay-in-touch program.

The biggest mistake sales teams make is discounting the importance of a given prospect. Web leads are very different from traditional leads because they've already done their homework. Traditional sales leads, who do not research online, may take more sales time and are usually not as prepared. A sales lead is not necessarily a better qualified prospect.

Sales teams should spend more time listening and understanding the prospect and less time explaining what the prospect may have already read or seen. This can shorten your sales cycle and save time and money.

The second biggest mistake companies make with web leads is not having a structure or method for dealing with leads and follow-up. Salespeople should report on the status of leads and your website stats should track all conversions. Sales management should know how much time it takes to get back to leads and the process for follow-up. Make sure your sales team is trained to manage leads effectively and take them seriously.

Respond immediately for better results. The faster your sales team can respond to a lead, the more trust is built in the firm and the higher the chances of closing. Web users appreciate this, and you can catch them while you're fresh on their mind. In fact, CRM software even allows you to respond to leads while they're still on your website!

In my book with Karl Becker, *Sales and Marketing Alignment*, we go into great detail on how to get your sales team working with your marketing team to move people through your intentional sales funnel and to a close.

Questions to Ask the Sales and Marketing Team

Here are a few questions to ask your sales team about how web leads are handled:

- What is our strategy for handling website leads?
- What is the average length of time to respond to a web lead?
- What are the steps in converting web leads?
- What is our conversion rate on web leads?
- Where do web leads fit in our sales process?
- How do you follow up with leads and sales from the web?
- What content areas and pages on the website generate leads?
- Can we use live chat on the website?
- What happens after the sale is closed from our website?
- Asking your sales and marketing managers these questions will lead to action items that improve their process and greater success with web leads.
- Coordinate the conversion and stay-in-touch process with your sales team.

Website Drives Growth for Card Lock Company

"Before we started working on our digital marketing strategy, we did not give much thought to our website," says Walker. "We did not think our target market used the . We were wrong about that."

Card Lock Company is a manufacturer of custom keyless entry systems for very specific target markets. Their website has become a major source of leads for the sales team and has been the key to business growth.

The company developed a professional website with clear instructions about the buying process. This resulted in a dramatic increase in submissions and requests for products. The site has a conversion rate of 2%, and traffic has doubled in the past two years. Both new customers and the activation of lapsed customers are driving this trend. We also developed a mobile website because 25 of their visitors were coming from mobile devices.

"I know the website is working for us because I can see the increase in phone calls, emails and new business signups. This was not happening before we launched the new website," says John Walker, the CEO of Card Lock Company.

Card Lock Company built a professional website, without making assumptions about how people use it, that clearly explains the buying process to new prospects and to customers looking to reorder. Make strategic decisions based on data.

"We didn't think so many of our inactive customers would use the website to place new orders and reactivate their accounts," continued John. "This has really helped us get current customers to reorder in larger numbers than we expected. It also keeps them away from our competitors. We saved a lot of money by getting rid of a 50,000-piece mailer and focusing on the website."

They now use the website to teach current customers how to place orders. Include content in a variety of areas related to the industry and the needs of the target market.

Card Lock Company targets SEO for the company brand and related keyword terms used by actual customers. Develop linking strategies from key association websites used by the target market.

The leadership team meets monthly to review web stats and how conversions happen. They continue to simplify content to improve conversions.

Card Lock Company has seen steady growth in revenue from an increase in former customers placing new orders and reactivating their accounts.

How to Modify Your Digital Strategy When Needed

One of the biggest mistakes made by business leaders is thinking their website strategy or design is complete and does not need on-going attention after the site goes live. You may not need to over-haul web strategy in each digital marketing meeting, but you do need to react to the data from your web stats and constantly find ways to improve results and modify the strategy. These strategy modification efforts are key to increasing website traffic and max-imizing conversion rates.

The driving factor behind Step Four of the Four-Step Process is the ability to successfully modify a business digital marketing strategy based on the available web stats and feedback from your site's vis-itors. This is usually done in the team's digital marketing meetings and implemented through the team's action plans generated as a result of these meetings.

How Often to Update the Homepage and Key Taglines

For the most part, your homepage design does not need to change very often. However, after two or three years the design will be stale and will need an update. Work with your designer on this process and observe design trends among your competitor websites and other sites you frequent online.

The content focus and key messaging on your homepage should be updated more frequently. What are the most important things hap-pening at your company that you want website visitors to know about? This should be updated monthly or even weekly. We don't recommend a "what's new" section because few people click on those pages, and most companies are not able to keep it current. Rather, place new homepage content in a brief tagline in your main banner or just below the banner or homepage images. Your website homepage is usually the most popular web page on your site and it's a great place for content updates.

It's important to note that internet users are very observant o the look of a website's homepage. They'll know if you have an old de-sign or if your design is fresh and up to date. Olderlooking websites do not communicate a strong brand, especially to younger site visitors who've grown up with the Internet. This is another reason to make regular design updates and keep the site fresh and modern.

When to Change the Focus of Website Content

As we discussed in previous chapters, content is critical to your website's and you must have a plan for regular updates through your blog and in other areas. You may find a need to change the focus if your stats do not show strong engagement. For example, if your pages have bounce rates over 50%, fewer than three pages per visit, or low time per page visit, these are indicators that your content is not appealing. This would be a good time to reach out to a few people in your target market for feedback on the type of content with higher value. Higher-value content drives more traffic and conversions, and all this is reflected in your web stats.

The most active content area of your website will be the blog. However, new product and service pages should be updated as needed and highlighted in your main navigation menu.

When to Update Website Navigation

The effectiveness of your website navigation is also measured in your web stats. Your site should include a well-thought-out navigation menu and site map that's intuitive to users and have easy-to-understand link titles. You should see a fairly even distribution of visits among the website's pages. If you find that a handful of pages are dominating the user's time, then your navigation may be making it difficult for users to access multiple pages. You may need to consolidate pages and possibly simplify the navigation structure. Remember, website navigation is one of the most important parts of your website and can make or break your digital marketing goals. Make sure your main navigation covers your services and products, resources, about and contact us.

Search Engine Landing Pages

Review your digital stats for key search engine landing pages and check user engagement on those pages. These are the first pages visited by users. They're driving visits from Google and are important entry points. Google has indexed these pages and they're very important to driving results because they're a key branding point. You can never change the first impression, and often that first impression doesn't come from your homepage but from an interior landing page.

Promotions, Special Offers, and Incentives

These action items are an ongoing part of your implementation, and it's best to use what's worked offline and test various approaches. Any promotion or special incentive should be tracked in your web data and measured in your conversion tracking. This will take the guesswork out of determining what works best for your business. If promotions are a part of your marketing plan, then include them in your digital marketing meetings and update your website accordingly.

Make sure to coordinate your offline efforts with your online marketing.

Action Items:

- ❑ Look for red flags in your data that suggest modifications to your website.
- ❑ Make this a part of your digital marketing meetings and your culture so your website is constantly improving.
- ❑ Review your homepage weekly and develop a plan for regular updates.
- ❑ Check your web stats to determine the landing pages or entry points for website visitors other than the homepage.
- ❑ Include website usability improvements as part of your site's regular updates and reach out to your current and prospective customers for feedback.
- ❑ Understand that your website is always under construction.

Tracking Ongoing ROI

We've discussed in great detail the importance of ROI and how it connects to a successful strategy. Here are some ROI examples and a system for tracking the ROI from digital marketing. Tracking ROI is a necessary part of a successful digital marketing strategy. This is easily done, thanks to Google Analytics and other web data tracking tools.

It's important to develop a method to accurately calculate ROI. Below are two ROI examples following a proven method based on the Four-Step Process. This method can be applied to your company using your web stats and data from your sales team. You may think this tracking is common sense and used by most companies. However, most businesses do not track digital marketing ROI or have a process for accurately measuring online results.

Tracking ROI and Monitoring Results

The fourth step is important because it quantifies and defines your success. It's the glue holding the process together and drives results and accountability. The final step brings the first three together and is used to receive and update the action items in the first three steps. This involves a process for tracking digital marketing results in your web stats, meetings to review digital marketing efforts and online conversions, and a method for tracking ROI. From this step will come modifications to the Digital Marketing Strategies and Action Plans to improve conversions and drive a strong, measurable return. Step Four sets the digital marketing priorities for your team based on clear data and feedback from users.

Action Items are the Key Value of Step Four

It may be that you'll start with the action items in Step Four and use them to update your strategy, which in turn leads to website updates and traffic generation updates. Any way you look at it, Step Four is critical to success because it drives the review and analysis that brings about action plans to improve the first three steps. The action items in Step Four are composed of the daily and weekly digital marketing work used to improve results. Most of the digital marketing team's time will be spent in Step Four activities.

Digital Marketing Needs Constant Attention

Don't take Step Four lightly just because it's the final step in the process. Many web marketers spend less time on Step Four than they should. This is especially true after they redesign and launch a new website. Websites are not like printed brochures which are completed when sent to print. Websites must be constantly updated with fresh content. They are always changing and adapting to better meet visitor needs, and those change over time.

The first example is ROI tracking from a typical lead generation website.

Wiggam Law Increases Lead Flow by 100%

When you're looking to get ROI from your digital marketing and your website, it's important to know where to start with the cost. What does this work cost to get done? Well, because of our experience working with contractors, employees, part-time folks and all the people who work for our clients, we have a very good sense of what it costs to get this work done. You're going to spend about $20,000 or more to build a really decent WordPress website, using a professional team. Digital marketing services are going to cost around $85 an hour or more, and even if you hire these people internally, with your overhead and benefits, it's going to cost about the same.

When using an agency, you're hiring professionals who have to know about technology, content and marketing. These skill sets are in high demand, so these are the prices that you're going to pay.

If you know what you're going to pay, and you can get a sense of what the budgets are, then you can run an ROI analysis based on specific campaigns and specific things you do to generate traffic and queries.

Wiggam Law is an interesting case because we had to build a website and launch their new brand starting from scratch. When we started to put together the ROI for Wiggam law, one of the first things we wanted to know was, if a client comes in, what's the average billing from their engagement? In this case, it was about $6,500. The *lifetime* value of a client is higher because clients come back repeatedly, and this doesn't really include the big whales.

And a big whale for Wiggam might be a corporate account that comes on and might be a $100,000 account. Those do occasionally happen as a result of digital marketing, but we took them out of the equation.

Once you know the average order, you can start to break down the costs and get to the ROI. In this case, Wiggam law spent about $40,000 with Intuitive Websites to build and launch their website, which you can see at www.WigamLaw.com.

They're currently on a retainer of $5,500 per month for the ongoing work we do. This includes website updates, content, social media, email marketing, SEO and ad budget management; all the things the digital marketing team does to build traffic. The monthly digital marketing spend also includes $25,000 a month for Google Ads.

And you might be thinking, "That's a lot of money for Google Ads!" Here's the kicker. This covers the marketplace for *any* searches done for the keywords "tax resolution attorney." Wiggam Law would spend even more to get even more traffic from Google Ads, but there are only so many searches done every month. They only pay when a visitor clicks through on their ad, so they're maximizing the market opportunity at $25,000 a month. If there were more searches, they would gladly pay more to get that traffic.

These efforts have built average traffic to around 3,000 visitors a month. It's worth noting that when the project started, there were *zero* visitors a month. This investment is what brought people to the website. Of those 3,000 visitors, about 8%, or about 240 people, decide they want to talk to someone at Wiggam Law. They either submit a form on the website, email directly, place a phone call or chat with someone online.

But the real question then becomes, what percentage of these turn into a client? In the case of Wiggam law, about 6 percent, between 14 and 15 people, turn into a sale. That's a fantastic conversion rate. Anytime you can get a conversion rate of 5 percent or more, you're doing really well. If you can convert between 5 and 10 percent, you're at the top of the industry.

So now that you have that number and you have the conversion rate, we know that they get 14 new cases that generate, on average,

$91,000 gross, every month. That turns into a $60,000 gross margin after what they've spent on marketing. This doesn't include the *net* margins for Wiggam law. It also doesn't include whales. This is a winning formula. Now, when you look at this ROI example and plug different numbers into these equations, the question then must be, what can you control?

What can you control in this equation to improve results? You can control a lot of things. You can certainly get more people to the website by doing better SEO, generating more content and just flat-out asking people to come to the website.

You can also find ways to convert even more customers by looking at the data, heat mapping the site and seeing how you can maximize that conversion rate. However, in this particular example, the low-hanging fruit is the ratio of conversions to sales. Eight percent is a pretty low number. We'd love to see more of those inquiries become clients. So the question might be, is there another service that you should offer? Should you do sales training? What is causing 94% of people not to purchase? And what are those people doing instead? Are they going to another firm? Or just not doing anything? Or might there be another service you can provide that helps them with their tax issues?

This is an example of how you should monitor your return on digital marketing. Take this example and start applying it to campaigns that you run, especially if you're going to spend money on Google Ads. But even if you don't invest in Google Ads, you can run these numbers. And there are many companies that have a small monthly ad spend but are getting enough visitors to more than recover the cost. A little bit of effort put toward improving conversion rates can go a long way to driving ROI.

ROI Example: Lead Generation Website

Most websites are looking to generate leads for the sales team based, for the most part, on static content. Here are the key components, with sample dollar amounts and conversion rates included, of ROI calculations for lead generation websites. You will need this information to accurately track the ROI from your company's lead generation site.

Let's start with an example. You can do the same using your metrics.

Average Order: $2,500
This is the average order amount from individual sales. In this example, the average order value is $2,500, but in most cases, average order amounts can be much higher, and this does not consider the lifetime value of a new customer or client.

Website Design and Development Cost: $20,000 and up
This budget is the one-time spend to develop a basic website structure and the foundation for online marketing action items. This can include design, technology, content, photography and all other costs needed to launch the website and social media sites. This does not include the ongoing digital marketing work for content, website updates and other digital marketing costs.

Monthly Digital Marketing Spend: $4,500
This is the amount of money spent monthly to market and maintain the website and on other online marketing efforts, such as social media, email and Google Ads. Traffic generation is an important part of this budget, and it should include staff time and external contractor hours. This budget may vary based on conversion results.

Total Monthly Website Visitors: 2,000
This is the total number of monthly, unique visits to your website. This number can be either total visits or unique visitors. It's generally best to monitor total visits or sessions as the key indicator. This is part of the ROI equation controlled by digital marketers. Generally, the higher the targeted traffic, the greater number of leads for the sales team.

Conversion Rate to Leads: 2.5% (50 leads)
This is the conversion rate of visitors to sales leads. The number of leads divided by the site's traffic equals your conversion rate. In

this example, a 2.5% conversion rate generates 50 qualified leads per month on average.

Keep in mind that there are many ways to convert website visitors into sales leads. The key factor here is that they've contacted your company and are now in touch with your sales team. Strive for a conversion rate of 1 to 5% for lead generation websites. The better your website converts, the higher the number of sales leads. This is an ROI factor you and the digital marketing team can influence with excellent content and a high-performing website.

Lead Conversion Rate to a Sale: 20%

This is a measurement of how successful your sales team is at closing the sale. If one out of every five sales leads convert into a sale, your conversion rate is 20%. Calculate this number by dividing the total number of sales orders by the total number of leads in that same time. Most sales teams convert at higher than 20%, and this is a conservative number for this example. Sales teams with strong performance convert at 50% or higher, depending on the average order. Higher price points tend to convert at lower conversion rates.

10 Sales per Month = $25,000

This is the total number of monthly sales in gross dollars, given the volume of sales generated by the sales team. This is your average order amount times the number of sales, which equals gross sales volume. Remember, this represents gross sales and not profitability, which is a separate formula based on how you manage and monitor expenses.

ROI FORMULA: Lead Generation Website

Here is the ROI formula for lead generation websites. Keep in mind this data is measuring gross sales or top line revenue. You may find other factors that are unique to your company to help calculate ROI, and these numbers will change based on your costs and other factors.

Total Website Traffic x **Online Conversion Rate** x **Average Order Amount** x **Lead Conversion Rate** = **Total Gross Sales**

— or —

Here is what the formula looks like when we put in the numbers from the example above.

(2,000 x 2.5%) x $2,000 x 20% = $25,000

Divide this number by your total spend to determine your ROI percentage.

You can see from this example that $4,500 per month in digital marketing spend is producing $25,000 per month in gross sales.

ROI Example: E-commerce Websites

The second ROI example is for e-commerce websites generating orders directly from an online store and shopping cart.

Here are the key components of ROI calculations for e-commerce websites.

Average Order Amount: $150

This is the average order amount for individual orders placed on the e-commerce website. It includes groupings of various products and is a total order amount. Shipping costs should *not* be included in this number. E-commerce websites in general will need to produce healthy average order amounts to produce a solid return. Many e-commerce sites fail because the average order is too low and there's not enough traffic or sales to cover costs. The best e-commerce sites offer free shipping and build shipping into the product cost.

Website Design/Development Cost: $25,000 and up

The total price of an e-commerce website is usually higher than the cost of a content-based, lead-generation website, and $25,000 is a good benchmark for basic e-commerce sites. Complex online shopping sites require higher budget amounts.

Monthly Digital Marketing Spend: $4,500

In this example, the amount spent each month to market and maintain the website is $4,500 per month.

Total Monthly Website Visitors: 5,000

E-commerce websites survive on traffic generation and should work hard to grow website traffic while maintaining conversion rates. This is the number of total monthly visits to the site.

Order Conversion Rate: 2% (100 sales)

Target a conversion rate of at least 2%. Some e-commerce websites have conversion rates as high as 15% or more. Seasonality also plays a big factor in conversion rates. For example, conversion rates increase substantially during holiday periods.

100 Sales per Month = $15,000

The website's conversion rate is a direct indicator of online sales success. E-commerce sites with higher conversion rates are more profitable. The number of sales times the average order amount equals the total gross sales for the month.

ROI FORMULA: E-commerce Website

Here is the ROI formula for e-commerce websites:

Total Website Traffic x Online Conversion Rate x Average Order Amount = Total Gross Sales.

- or -

Here is what the formula looks like when we put in the numbers from the e-commerce example above. (5,000 x 2%) x $150 = $15,000

Divide this number by your total spend to determine your ROI percentage.

These calculations do not account for shipping costs and other factors that may impact conversion rates, average order amounts and profitability.

CHAPTER 12:
Building a Digital Marketing Team

Build a Digital Marketing Team

You cannot go it alone when executing a winning digital marketing strategy. There are too many skill sets that must come together to make this work, and anyone who tells you that he or she has *all* the skills to get it right will most likely fail. In companies of all sizes, developing a successful digital marketing team is one of the greatest battles fought by business leaders.

Marketing Versus Technology Versus Design
Three distinct disciplines must come together to get results from digital marketing. Look at the graphic below. Can these skill sets be any more different? Marketing is concerned with business growth and sales. Technology teams need to make technology work. Designers are creative and artistic. They're interested in colors, graphics, photos and how things look. Marketers have to grow sales and drive growth.

Many website problems happen because these three skill sets can't come together to get results. In the center is project management, the key to bringing these three disciplines together and completing the project.

Three unique disciplines must work together in digital marketing.

The differences in these three areas can lead to all sorts of conflict. These three skill sets must be managed by a strong Project Manager. In many cases, the project lead is the CEO or business leader.

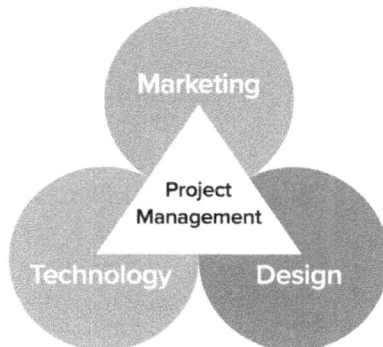

Many business leaders have been frustrated by this process, and in many cases, it's the reason so many websites are delayed or get poor results. You need an excellent project manager. You also need an understanding of the many hats people wear in making a website successful, and provide the right leadership and direction in each area.

The Hats People Wear in Digital Marketing

There are eight different job functions found in successful digital marketing teams:

1. Digital Marketing Director/Manager
2. Digital Marketing Project Manager/Coordinator
3. Digital Marketing Funnel Manager
4. Digital Marketing Google Specialist and SEO
5. Content Writer for Digital
6. Photography, Video and Other Media
7. Graphic Designer
8. Technology Professional

You don't need to hire eight employees to do this work, but you *do* need to assign someone to *each* of these roles, whether it be a contractor, an employee, a part-timer or an agency.

How to Develop and Assign Work

Each major job function or role has been broken down into eight distinct areas. As we mentioned previously, the position titles can change as needed, but the core functions remain the same. In this section we will review the action items for each separate job function.

Here are brief job descriptions and a summary of their responsibilities:

Digital Marketing Director/Manager — This person is responsible for the overall direction and strategy and prepares a budget. He or she reports to upper management and may be part of the company's senior marketing or management team. This person should have the final say on the site's development. Never make digital marketing a democratic process. Give this Director the span of control needed to make decisions quickly in accordance with an approved budget and strategic plan. The Director is also responsible for coordinating all *offline* marketing activities. This position is responsible for measuring the return.

This position is fully accountable for digital marketing results. This job might have different names, but ultimately, this is the person who is responsible for digital marketing.

I've seen too many companies where this position is not well-defined. Sometimes it's the CEO. Sometimes it's a sales manager or a marketing manager. The Digital Marketing Director is responsible for all the tasks overseeing the team to bring it together. This is one of the most important job functions you'll have at your company.

Action items for this position deal with leadership, strategy and building a winning team, as well as the following:

- Researches and writes the digital marketing plan
- Sets the strategy for digital marketing efforts
- Ensures the strategy is being followed by the digital marketing team
- Leads the digital marketing meetings
- Suggests improvements to the strategy to improve results
- Reviews digital marketing data weekly or monthly
- Asks questions of the digital marketing team regarding results
- Evaluates the digital marketing team's performance and results
- Makes the final decisions on digital marketing action items when necessary

AI is a fabulous tool for the Digital Marketing Director. They can use AI to develop a marketing scorecard, help track ROI, source content topics by persona and market segment, and develop the sales funnels. They can track conversion sources and rates and as a result learn what good digital marketing action plans and strong campaigns look like. AI can support all those things for digital marketing leadership.

Digital Marketing Project Manager/Coordinator — This staff member reports to the Director and is responsible for coordination of all activities and communications from the web team, handling schedules, action plans, time frames, meeting coordination, and all aspects of bringing the process into a cohesive plan. Project managers see that things get done, and this work can make or break your results.

Many digital marketing projects fail because of poor project management, or no project management whatsoever. It's best if this position is not outsourced. The email has to be set up, the content has to be provided, and then the graphic designs have to be put in place. All these different roles come together to accomplish any task in digital marketing.

That's why the Digital Marketing Coordinator is so important. I recommend hiring a digital marketing coordinator first. If you don't have a Digital Director, start with the Coordinator.

The Coordinator can report to the Digital Marketing Director, the CEO or another key manager. Then, as you start to work with contractors or agencies, you can bring in more internal teams.

In fact, all of these positions can be either contracted, part-time or provided by an agency. You can start with one or two positions, but eventually you'll want to round out your marketing team.

Here is a summary of a few key action items in this critical position:

- Schedules and organizes digital marketing meetings
- Organizes and follows up on action plans
- Is the taskmaster for communication between the digital marketing team members
- Updates online project management software for improved team coordination
- Looks for inconsistencies in team member action items
- Checks the website for broken links and other errors

- Prepares due dates for action items
- Helps recruit and replace team members as needed
- Communicates with contracted team members and other subcontractors
- Organizes website content timing and placement on the website and in social media

Digital Marketing Funnel Manager — Gathering feedback from users, analyzing web stats and online surveys and reporting findings and suggestions are key tasks for this position. This person should stay on top of trends and changing technologies that can impact the project. This position should report regularly to the Digital Marketing Director and work closely with the design and development teams to ensure the website is usable and generating conversions.

This person handles marketing automation, so they're going to be doing all things HubSpot, CRM and email. They help build and manage the funnel. They're concerned with mid-funnel assets like webinars and eBooks and bringing content together to move into the funnel. They schedule and write the emails. They might also do social media calendars. They are, in many cases, responsible for managing the content writers, but the Funnel Manager manages the funnel and uses a tool like HubSpot to automate all of that.

Be careful not to combine the Digital Marketing Funnel Manager with the Digital Marketing Specialist. Those are two different roles. It's very difficult to ask someone to know everything about Google and everything about email marketing and HubSpot. Those are two separate roles.

Accurately tracking website data and the site's overall usability is the responsibility of this position and may be combined with the Internet Marketing Specialist. Key tasks are focused on collecting data and research to improve results and reporting those findings to marketing and sales leadership.

- Reviews web stats weekly or monthly, comparing them against previous months/years, and spots trends in the data, making recommendations
- Develops user testing programs to gather feedback from website users
- Sets up marketing automation to nurture buyers through their buying journey
- Writes emails and tracks their results
- Reviews stats and data from email campaigns
- Sets up and reviews data and interactions from social media efforts
- Develops reports for the digital marketing team and company leadership
- Researches and analyzes digital marketing software and reports to constantly improve digital marketing results
- Sets up tracking for all relevant website conversion points

Digital Marketing Specialist – This person is responsible for driving traffic to the website through all sources, including search engines, pay-per-click, email, affiliates, ads, link exchanges, offline marketing, all things Google and all other functions that drive traffic.

This position will have some crossover with the action items for the Digital Marketing Funnel Manager. This position may also be broken into several job functions based on the variety of skills and action items needed to drive traffic. This position may be internal or outsourced, depending on the necessary skill levels.

This role may spill over a little bit into social media, but they need to know all about SEO, Google Ads and all the different factors that drive traffic to your website. They understand Google Analytics and Google Ads Keyword Tools and they're great at bringing together traffic generation and monitoring. This may start out being a contractor or agency-filled role.

- Prepares and implements a traffic generation plan for the website and social media

- Conducts keyword research and the development of keyword themes
- Responsible for the development and placement of title tags and meta descriptions for all website pages and modifications as needed
- Provides search engine optimization (SEO) of website code and content
- Conducts on-page content review to drive SEO with targeted keywords
- Setup, management, and review of AdWords and all online advertising programs
- Management of the monthly email newsletter and other email marketing efforts
- Oversees and sets up all social media for consistent design, content postings and distribution
- Works with the content writer on regular blog post topics and SEO coding for all blog posts and other content pages
- Develops and requests links from websites visited by the target market to the company website and oversees the link-building programs, both locally and globally
- Makes sure offline marketing efforts are coordinated with online marketing and traffic generation and tracks direct traffic from both marketing efforts
- Reviews and prepares analysis of website traffic sources as reported in web stats
- Sets up and monitors Google Analytics and Google Search Console
- Prepares reports on conversion rates by traffic source

Content Writer for Digital — Writing content for your website and email campaigns is the key task of this position. This person must know how to write scannable content for the web and be able to tell a story with 50% fewer words. The person in this role must be able to write scripts for online videos and podcasts, interview key people in the organization, and write effective copy for the web. This is one of the most active positions on the team.

This person can use AI tools to help write first drafts. They can use AI to proof content, edit content, and write content for different channels and personas. Digital content writing tends to be outsourced, and often they'll be contracted, but they're an essential part of your team.

These are the folks who execute the content calendar. People procrastinate when it comes to writing content, and if you don't have a Digital Content Writer, then content can get put off.

This position is responsible for writing service and product descriptions, articles, blog posts, social media content and other forms of content. This position can be internal or outsourced, depending on the amount of content needed.

- Meets with the digital marketing team on a content plan that includes topics, distribution channels and a schedule for writing content
- Recommends content approaches for both length and use of headers by content type
- Reviews web stats on the most popular content and how it's being read by website visitors and recommends new content topics
- Ensures all written content is in a format easily read and understood by online visitors

Photography, Video and Other Media — This position may actually be a team of people, and they're responsible for photos, video, webcams, interactive tours, slide shows, podcasts and all other media on the website. These team members follow direction from the digital marketing team and are most likely outsourced contractors who are specialists in each area.

- Prepares photo shoots, captures the photos and edits them for online placement
- Prepares the storyboard and script for video production work
- Shoots videos, mixes sound and edits online videos
- Records and edits audio recordings, such as podcasts, music and other audio clips

- Works with the graphic designer on the layout and placement of all media elements
- Ensures all media is easy to use on the website and provides value to visitors

Graphic Designer — This person is tasked with designing the graphic and artistic elements of a website including the logo, navigation, content placement, photo placement and all other graphic elements on the website. These last few functions are almost always outsourced.

The graphic designer's ongoing action items include several key areas.

- Prepares the homepage and interior page designs
- Updates the homepage rotator and graphics as needed
- Integrates the website's messaging and taglines into the graphics of the website
- Ensures all photos, videos and other graphic elements have the proper copyright licenses for use on the Internet and that they look professional on the website
- Works with the technology team so graphic elements are properly added and coded for SEO
- Provides design elements for all social media sites and other online graphics, keeping them consistent across all platforms

Technology Professional — The technology position is responsible for the structure of the website and how it operates. This includes the technology platform, hosting, CMS, e-commerce, HTML, site coding, how updates are made and all key technological functions. Obviously, the technology person is critical to the website but should not lead the process. This staff member should take direction and follow the strategy.

The technology team converts graphic designs to website code, handles the website's hosting and is responsible for the website's hosting platform, security and all other technical issues. This position is best outsourced.

- Selects the appropriate website platform that meets the needs of the website strategic plan and can also be edited by internal team members
- Establishes the hosting environment for the site, along with email accounts
- Sets up access to the website's administrative sections with passwords and training for making website edits and updates
- Sets up and oversees the security functions for the website and other spam and malware protections
- Oversees the integration of the website with any company software modules such as accounting systems, CRM software, inventory or other types of software
- Other technical issues that impact the usability and success of the website

External Versus Internal

All these tasks can be handled internally or outsourced based on the available talent and expected results. More than likely, the people at the top of this list are internal to your company. This includes the Digital Marketing Director, Digital Marketing Coordinator and Project Manager. Some of these tasks are best outsourced because of the level of expertise needed to run a successful program. The marketing and research specialists may also be internal but will likely need some outside help. Content writers, photographers, videographers, graphic designers and web technology specialists are usually external contractors.

This is especially true in the area of search marketing. It's also a good idea to outsource tasks where the organization can benefit from the combined experience of a variety of people.

How can the digital marketing team use AI tools to do their jobs better?

Let's start with the Digital Marketing Coordinator. This person can do a lot with AI tools. This is a person who can take their project plans, put them into AI and find ways to improve. They can make sure the team uses tools like Fathom to record meetings and automatically generate meeting notes for everyone who was there. The Fathom AI tools track everything, and project managers and coordinators should be using Fathom AI to hold all of your digital marketing meetings.

The AI tools that can record meetings are mind-blowing. They prepare amazing summaries. They pull all the action items into a bulleted list, and they help meetings to be much more productive. There's no need to go back and look at notes or try to remember what was done in the meeting.

You can use AI to improve every step of the digital marketing process. You can use it to help organize the team to minimize project risk and deliver returns.

The Digital Marketing Specialist can use AI in a variety of ways. AI is a great tool for experimenting with keywords and SEO. Imagine having your own personal SEO consultant right at your fingertips to talk about what would work best for you to get found and get heard.

You're still going to need the Google Search Console and tools like SEMrush, but having ChatGPT or Gemini to talk with about keywords and SEO insights is very helpful.

You can also use AI tools to build pillars of thought leadership, understand CTAs across various platforms, understand conversion data, interpret marketing data and identify the biggest challenges.

And you can use AI-generated content to build the pillars of great content for SEO: experience, expertise, authority, and trust.

The Funnel Manager can use AI to help build the funnel, develop content schedules, find out what kind of emails and headers are effective, write first-draft emails, analyze email results and come up with hot-button ideas for an email blast. You can also use it to pick great topics for social media posts and content calendars by channel.

You can use it to brainstorm ideas to get traction with your content. You can convert social media content into brief video scripts for YouTube, Instagram or YouTube Shorts.

And you can use AI tools to analyze the data and engagement you're seeing in the funnel. You can use it to build out development tools and plugins for WordPress, with coding support and insights.

You can build mid-funnel assets like calculators and conversion forms. You can build search tools or extract insights from the data coming from Google Analytics. You can also use AI to add apps and code to your website and your mobile site as well.

Building the digital marketing team is a key part of executing digital strategies. If this is done effectively, you'll see great results. If not, you'll have confusion and delays. Everyone on the team can use AI to supercharge what they already do well and drive more results.

Where to Find Resources

The Internet is an excellent resource for digital marketing information, and there are dozens of excellent websites where you can find help. Most of this work can be done remotely, and it's best to find external specialists who will respond in a timely manner and are able to connect with your website's strategic vision. Those with a proven track record are your best bet. Set up a phone call and ask for three references. Don't worry if they don't have specific knowledge in your industry because that can actually be a hindrance and keep you in a box. Start with a small project and gradually add on work as you see the results.

Avoid the Jack-of-All-Trades

These are the key staff functions required to run an effective digital marketing program. People will often combine these tasks, which can lead to poor results. The key challenge is to ensure that the right people are handling tasks based on their level of expertise and skill in that area. A common mistake in digital marketing is to delegate tasks to employees who do not have the proper experience. The most common example of this is having a technical person responsible for creative design or writing content.

These eight areas are very distinct from one another and should not be merged without careful analysis and a clear division of roles and tasks. Your website is a valuable marketing resource and will need attention each month from this team of specialists.

A winning digital marketing team must bring together professionals from marketing, technology and design to work together with a common purpose. Many companies make the mistake of having design teams lead the digital marketing strategy. Digital marketing strategy must come from marketing, which leads the three disciplines.

We've covered many ideas you can use to improve your digital marketing and many ideas for using AI to supercharge your efforts. But regardless of what action items you take from this book, you're going to need people to execute these tasks.

Be aware of the three major disciplines of digital marketing: marketing, technology and design, as these are very different types of people. Trying to bring them together and work as a team is very, very challenging. That's why it's critical that you know who leads the team and who's accountable for the results. Project management is the glue that holds this all together.

Digital marketing is a *marketing* led initiative. I still see too many companies that put their digital marketing in the hands of their graphic design agency or in some cases, their IT department.

Action Items:

❑ Develop your digital marketing team and assign tasks to each person. Start with a project manager.

❑ Schedule time to meet with each team member to review their assigned action items and to build accountability for results.

❑ Determine who is needed in regular digital marketing meetings.

❑ Schedule and run regular digital marketing meetings to keep the team on track.

❑ Use the content in this book to write job descriptions, assign tasks to internal employees and recruit contractors to build your digital marketing team.

❑ Adjust budgets as needed based on digital marketing ROI to determine which team members are internal to the company and which are outsourced as contractors.

Digital Marketing and the Sales Team

Sales and Marketing Alignment

In our book, *Sales and Marketing Alignment*, Karl Becker and I go into great detail on the importance of aligning sales and marketing teams to best leverage results and why this is critical to marketing success in the age of AI.

Merging digital marketing action items with the efforts of the sales team is critical to success because it's the sales team who usually closes sales and builds long-term relationships with clients and customers. Online marketing will attract prospects, but it's the sales team's job to close the sale and build the customer relationship.

In this section, we will cover how the Internet changed personal selling, how to transition a web conversion to the sales team so it can be closed and how sharp, web-savvy salespeople may be the best individuals to include on the digital marketing team. Let's start with how the Internet and digital marketing have changed sales.

Selling and Marketing Turned Upside Down

The arrival of the Internet caused a selling revolution by putting a greater amount of purchasing and decision-making authority in the hands of prospective buyers. If your website doesn't have what prospects want, another website will meet their needs. Today's sales force is no longer the company's primary source of new prospects for products and services. Now prospects can find your company online in great numbers without first talking to a salesperson. This has put an end to much traditional sales prospecting and has driven many lead generation efforts online.

As people strive to be more efficient with their time, prospects in your target market don't make time for meetings with sales reps to learn about products and services. In fact, sales managers and reps who have time for fact-finding meetings will not be at their jobs very long. Their focus should be on lead generation and attracting prospects.

It's much faster and easier for people to research solutions on the web and make contact when they're ready to buy. Companies must adapt to this changing environment, which has changed traditional sales roles in many ways.

Traditional Sales Roles Have Changed

Traditional selling models involved the basics of prospecting, qualifying, presenting, handling objections and closing. Old-school salespeople spent most of their time finding prospects they could meet and qualify. This process is becoming obsolete, and the roles have changed as the prospective customer or client is now in charge of qualifying *themselves* via web searches and online content.

In the majority of cases, the company website has become the first stop in the sales process. This is the vital first step in moving a prospect toward a sale.

So, what is the role of salespeople? Are they necessary? Absolutely! With the exception of e-commerce websites, many sales leads generated by digital marketing will involve contact with a company sales representative or will be included in stay-in-touch programs. In addition, salespeople can be excellent at digital marketing. The challenge is to extend the Four-Step Process into the company's sales process and train salespeople to market online.

Digital Leads and the Sales Strategy

It's important to develop a sales strategy and process for handling web leads and sales. The sales team must be trained in this process and there must be accountability for closing web leads. This is critical to digital marketing ROI, and a strong sales team should be able to close 25 to 50% of all web leads. Those that do not close should become part of the company's stay-in-touch program. The sales team should clearly understand how people become sales leads from digital marketing, and they should take these leads seriously. It's important to include sales management in the digital marketing meetings and explain how people use the website and how they convert to leads. This will help the sales team better understand their online prospect and develop a strategy to close more sales. It will also provide the digital marketing team with valuable insights on how to convert more site visitors into leads.

Response Times

Extending your digital marketing process into the sales process starts with recognizing the value of a lead. This should go without saying; however, many sales organizations still do not respond fast enough or recognize how important they are to closing sales.

This should be part of the sales team's culture and personality. This guidance will come from the sales and marketing leadership.

People expect fast response times from salespeople, and if you don't do it, your competitors will. Web technologies allow for quick response time, which has improved dramatically within successful selling teams. The sales team should respond to web leads immediately or within a few minutes. In fact, live chat and other web technologies allow salespeople to respond immediately to inquiries and other requests from prospects. This is the best way of showing just how important a web lead is to the company's growth. Salespeople can also play a role in lead generation and prospecting by contributing to the digital marketing team.

Visitors want fast response times but don't want to deal with intrusive salespeople. The sales team must find the right balance with live chat and other resources to maximize sales conversions.

Salespeople as Marketers

Salespeople can make great web marketers. This is true because they understand the customer best and are on the front line of the customer relationship. Salespeople must be integrated into digital marketing because it's one of the primary drivers of sales leads. It's critical to their success.

Web leads and prospects are usually highly qualified. Prospecting, historically the most time-consuming part of the old sales process, can be skipped in its entirety, and the focus can be placed on generating leads from the web. The sales rep can move right into highly qualified selling and closing with an educated prospect who has researched online.

Great Salespeople are Perfect for Digital Marketing

A sales rep's value and the overall marketing ROI will increase dramatically if salespeople can market online. The good news is the fundamentals of digital marketing are similar to the basics of selling. Your company's website is now a key sales tool and needs to function like a great prospector and presenter. The website should be easy to use and simple to understand with a focus on key benefits. The site should push visitors to hot buttons to drive inquiries. The best salespeople on your team have an intuitive understanding of how to get this done. It's too expensive to pay for prospecting efforts when they produce such poor ROI. Businesses that take a web-savvy approach to selling will outpace competitors, and the changing role of the company sales rep can make an impact.

The Role of Salespeople Starts with Education

If salespeople are to make the transition from traditional sales roles to web marketers, they must first learn the basics of digital marketing. This is a personal choice and if they're not willing to learn there's not much hope. The necessary skills will not come from a college or university.

Internet marketing skills are developed by doing, watching and acting on results. It's critical to stay on top of changes, which can literally happen overnight. It takes time and effort to optimize digital marketing efforts. This effort will pay off many times over with increased leads and sales. Anyone can learn these skills from the many free resources available online and the content of this book. The biggest challenge is finding the salespeople with the desire and motivation to make the change and learn a new approach. Let's take a look at the specific skills salespeople need to become effective web marketers.

Salespeople and Digital Content Distribution

Each of the Four Steps leads to a lengthy list of action items. Once the website has an excellent strategy and great design, the next step is driving traffic. The salesperson's role in driving traffic is mostly based on written content. In fact, content preparation for the website and social media may be the most common tasks performed by salespeople. This content can be posted on the company website and blog, written in articles, used in email marketing or spread throughout the Internet on a variety of websites. Salespeople should be able to write excellent customer-focused content.

Content preparation is the most time-consuming, yet most effective role of a web marketer. Website content comes in a variety of formats.

Here are a few examples of content types perfect for sales professionals:

- Email newsletters
- Blog posts
- Podcasts
- Webinars
- Informational articles
- Social media postings
- Product and services descriptions

This is how salespeople must sell today and in the future. The traditional sales pitch has been replaced by carefully crafted, inviting websites, informative email contacts and the effective use of social media content and resources. Salespeople must become experts on their products and services, facilitate expert discussions, tell stories and have a deep understanding of how targeted markets use the Internet.

How to Find and Train Salespeople to Market Online

Hiring is the greatest challenge in developing an effective sales team. Finding a sales rep with online marketing skills, or the desire to learn those skills, makes hiring an even greater challenge. However, finding a salesperson with those skills is a real benefit to the company and the salesperson. The organization gets more sales and leads, and the sales rep gets more enjoyment from the work. The challenges are finding salespeople with those skills or finding ways to convert current sales team members into web marketers by providing access to digital marketing job functions or marketing training. It's difficult but not impossible.

Hiring and Training Recommendations

Look for salespeople who are comfortable on the web and good at writing content. People who have attempted to build a website or frequently use LinkedIn and other social media sites are good candidates and will naturally want to learn more about digital marketing and look forward to posting content.

These salespeople should have a high comfort level with technology and a passion for the Internet and digital marketing. Without this passion, there may be little incentive to learn and practice new skills.

Encourage learning about digital marketing from proven web resources. You can find nearly unlimited resources online. Make the time for salespeople to try out what they learn and convert natural selling skills to digital marketing. Set up web stats and ROI tracking to measure their performance.

It's important to modify incentives and rewards around digital marketing activities such as lead creation, online conversions, understanding web stats, email marketing and more.

Some of the best candidates for digital marketing positions may already be a part of your team. Look internally to find skills that go beyond traditional selling and into a more effective digital marketing approach to drive leads. Watch out for non-technical salespeople because they will find it more difficult over time to generate leads and close sales, although, they may have excellent writing skills.

Follow-Up and Stay-in-Touch Programs for Web-Based Sales

Digital marketing is tremendously powerful not only for creating sales leads, but also for cost-effectively staying in touch with a large universe of potential customers at a very low cost. However, the best lead generation in the world is meaningless unless salespeople are prepared to make multiple contacts with their prospects. In this way, salespeople are a major factor in successful stay-in-touch programs as part of their sales process. Get the sales team involved in email blasts, online content, and other stay-in-touch programs.

Most Salespeople Give Up Too Early

Research with salespeople has shown that prospects need multiple contacts before they're ready to buy. Most salespeople fail because they do not communicate enough with prospects until they're ready to buy. Salespeople often give up because of assumptions they make about prospects and the amount of work needed to close a sale. It's not enough to train salespeople to generate leads without also learning how to keep in touch until the sale is closed.

Stay-in-Touch Methods

As we discussed in previous chapters, staying in touch with prospects revolves around online content. Content serves the dual purpose of driving traffic and keeping in touch with your target market. The major rule of thumb is that the content must be *relevant* and *highly interesting* to the prospect, or it will be ignored. Content must either improve the quality of life or help people do their jobs more effectively.

Here are examples of how salespeople can use content for stay-in-touch programs with web leads:

- **Email Newsletters** – Collect email names and addresses and send monthly newsletters.
- **Webinars** – Develop a free 45-minute webinar to present quarterly.
- **Podcasts** – Reach a massive audience for free on iTunes with ten-minute audio segments.
- **Blogs** – Keep a running journal of value-added content that informs and tells a story.
- **Website Content Updates** – Develop a process of regular updates to your website.
- **Facebook, LinkedIn and X** – Communicate small nuggets of information and build discussions on all major social media sites.

CRM and Google Analytics

Search engines love content. CRM tools such as HubSpot and SalesForce can help track content used in stay-in-touch programs and provide data on prospect responses. Google Analytics reports on which content is most popular and provides a wealth of information on the results of content distribution strategies. These strategies will not only help you keep in touch with prospects but also improve your organic search rankings. The goal is to focus on automation and reaching the maximum number of people possible with content they want to read and share with others. This is part of the sales process, and your sales team will play an important role in writing and distributing this content to the right prospects.

Give this book to sales managers and to each member of your sales team.

Marketing is a team effort. Team members at all levels will get value from this book. Also, make sure to read *Sales and Marketing Alignment* for more on building your digital marketing team, coordinating those efforts with the sales team and building a winning sales funnel.

Action Items:

- ❑ Develop a list of digital marketing resources for training salespeople.
- ❑ Provide the sales team with digital marketing learning resources.
- ❑ Interview the sales team for web interests, skills and passion.
- ❑ Identify salespeople who should run digital marketing programs.
- ❑ Assign content and follow-up responsibilities to members of the sales team.
- ❑ Include the sales process or funnel in your digital marketing plan.
- ❑ Train the sales team on how to best handle web leads.
- ❑ Integrate the digital marketing process with the sales process through the company CRM.
- ❑ Involve key salespeople in the company's digital marketing processes.

CHAPTER 13:
Let's Get to Work

The purpose of this book is to get readers to act. You now have the action plans, tools and insights you need to excel at digital marketing and drive growth.

This book offers many ideas and suggestions so you can change what you are doing and get improved results, but you must act.

If you do the same things you have always done, you will get the same results.

A New Perspective for Growth

I hope you've begun to see digital marketing from a new perspective and as a process to be worked on and monitored. As your sales and marketing teams strive to increase sales, they're looking for competitive advantages and unique techniques to reach their goals. The Four-Step Process will help provide the direction they need to accomplish those goals. This book is a competitive advantage for those companies choosing to follow the Four Steps and find ways to rise above the competition.

Five Critical Questions

Awareness leads to growth and awareness is fueled by asking questions. These five questions are key to your marketing success and are the core of this book:

1. Who's visiting our website, and what is their intent?
2. What are the conversion rates, and how do we measure ROI?
3. Is our digital content benefit-focused or company-focused?
4. Are the digital marketing metrics improving?
5. How do we improve our sales funnel to grow?

If your team doesn't know the answers, or if you feel their answers are off, it's time to have them read this book, or you may need a new team.

The Translation of Value

Business leaders are in a unique position to translate what their company does very well to the world's most important communication channel: the Internet. They need a clear understanding of how to do that, and an excellent digital marketing team to make it happen. These are the two most important keys to success in digital marketing.

This book has outlined processes, strategies and action plans to help you win at digital marketing. Use the tactics in this book to improve results from your website, expand your reach in social media and get email marketing right.

Digital Marketing in the Age of AI

This is the age of AI. It will be integrated into our lives as long as we use technology, and the time is right to start the process of integrating it fully into your marketing and sales efforts as an invaluable tool to help you reach your goals.

Good luck in your digital marketing efforts, and I wish you great success in all your endeavors!

To schedule a complimentary discovery session about your digital marketing goals email me at tom@intuitivewebsites.com

For interviews, media or presentation inquiries, call me directly at 719-231-6916.

I'm also available to speak at your conference, convention or trade show about *Digital Marketing in the Age of AI.*

Digital Marketing Resources

There are too many online tools and resources to mention in this book. We've reviewed hundreds of websites and online tools and have summarized a few that are most important for the business leader. Many of these resources will contain links to many more tools to be evaluated as a possible fit for your business.

AI Tools

AI Large Language Model (LLM) Chatbots

ChatGPT	https://chatgpt.com/	The original by OpenAI
Microsoft CoPilot	https://copilot.microsoft.com/	AI Companion
Gemini	https://gemini.google.com/	AI Chatbot
Claude	https://claude.ai/	AI Chatbot
Perplexity	https://www.perplexity.ai/	AI Chatbot
Grok	https://grok.x.ai/	AI Chatbot

Multiple LLM Aggregator

Poe	https://poe.com/	LLM Aggregator
TheB.AI	https://theb.ai/	LLM Aggregator

Videos

Captions AI	https://www.captions.ai/	AI Creative video studio
Klap AI	https://klap.app/	Edit videos into video shorts

Content (Written)

Grammarly	https://www.grammarly.com/	Editing, grammar, spell check, plagiarism
Jasper AI	https://www.jasper.ai/	Copywriting, Marketing campaigns, social media campaigns

| Copy.AI | https://www.copy.ai/ | Prospecting, Sales content, Ad creation, Competitive reviews |
| Otio.AI | https://otio.ai/ | Read, write and more |

Meetings, Transcripts, Notes

| Otter.ai | https://otter.ai/ | AI Meeting Assistant |
| Fireflies.ai | https://fireflies.ai/ | AI Meeting Assistant |

Website Builders

Wix	https://wix.com	AI-based website builder
10web	https://10web.io/	AI-based website builder
Framer	https://www.framer.com/	AI-based website builder
Jimdo	https://www.jimdo.com/	AI-based website builder

Coding/Developers

GitHub Copilot	https://github.com/	Coding Copilot
Eden	https://www.edenai.co/	Coding Copilot
Amazon Code Whisperer	https://aws.amazon.com/codewhisperer/	Coding Copilot
Tabnine	https://www.tabnine.com/	Coding Copilot

(Compiled by Ed Valdez, Partner and CMO, Chief Outsiders)

AI Tools

Chat GPT 4 from OpenAI.com (owned by Microsoft) Gemini from Google Claude.ai

AI Websites and Resources

Many of the AI software tools on these websites use Chat GPT, but you might prefer having a different interface or functionality.

FutureTools.io

Futurepedia.io

SuperTools.therundown.ai

TopApps.ai

ebaqdesign.com/blog/best-ai-tools

GPTforwork.com

Estoreera.gumroad.com/l/chatgpt4mastery

Chatspot.ai

Capacity.com

Byword.ai

Undetectable.ai

Directory of ChatGPT Tools and Plugins

https://fosterinstitute.com/some-useful-artificial-intelligence-sites/

Database Websites

- ZoomInfo.com
- https://datavu.databaseusa.com
- https://www.apollo.io/
- https://sparktoro.com/

Essential Tools and Resources from Google

Google is the starting point for the most essential digital marketing tools and resources. Google has a variety of web tools that are the standard in digital marketing and statistics. They're also free. These tools can be found by setting up an account with Google using one username and password. Make sure you keep those Google login credentials in a safe place and that they always stay with the company.

You will find these resources discussed throughout this book. **Here are a few of the most important Google tools:**

- Google Analytics
- Google Ads
- Google Keyword Tool
- Google Search Console
- Google Alerts
- Google Insights for Search
- Google Think Insights
- Google My Business

Website Strategy Resources

- IntuitiveWebsites.com
- HubSpot.com
- Shop.org

Website Design and Development Tools

WordPress.org
MagentoEcommerce.com
Shopify.com
WhichTestWon.com
UserTesting.com
BuiltWith.com

SEO Tools and Resources

SearchEngineLand.com
SearchEngineWatch.com
AdvancedWebRanking.com
SEMRush.com
MOZ.com
Google Keyword Tool in AdWords
WordTracker.com

PPC (Pay-per-Click) Resources

Google Ads
WordStream.com
MSN - BingAds.com

Must-Have Social Media Websites

Facebook.com
LinkedIn.com
YouTube.com
Twitter.com (now called X)
Google My Business
Pinterest.com

Social Media Tools and Resources

SocialMediaExaminer.com
Google Alerts
SocialMention.com
HootSuite.com

Email and Marketing Automation Tools

HubSpot
MailChimp
iContact
Constant Contact
Marketo

Content Marketing Resources

Checklist of Content Marketing Types
Checklist of Content Marketing Channels
Content Marketing Packet
ContentMarketingInstitute.com

Online PR Resources

PRWeb.com
PR.com
PRNewswire.com

Website Stats and ROI Resources

Sales Lead ROI Worksheet
Online Sale ROI Worksheet
ROI Calculator for Online Conversions (link to IW calculator)
LeadLander.com
Google Analytics
Alexa.com
BuiltWith.com
Agency Analytics

Five Great Books

Sales and Marketing Alignment, by Karl Becker and Thomas Young

Don't Make Me Think, by Steve Krug

SPIN Selling, by Neil Rackham

Building a Story Brand, Donald Miller

This is Marketing, Seth Godin

ROI Worksheet: Online Sales Lead

Use this ROI worksheet to determine your return from online sales leads from digital marketing.

Marketing ROI Worksheet for Lead Generation

Timeframe: (The time frame is the amount of time for the ROI calculations. Monthly time frames are common.)

Total Website Visits:

Conversion Rate to Leads: (Target a 2-5% conversion rate)

Total Digital Leads: Conversion Rate to Sales: (Target 30% or more). (This is the conversion rate measurement for your sales team converting sales leads into closed business.)

Number of Orders:

Average Order Amount:

Total Sales:

Digital Marketing Spend:

ROI: (Marketing Spend/Total Sales)

Cost per Customer Acquisition:

ROI Worksheet: E-commerce Sale

Here is a sample ROI worksheet for determining return on direct online sales from an e-commerce website.

Marketing ROI Worksheet for eCommerce

Time Frame: (The time frame is the amount of time for the ROI calculations. Monthly time frames are common.)

Total Website Visits:

Conversion Rate to Orders: (Target a 3% to 5% conversion rate)

Number of Orders:

Average Order Amount: (Target an average order amount of at least $75 for eCommerce sales.)

Total Sales:

Marketing Spend:

ROI: (Marketing Spend/Total Sales)

Cost per Customer Acquisition:

About the Author

Thomas Young is a business owner, consultant, speaker and author. He's the founder and owner of Intuitive Websites, a Colorado-based digital marketing agency.

Tom has been a Vistage member and Vistage speaker since 2001. He has more than 30 years of experience in marketing and sales, including digital marketing and website usability research. He has helped thousands of companies increase their sales through his speaking, consulting and digital marketing services provided by the Intuitive Websites team. He's passionate about helping clients succeed at digital marketing and grow their sales.

Tom has presented around the U.S. and Canada on digital marketing. He's the author of three other books: *Intuitive Selling, Winning the Website War* and *Sales and Marketing Alignment*. Tom has a BA in communications from the University of Northern Colorado and an MBA from the University of Colorado. He is the father of two sons and an avid tennis player and musician.

Visit www.IntuitiveWebsites.com to learn more.

To schedule a complimentary discovery session about your digital marketing goals, email me at tom@intuitivewebsites.com

For interviews, media or presentation inquiries, call me directly at 719-231-6916.